19th Century woodcut by Ludwig Richter (1803-1884)

The
Beer Drinker's Guide
To Munich

Larry Hawthorne

Sixth Edition
Revised and Updated

www.beerdrinkersguide.com

Freizeit
Publishers

THE BEER DRINKER'S GUIDE TO MUNICH
Copyright © 2008 by Larry Hawthorne
First Edition 1991
Second Edition 1992
Third Edition 1995
Fourth Edition 2000
Fifth Edition 2005
Sixth Edition 2008
Printed in the United States of America

Published by
Freizeit Publishers
1035 S. Lyon Ave.
Hemet, CA 92543

—————————————————

Photos by author and Eliska Jezkova, or as indicated

Illustration by
Heather Goodwin, pg. 23

ISBN: 978-0-9628555-3-5

About the cover. A night at Munich's annual spring Frühlingsfest is featured on the cover of the 6th edition. The festive fervor is captured in a window that only begins to describe the wild and crazy atmosphere of the Augustiner tent. Those folks dancing on the tables don't appear terribly upset at having to wait another five months for the Oktoberfest to be unveiled on the same stage.

And what about Wolfgang? Wolfgang Schad, and fellow beer-drinker members of his Prinzregent Luitpold Verein, have graced the cover of the past three editions of *The Beer Drinker's Guide to Munich*. Wolf and friends are doing just fine, thank you, and remain perennial weekend *Stammgäste* (regulars) at Viktualienmarkt, the Hofbräuhaus and an evening *Stammtisch* at the Bräustüberl of the Bier und Oktoberfest Museum. As always, these folks are for real and they really know how to drink beer. Stop by and have a brew with them if you get the chance.

Wolfgang Schad (l), Ria Scheibenzuber, and Lukas Bulka, hoist a beer at the museum's Bräustüberl Stammtisch.

To all those, over the years,
who have come to
Munich as strangers
and left as good friends.
Zum Wohl!

for Jimbo

Contents

M unich is a kind of German heaven . . . A great Germanic dream translated into life . . . . The best beer in Germany, in the world, is made there, and there are enormous beer cellars that are renowned throughout the land. The Bavarian is the National Good Fellow. He is supposed to be a witty and eccentric creature, and millions of postcards are printed of him in his national costume blowing the froth away from a foaming stein of beer. In other parts of Germany, people will lift their eyes and sigh rapturously when you say you are going to Munich: 'Ach! München . . . ist schön!'

American Novelist Thomas Wolf
The Web and the Rock

A Word About the Rating System

We employ a rating scheme to go along with our individual reviews and profiles of the establishments in this book that needs some explanation. Our opinions are subjective, to be sure, but we also factor in the views of literally hundreds of past users of this book. They have not been too shy to let us know over the past five editions just how they would rate these same establishments if only we had asked. And we did. So consider these ratings a benchmark and a tool that can save you some time and help you experience and enjoy Munich at its best. The rating for each establishment employs a 10-point scale, 10 being best, in "half-beer" increments. Thus a 5-beer rating is tops on the list. In writing this book and over the years, we have visited literally hundreds of beer halls and beer gardens. (Literary research is full of personal sacrifices like that.) If they didn't rate at least a five (2 1/2 beers) on our scale of suds, they didn't make the pages of this book. Some are better than others, but be assured that every establishment listed here is worthy of your patronage. We hope you enjoy them as much as we do. Cheers!

Beer Drinkers only think they're perfect!

As with each new edition of the BDG2M great care was taken to verify the information and assure the accuracy of this guide at the time it went to press. However, along with the inevitable passage of time will come change.

The printed page will never keep up with it all and there will always be some errors likely to occur. The price of a beer, opening and closing times, the *ruhetag* "rest day" each week when some (but not many) establishments close are always subject to change.

Smart travelers will call and double-check important items before committing to travel. We've tried to give you plenty of FAX and telephone numbers in case you need them and Internet addresses as well. Also, exact dates of Munich's annual events are sometimes locked in only a year in advance. The out-year dates listed in the five-year fest calendar are probable and could shift slightly, depending on the city's final scheduling. They should be reconfirmed with the Munich Tourist Office prior to traveling:

Tel: (089) 233-96-500; **FAX** (089) 233-30-233 (from U.S. dial 011-49-(drop the 0) 89- phone number.)
Internet: www.muenchen-tourist.de
E-mail: tourismus@muenchen.de

The Beer Drinker's Guide to Munich is constantly being revised and updated. Your own personal experiences in using this book — the good and the bad — can help greatly in confirming or revising the opinions and information in this guide.

Send your letters to Freizeit Publishers, 1035 S. Lyon Avenue, Hemet, California 92543, or log on to our Internet site at beerdrinkersguide.com and send us an e-mail.

Thanks, we'd love to hear from you.

Introduction
to the sixth edition

Welcome to the sixth edition of *The Beer Drinker's Guide to Munich.* This edition is fully revised, updated and expanded with more beer gardens and beer halls than ever before along with honest assessments, ratings and reviews. There are maps to take you there and where there's a story behind these fascinating establishments, we try to tell it. A good number of those stories revolve around Oktoberfest and the city's other worthwhile festivals. In the back there's an updated calendar projecting events out to the year 2012. The book is not so much about beer — all Munich beer is great — as it is about where to find and drink it. And that's why this is the "beer drinker's" and not just the "beer" guide to Munich.

Beginning with the fourth edition, members of the "5-Beer Club" — those establishments that earned an ultimate 5-beer rating and "best of the best" among Munich's beer emporia — extended the welcome mat where it matters most. They agreed to a "buy one, get one free" beer offer that makes a visit to Munich easy on the pocket book while you enjoy the best the city has to offer. Continuing with this sixth edition are tear-out coupons in the back of the book, although naturally those participating vary along with their ratings. Use the guide and the coupons just a couple of times and the book has more than paid for itself in free beer. Prosit!

Those familiar with earlier editions of the BDG2M should know this book is a true labor of love. It began as a notion one day nearly 30 years ago while sitting alone in the Hirschgarten along with the usual crowd of 8,000 or so Münchners in attendance. Struck that nowhere in the din of conversation was a word of English to be heard, I realized then that visitors from around the world love Munich. They love the food, the beer, the museums, the churches. They are fascinated by the friendly, fun-loving Bavarians and are sure to include Munich on every tour itinerary. But when it comes to a knowledge of the city, they're like Columbus in search of the New World: not sure where they're going, or how to get there. And then they have trouble putting their digital stills together when they get back because they're not certain where they have been.

This guide is an answer to that, although the natural restrictions of time and writer's cramp have winnowed the field of worthy beer establishments down to just the very best.

The best, as you will see, does not always mean the biggest, or the most famous. But it does mean the ones where the adventurous traveler can expect to find the most fun. It will lead you to those places that, as though they were some closely guarded state secret, are overlooked by most visitors to Munich. More than addresses or landmarks on a map, each beer garden, beer hall or beer pub has its own compelling story and colorful history, often closely linked with Munich itself.

There is life after the Hofbräuhaus. You only have to find it!

Getting Around Munich with MVV

Navigating Munich by car is a bad idea. City traffic is heavy, it's too easy to get lost and there are too many one-way streets to recover quickly. When you reach your destination, finding a parking space is a lot like waiting for the leaves to turn. But not to worry. There is a terrific alternative because Munich is blessed with one of the most accessible and efficient public transportation systems in the world. The four-tiered network of suburban railways (S-bahn), subways (U-bahn), streetcars, and buses makes getting around a breeze. (Note: If you're traveling on a Eurail, Germanrail or similar rail pass, it's good for the S-bahn system, but not the U-bahn, streetcars or bus lines in Munich.) Here are a few reasons to leave the car at home or parked in one of the city's many indoor parking structures and rely on MVV (*Münchner Verkehrs- und Tarifverbund*) to visit all the beer gardens, beer halls, lokals and restaurants in this book.

❏ **MVV is safe, clean, and fast.** You won't get mugged, you won't get dirty, and you'll get there in a hurry. Simple as that.

❏ **It's dependable.** The trains, trams and buses run on time. Schedules are clearly posted and universally adhered to. Also, the city has gone to digitized information boards that will give you all the information you need at a single glance.

❏ **It's flexible.** There are often several alternative routes to the same destination, with overlapping bus, streetcar or other rail service.

❏ **It's getting better.** The city is continually expanding and improving the system. Outlying areas that were inaccessible just a few years ago are now easily reached.

❏ **It's incredibly cheap.** With the special all-day group and extended stay tickets now available, shoe leather is more expensive.

❏ **It's smart.** Using public transportation means full enjoyment of the beer gardens, beer halls and lokals. No one should get behind the wheel of an automobile even after one beer. It's illegal, it's dumb, and it's unnecessary. A relatively low blood-alcohol level of .08 is the legal limit to operate an automobile in Germany. While German authorities are very tolerant of pedestrians who celebrate too much, they throw the book at anyone who drinks and drives. It means time in jail, a heavy fine, automatic loss of license, and a lot of embarrassment. If this were the only reason to stay with the public transit system, it would be enough.

'Wo ist der Hauptbahnhof?'

The concept of this book is simple. Detailed directions to each beer garden or beer hall begin at the Hauptbahnhof, the main train station. In Munich, like few other German or European towns, the central station is the hub of the city's spoked transportation network. Six underground systems, eight suburban rail lines, and dozens of bus and tram routes all converge at the Hauptbahnhof. It is the logical and most convenient starting point for any trip within the city or to nearby suburbs. With the Hauptbahnhof as a base, each route is carefully mapped with full graphic and written instructions. In most instances, one or possibly two modes of transportation are required, followed by a short walk (usually only a couple blocks) to the designated establishment. Careful attention should be paid to whether a U- or S-bahn is used. The two train systems are similar in many respects. In some cases, they traverse similar routes and stop in the same stations. However, the two systems are completely separate and are accessed from different levels. The subterranean U-bahn is usually one level below the S-bahn and services a much smaller area.

Signage

Munich's stations are filled with clues to help travelers stay on the right track or find the correct exit to the street they need or the next mode of transportation. This is cleverly accomplished through the use of pictures of buses, streetcars, etc., posted in conspicuous places. The Europeans have perfected this system of pictographs to minimize the need for multiple languages. The system is extremely easy to follow without the need to know more than a smattering of German. At transit terminals, such as U- or S-bahn stops, posted signs point the way to nearby street exits and connections for continu-

The sign at the right helps travelers find their way. This one in a U-bahn station indicates the stop (Marienplatz) and that S-bahn and bus connections can be made by exiting to the right.

MVV has modernized and digitized. The latest innovation are digital monitors in the city's fleet of buses. They keep an updated running list of upcoming stops, providing passengers with advance warning to make the correct transportation decision.

ing travel.

With just a little practice, one can also interpret the wealth of information available at every boarding point. It usually consists of a posted time schedule, a complete map of the route, a sequential listing of stops and travel times between them, as well as available transfers. As if that weren't enough, on board the train, tram or bus is another easy-to-read annotated map, usually plastered on the ceiling. It provides a running reference of points along the route. The latest techno-wrinkle is a continually updating monitor on buses that displays the current and upcoming

stops, three or more at a time. Bus and tram stops are easily identified by the ubiquitous green "H" on a yellow background. The "H" stands for *haltestelle*, the German word for stop.

S- and U-bahn Systems

Most subway and suburban railroad systems in the world's major metropolitan areas follow a common code in identifying transit routes and directions. Any frequent urban traveler will recognize Munich's "last-stop" identifier system. Basically, the last stop on any given line will serve as the direction (*richtung* in German) to look for. Thus, if you want to

A trans-European train arriving in Munich's Hauptbahnhof (Main Train Station) in 1897 was a big event. Today the city's multi-tiered modern transit system makes getting there and back a routine undertaking.

14

reach Heimeranplatz from the Hauptbahnhof, you look on the MVV map (printed in this book) and find that two U-bahn lines serve Heimeranplatz, U-4 and U-5. Either will take you there. However, to make certain you head in the right direction you would take U-4 toward Westend Str. (last stop in the same direction you're headed) or U-5 toward Laimer Platz (last stop on the U-5 line). The last-stop-indicates-direction formula works for every other MVV mode of travel. Occasionally, major intermediate stops are also used to indicate direction — such as "Richtung (direction) Marienplatz" or often you'll read "Richtung Hauptbahnhof". In suburban areas you will often see "Innenstadt" to indicate the direction of travel is toward the city center (Hauptbahnhof).

Since most U- and S-bahn stations are at major crossroads throughout the city, it isn't unusual to find three or four different exits to choose from. The maps in this book try to anticipate the need to exit the station at the right spot. When a particular exit is required, it is highlighted.

Tageskarten - Single and Partner

The folks who run MVV seem to never rest until they've refined and revamped the fare structure to accommodate the greatest number of travelers with the best deal possible. One result has seen the venerable Tageskarte split into a single and group version called, predictably, the Single-Tageskarte and the Partner-Tageskarte.

If you're traveling alone or in a group with each member minding his own budget, then the Single-Tageskarte is the one for you. This entitles the holder to travel any mode of conveyance MVV has to offer (U-bahn, S-bahn, Tram, Bus) from the time the ticket is validated to 6 a.m.

the next morning. You can buy a ticket for the inner zone, or the expanded "Munich XXL" zone (we recommend this one) or the entire network. Current prices for the Single-Tageskarte are € 5 for the limited inner zone, € 6.70 for the XXL zone, or € 10 for the entire network.

Almost all of the beer gardens and beer halls in this book are within the two inner zones (white and green on the map) that MVV's marketing folks call "Munich XXL." Only those beer gardens listed as day trips are beyond the zone (except Dachau and Leibhards, which are just inside the XXL zone). Thus, in most cases the € 6.70 single or the € 11.80 partner Tageskarte will be sufficient. With these tickets you can travel most everywhere in Munich, take all four modes of transportation, make as many stops as desired, travel the entire morning, evening, and into the next morning, for a lot less than the cost of a half-mile taxi ride.

With the Partner-Tageskarte, the time and zone restrictions remain the same, but the number covered by the ticket is significantly expanded. This group ticket covers up to five adults (related or not) traveling together. Two children ages 6-14 count as one adult, so theoretically 10 kids can travel on one Partner-Tageskarte. Thus, you and a friend, or a spouse and your six kids, or somebody's kids, can ride the roads and rails all day long for around the cost of a beer where you're headed. Current price of the Partner-Tageskarte is € 9 for the inner zone (Innenraum), € 11.80 for the first two zones (München XXL) and € 18 for the entire network (Gesamtnetz).

Additionally, MVV now sells a 3-day Tageskarte at a similar savings for those who plan to be in town for a long weekend. However, the 3-day pass is only good for the inner zone (Innenraum) and not the entire network. It currently runs € 12.30 for the single and € 21 for the partner.

IsarCard9Uhr (and IsarCard60)

Worth mentioning for those who are planning an extended stay in Munich is the IsarCard9Uhr. We love this ticket because it covers an entire calendar month, or part thereof, depending on when you buy it. If you buy it in the middle, it's good for about two weeks, and it's still a bargain. If you can buy it around the beginning of the month, there is nothing equal to it in terms of savings. The IsarCard9Uhr costs € 59 for the entire MVV network for the whole month! Think about that savings. The only restriction with this card, as its name suggests, is you must wait until after 9 a.m. during the work week to use it. Oh, well, if that means sleeping in a little longer and arriving at beer gardens *after* they're open, that's a sacrifice we're willing to make. Weekends and holidays, you can use the IsarCard9Uhr any time. Also, if you happen to be 60 or older, you get a break and only have to pay € 50 for the IsarCard60, with the same provisions of the month-long IsarCard9Uhr. Either IsarCard is valid the remainder of the month for which it was purchased until 12 noon the first working day of the following month.

It's hard to imagine any better transportation bargain than the Tageskarte in either form, or even the IsarCard if your circumstances permit. These passes can be bought through vending machines at most stations or ticket counters. They are also available at reception desks in many hotels, tourist bureaus and city information offices, and a number of Munich's shops and department stores.

The tickets are good as soon as validated in one of the blue time-and-date clock machines (they have a large "E" on their face) at the entrance to U- and S-bahn tracks, and at bus and tram stops. The IsarCards do not require validation, since they already have their month of validity stamped on them.

Once you've validated a ticket and are on board, you may be surprised that nobody wants to check it. The honor system is in force in Germany and is seldom violated. Although verification is infrequent, it does happen.

By our reckoning — very unscientific, but infallible nevertheless — you will be checked on average about 10 percent of the time. When a "kontrol" is made, those who can't produce a validated ticket face a stiff on-the-spot € 40 fine and a lot of embarrassment in a crowded car filled with paying customers. Buy the Tageskarte or IsarCard, stamp it, and forget about it.

About the Maps in the Sixth Edition

The maps in this book are hand drawn, from the perspective of someone actually on the street, walking the route. They're the end product of more than a few wrong turns and false starts. By design, they're not to scale nor exact in every detail of every nearby street. We've tried to eliminate superfluous information to make the maps practical and easy to follow, including a number of landmarks seen only from the ground. Each map represents the easiest way to get to a particular Munich beer garden or beer hall, devoid of excess detail that detracts from clear understanding. The maps reflect many changes since the previous edition, including a complete renumbering of the bus system and some redesignating of the U- and S-Bahn lines. We follow these maps ourselves when we revise each edition of The BDG2M because we know that if they don't work for us, they won't work for you.

Getting There: Line by Line at a Glance

Primary public transportation stops are listed below, with secondary travel modes to individual beer gardens. Refer to MVV system map on inside back cover and next two pages for a map with cross-referenced beer gardens and U- and S-Bahn stops.

1. Hauptbahnhof:
Park Cafe - walk
Augustiner Keller - Tram 17 to Hopfenstr.
Zur Schwaige -Tram 17 to Schloß Nymphenburg
Fasanerie - Tram 17 to Amalienburg Str.
Concordia Park - Tram 20/21 to Olympiapark West
Bräustüberl Tegernsee - Track 33/34 (at 42 after the hour) to Tegernsee
Augustiner Bräu (Salzburg) - Two-hour train ride to Salzburg, Austria

2. Karlsplatz:
Augustiner Großgaststätte - walk

3. Marienplatz:
Donisl/Andechser am Dom - walk
Weisses Bräuhaus - walk
Hofbräuhaus - walk
Viktualienmarkt - walk
Siebenbrunn - Bus 52 to Tierpark

4. Isar Tor:
Bier-und-Oktoberfest Museum - walk

5. Sendlinger Tor:
Altes Hackerhaus - walk

6. Hackerbrücke:
Augustiner Bräustuben - walk

U-Bahn 1:
7. *Löwenbräu Keller* - Stiglmaier Platz
8. *Taxisgarten* - Gern

U-Bahn 2:
9. *Franziskaner Garten* - Trudering; Bus 192 Vogesen Str.
10. *Menterschwaige* - Silberhorn; Tram 15 or 25 to Menterschwaige
10. *Paulaner Keller* - Silberhorn; Tram 15/25 to Ostfriedhof

U-Bahn 3:
11. *Flaucher* - Brudermühle Str; Bus 54 to Schäftlarn St.
12. *Hinterbrühl* - Thalkirchen; Bus 135 to Hinterbrühl
12. *Mangostin* - Thalkirchen

U-Bahn 4:
13. *Am Hopfengarten* - (Also U-5) Heimeranplatz; Bus 133 to Siegenburger Str.
14. *Hofbräu Keller/Unionsbräu* - Max-Weber Platz
15. *Im Grüntal* - Richard Strauß Str; Bus 187 to

Rümelin Str.
U-Bahn 5:
16. *Michaeligarten* - Michaelibad; Bus 195 to Heinrich-Wieland Str.
17. *Leiberheim* - Neuperlach Zentrum; Bus 55 to Waldperlach
18. *Am Rosengarten* - (also via U-4) Westend Str.; Tram 18 to Stegener Weg

U-Bahn 6:
19. *Max-Emanuel Brauerei* - Universität
20. *Englischer Garten (Osterwald, Chinesischer Turm, Hirschau, Seehaus)* - Münchner Freiheit
21. *Aumeister* - Studentenstadt
21. *Sankt Emmerams Mühle* - Studentenstadt; Bus 50 to Sankt Emmerams
22. *Paulaner Bräuhaus* - (also U-3) Goetheplatz

S-Bahn 1:
23. *Hirschgarten* - Laim
24. *Oberschleißheim* - Oberschleißheim
25. *Weihenstephan/Plantage* - Freising; Bus 638; Bus 620/621 (Plantage)
26. *Airbräu* - Flughafen
(in Airport Center)

S-Bahn 2:
27. *Insel Mühle* - Allach; Buses 160, 164, or 165 to Friedhof Untermenzing
28. *Schlossberg Biergarten (Dachau)* - Dachau; Bus 720 or 722 to Rathaus

S-Bahn 4:
29. *Deutsche Eiche/Bienenheim* - Lochhausen

S-Bahn 5:
30. *Aubinger Einkehr* - Neuaubing
31. *Kloster Andechs/Seehof* - Herrsching
32. *Kugler Alm* - Furth

S-Bahn 6:
33. *Kraillinger Brauerei/Heide Volm/Alter Wirt* - Planegg; Bus 967 to Mitterweg
34. *Forschungsbrauerei* - Perlach
35. *Liebhards (Ayingerbräu)* - Aying

S-Bahn 7:
36. *Spektakel* - Harras; Bus 53 to Sendlinger Kirche
36. *Waldheim* - Harras; Bus 54 to Lorettoplatz
37. *Münchner Haupt* - Mittersendling
38. *Waldwirtschaft Großhesselohe* - Großhesselohe
39. *Brückenwirt* - walk from Höllriegelskreuth

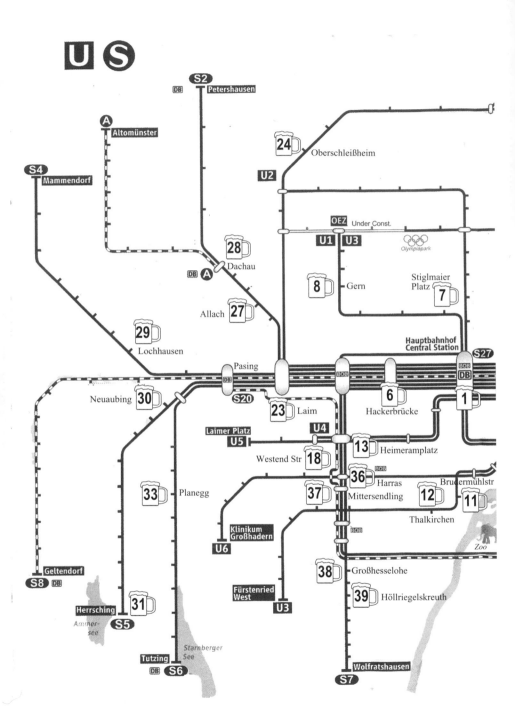

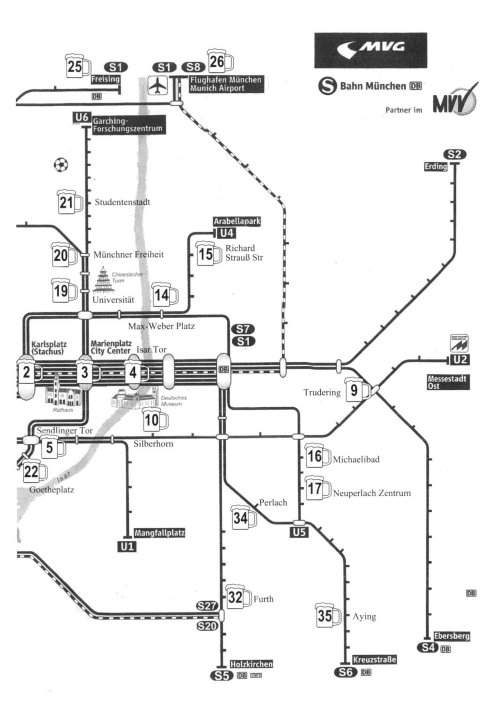

S-Bahn Lines - Primary Stops

S-1: Freising/Flughafen München • Laim
• Hauptbahnhof • Marienplatz • Ostbahnhof
S-2: Petershausen • Laim • Hauptbahnhof
• Marienplatz • Ostbahnhof • Berg am Laim • Erding
S-4: Mammendorf • Pasing • Laim • Hauptbahnhof
• Marienplatz • Ostbahnhof • Berg am Laim • Haar • Ebersberg
S-5: Herrsching • Pasing • Hauptbahnhof • Marienplatz • Ostbahnhof
• Giesing • Furth • Holzkirchen
S-6: Tutzing • Pasing • Hauptbahnhof • Marienplatz • Ostbahnhof
• Perlach • Aying • Kreuzstrasse
S-7: Wolfratshausen • Donnersbergbrücke • Hauptbahnhof
• Marienplatz • Ostbahnhof
S-8: Geltendorf • Aubing • Pasing • Hauptbahnhof • Marienplatz
• Ostbahnhof • Ismaning • Flughafen (Munich Airport)
S-27: Deisenhofen • Solln • Harras • Heimeranplatz • Pasing

U-Bahn Lines - Primary Stops

U-1: OEZ • Westfriedhof • Rotkreuzplatz
• Hauptbahnhof • Sendlinger Tor • Kolumbusplatz
• Mangfallplatz
U-2: Feldmoching • Dülferstraße • Hauptbahnhof
• Silberhorn Str. • Innsbrucker Ring • Messestadt Ost
U-3: Olympiazentrum • Münchner Freiheit • Odeonsplatz
• Marienplatz • Thalkirchen • Forstenrieder Allee • Fürstenried West
U-4: Arabellapark • Max-Weber-Platz • Odeonsplatz • Karlsplatz
(Stachus) Hauptbahnhof • Theresienwiese • Westendstraße
U-5: Laimer Pl. • Schwanthalerhöhe • Theresienwiese • Hauptbahnhof
• Karlsplatz (Stachus) • Odeonsplatz • Max-Weber-Pl. • Ostbahnhof
• Innsbrucker Ring • Neuperlach Süd
U-6: Garching-Forschungszentrum • Fröttmaning • Kieferngarten
• Münchener Freiheit • Marienplatz • Harras • Holzapfelkreuth
• Klinikum Großhadern

Beer Drinker's Etiquette

Maybe not manners, that would be going too far. Yet there are certain customs, traditions and standards of acceptable behavior that prevail in most Munich beer establishments. Here are a few of the more notable ones that may save the first-time visitor some unnecessary embarrassment.

Table Ownership

The notion of table ownership has been modified in Munich's crowded beer establishments. In fact, reservations are seldom taken and available seats are usually fair game, on a first-come-serve basis. Thus, new arrivals are welcome to join occupied tables where there are empty chairs by inquiring politely if the seat is "noch frei." Also, there is no obligation to carry on conversations with new-found table partners although after a couple beers it's a golden opportunity to break the ice. Chances are they're tourists, just like you.

The Stammtisch

An exception to the above is the *Stammtisch*. Clearly marked, usually with a sign or wrought-iron work, the Stammtisch is reserved for regulars. By definition, you are not a regular. Every beer hall and most beer gardens have one or two of these specially reserved tables. Even established patrons will assume nothing for granted and usually knock politely on the table as if to gain permission from the other Stammtisch regulars before sitting down.

Etiquette for Munich's beer drinkers is heavy on fun, but light on public drunkenness. Good news is there is much latitude between the two.

If you sit at a Stammtisch by mistake (it's easy to do since it's often the only table with any available seating) you'll soon know it. Others at the table will consider it their duty to instruct you in this quaint custom. Usually they do this by treating you as though you have a social disease. If you're so unlucky to sit in a particular favorite chair of an arriving regular he may sit in your lap. Again, look for the signs or be prepared to spend the evening talking war stories from a completely new point of view.

Self-Service or Not

If no one seems to want to wait on you, and you are not broken out in some form of skin rash, see if your table has a table cloth. If none, you may be sitting at a *selbstbedienung* (self-service) table where you will be expected to fend for yourself in securing your own beer and food. The roots of this custom go back several hundred years and are usually enforced in beer gardens more than in beer halls.

It seems that during the time of King Ludwig I, Munich's brew masters decided it would be a good idea to branch out. Instead of just selling their beer at indoor *bräustuben* they beseeched the monarch to allow them to establish outdoor gardens or *bierkellers*. (When you see the term "keller," by the way, it usually refers to the cellar

where the beer is kept cool and not where it is dispensed. Thus bierkellers are in reality beer gardens.) The king agreed to the idea and soon beer barons all over Munich were reaping huge profits through skyrocketing sales of their foamy product. In time, the poorer citizenry of Munich found that it was cheaper to bring their own lunch to picnic under the flourishing chestnut trees. Again, sensing a disappearing market, the beer-hall-now-garden proprietors petitioned their king to let them ban this practice that was cutting into their margins. In one of Munich's great compromises the king decreed brown-baggers would still be allowed, but only at tables without table cloths. That unwritten law exists today. Most beer gardens allow patrons to bring their own food but they must be content to sit at uncovered tables (resourceful Münchners bring their own table cloths).

In some of the more traditional beer gardens, you will be required — if opting to take the self-service route — to select your own liter glass mug from a wooden rack, wash it and then dutifully take it to the nearest *bier ausschank* to be filled. The Hirschgarten, Munich and Augustiner Bräu, Salzburg, Austria (see day trips) are examples of this still-surviving custom.

Paying the Bill and Tipping

A favorite and telling cartoon has a typical restaurant patron clutching desperately at the leg of a smug waiter with one hand, a fist full of money in the other, in a futile attempt to pay his check. Like

A sign at the Hirschgarten says it all: "Dear Guest, It's a tradition in Bavaria that all drinks in a beer garden must be bought from the Wirt. It's another tradition that in a genuine Munich beer garden, one is allowed to bring his own food or buy it from the Wirt. Please hold true to this Bavarian custom."

most caricatures, it exaggerates. But not much. For some reason, attracting the attention of a waiter in time to settle the bill invites the supreme effort. You announce your intentions by saying "zahlen, bitte." (Check, please.) Herr Ober will invariably answer with "sofort!", which loosely translated means "right away." Don't you believe it. "Sofort" sounds a lot like "go for it!" and that would be more to the point. Be patient.

If just ordering drinks, be prepared to pay when served. If ordering food along with beverages, the waiter or waitress will usually run you a tab.

Tipping is a relatively recent post-war innovation in Germany, but they learn real quick. Kellners automatically tack on a 15-18 percent "service" charge to the price of every item on the menu— beer, food, everything. The tip is now conveniently included, but unfortunately has little or no influence on the quality of the service. It's just there, and it's already added in when you pick up the check. Rounding up to the next Euro is the custom most Germans follow, although many will still pay the bill to the exact Eurocent without losing any sleep over it. What works for Münchners should work for you, too. An exception is taxis, where the driver expects a 10-15 percent tip.

Odds and Ends

When ordering from the menu, make sure all in your party know what they want. If anyone falters, the waiter will skip you and come back when all minds are made up, say in a half-hour or so. Don't be afraid to point, or order by the number. They're used to it.

Ask for an English menu if it helps and don't worry about any special, higher price for foreigners. Just doesn't happen in Munich.

Those neat, liter glass mugs make great souvenirs but there are guards at the door just waiting to nab anyone trying to liberate one. You can buy them in the gift shop or at the souvenir stand.

In an odd reversal of customs, the beer halls are closing when the lights are dimmed; open when the lights are at full blast.

Men, don't be shocked to find cleaning women permanently stationed in the restrooms. You'll get used to it, and they're usually more interested in reading their book. If you wash your hands and use a paper towel (and we hope you do) throw a couple 5 or 10 eurocent pieces on the plate. For women, the usual toilet fee is 20 eurocent. I don't know why it costs more.

If you know some German, try it. It's appreciated. On the same hand, don't expect everyone to know English. They won't.

If you can't meet the requirement to order a full liter of regular beer, you can side-step the provision by ordering a *Weizen*, or wheat beer. This style of beer always comes in a tall, half-liter, wide-mouthed glass.

Above all, remember that fun is tolerated and encouraged, public drunkenness is not.

The convenient way to handle a liter Maß of beer.

23

Beer

Beer. You may not know much about it, but you know what you like. And if you know Munich's beer, you already like it. There really isn't a whole lot of prior knowledge required to enjoy what's in the glass. But a couple of facts here and there add to the appreciation of Munich's best-known product and enforce its reputation as the world's premier beverage.

How Strong the Brew?

The short course on German beer begins with a comparison of potencies, because here is an area where confusion abounds. A popular myth ascribes German beer to be something akin to America's "White Lightnin'," a liquid tornado in a Mason jar. For example, folks new to Ger-

man beers will often estimate them to be two or three times the potency of their American, Canadian, or British liquid counterparts. The beer's heavy hops and malt content supports the illusion when a slightly bitter taste is mistaken for a higher alcohol content.

Adding to the confusion is the lack of international standards in measuring alcohol content of beers. Some countries measure alcohol by weight, others by volume. In Britain they gauge alcohol content by gravity. Thus, a "light beer" in Milwaukee would have 3.2 percent alcohol by weight (the infamous "three-two" beer of one's youth). But the same beer in Ottawa would measure 4 percent volume, and 1030 gravity in London (nobody really knows what that number means). Measuring alcohol content as a percentage of volume is the most common method, and this is what is seen on the label of most German beers. So, for purposes of comparison, alcohol contents of beers mentioned in this book are measured by volume. In the mishmash of conflicting data, it's a good yardstick to use.

Using that standard, most German brews, and 90 percent of those served in Munich, contain about 4.5-5 percent alcohol by volume, only slightly stronger than regular American and British beers ("bitters") that run around 4.4 percent. Not exactly the potent, fiery brew of popular mythology. Where the legend lingers is in the one-liter-fits-all approach to dispensing beer. In the typical Munich beer hall or beer garden, one orders a liter or nothing at all. Sometimes, in a restaurant or before 2 p.m. in the afternoon, half-liters are served. But normally it's the full ration, and any brew would seem industrial-strength when consumed in such quantities. Interestingly, only in Munich and a few other Bavarian cities are the compulsory beer servings so large. In the rest of Germany, the normal glass of beer is 3- to 4-tenths of a liter, or 10-13 ounces.

Not that there aren't strong German brews. There are some, but they are dispensed sparingly, and usually on special occasions. The best-known of the muscle beers are bock and doppelbock. Bock beers — also known as Maibock, Märzen or Oktoberfest beer — run a higher potency level of 5-6.5 percent. The highly concentrated Doppelbocks are a German beer-drinking secret weapon. They are most popular during Starkbierzeit, the strong beer season running from mid- to late March. Doppelbock beers run 7-8 percent alcohol and should be handled with care.

Why does it taste so good?

Although some have to acquire the taste, the most discriminating beer-drinker is usually won over to German beer with the first smooth and frothy gulp. The beer is just that good. Why? Two reasons: freshness and purity. The first attribute is due to the stubbornness of most German brewers to give in to the all-too-common industrial practice of pasteurization. The process, most often employed to sanitize raw milk products, requires hyper-heating the liquid long enough to kill all the bacteria. The treated beverage can then be shipped across long distances and remain stable, making it practical for over-seas markets. However, the longevity of the brew comes at a high price. "Authentic" German beers exported in this manner lose their distinctive qualities, since the pasteurization and use of preservatives kill the flavor. Also, exposure to light further damages the brew, giving it an acrid, excessively bitter and "skunky" taste.

And why pasteurize anyway? In Germany, where even the smallest village has its own brewery, "shipping" beer usually means delivering several kegs to the gasthaus or beer garden around the corner. Product equilibrium, when demand is matched by production, lets the brewer avoid having to resort to any manufacturing slight of hand to extend shelf life. Certainly, he would rather pour the beer down the drain than do anything that might alter the taste. As if that weren't enough, the integrity of the brew is further protected by a centuries old German law.

In 1516, Bavarian Duke Wilhelm IV decreed the world's oldest food purity law, the German *Reinheitsgebot*. A careful reading of the law reveals it was primarily concerned with fixing beer prices, a nagging public issue throughout German history. Yet, one small "rider" in the original royal ruling has had its impact over the centuries. It stipulated that beer will only consist of three ingredients: hops, barley malt, and water (yeast was still a scientific mystery). Of course, in 1516, that's about all there was, so it was no radical pronouncement. But while the price of beer has continued to rise over the centuries, the three-ingredient limit has not. To this day the purity law is in force, not just in Bavaria, but in all of Germany, including the reunited east German states. No chemicals, no preservatives, no sugars that don't occur naturally, no corn syrups or other sweeteners, and no substitute grains — just the three basic ingredients. (Special beers, such as Weizen or wheat beer, are allowed to be manufactured using alternative grains.) If there is any secret to the palate-pleasing quality of German beer, it is embodied in this ironclad law. It makes all the more impressive the ingenuity and creativity of German brewers who comply with the law and still produce distinctive, high quality beverages. It is both their trial and their salvation.

The purity law has been challenged on numerous occasions as making it almost impossible to compete in overseas markets. Thus, for export, the law has been relaxed, to the detriment of the product sold for foreign consumption. Yet, within Germany the law has been zealously guarded and each attempt to overturn it has been soundly rebuked by the German beer-drinking public.

As the beer brewing science has held fast to its three basic ingredients, the number of its practitioners has diminished. In 1790, Munich had 60 breweries. In 1819, stiff competition reduced the number to 35. By 1865 only 15 remained. Today, the "big six" dominate the Munich brewing scene: Augustinerbräu, Hacker-Pschorrbräu, Hofbräu, Löwenbräu, Paulaner-Thomasbräu, Spatenbräu. Belgian conglomerate Interbrew has winnowed the field once more with its 2003 purchase of the combined assets of Spaten and Löwenbräu. Hacker-Pschorr has also been absorbed by Paulaner. Still, the six distinct brands remain and combined they employ some 2400 people in the production of 123 million gallons of beer annually. Smaller breweries with avid followings if not huge national distributorships include Ayingerbräu, Schneiderbräu, Forschungsbrauerei, and also Weihenstephan.

"Gimmeabeer"

Ask simply for a beer in Munich and you will get a *Helles*, or pale-colored lager beer. It will have a heavy head of foam and come in a one-liter glass mug. It will have an aromatic, sweet, malty taste and be less bitter than other German beers.

The standard liter Maß of Münchner-style golden lager is the preferred brew in the city's thriving beer halls.

26

It will be cold, filling and thirst-quenching. Dieters take note that it will contain the equivalent of 400 calories, less than milk or most fruit juices. It will be a popular style of a particular type of beer that draws its distinctive characteristics from the way it is brewed.

In Munich or elsewhere, there are basically two categories of beer: bottom brewed and top brewed. This refers to beers where the yeast rises to the top, or settles to the bottom, during the fermentation process. Historically, the top brewing method came first. The biggest problem with this style of brewing was the instability of the beer. It would go bad quickly if it were not kept in a cold place. Thus, brewing was somewhat seasonal, with most production occurring during the winter and spring months. Then the brew was stored in cold cellars or alpine caves, in sufficient quantities to last through the hot and thirsty summer and fall months. In essence, this is how the *bierkeller* was born. The cellar was where the beer was kept; the garden where it was sold and drunk. Somehow the two have become interchangeable and a bierkeller in Munich is likely a beer garden whether or not there is a cellar on the premises. Shade-bearing chestnut trees were added to keep the cellar that much cooler and the tradition has stuck.

While the beer was stored for long periods in a cold environment, observers noted that after the yeast settled to the bottom the brew would keep indefinitely. Eventually a method was devised in Pilsen (today Czech Republic) and Vienna to brew the beer from the beginning with the yeast on the bottom. Pilsener and Lager (from the German word *Lager*, to store) beers were developed in this way and today they dominate the German (and majority of the European) beer market.

A good lager beer is stored for one to three months while it matures. The lagering is carried out at about 32-36 degrees Fahrenheit. The result is a clean-tasting, golden colored, thirst-quenching brew that abounds in Germany and in most beer-drinking countries around the globe. It's the most popular of all brews and the one you'll get if you simply ask for a beer anywhere in Munich.

A Spectrum of Beers

Among the bottom-brewed Munich beers in evidence, besides the Helles variety served everywhere, are the Pilsener, Dunkeles, Bock, Doppelbock, and so-called Diät Pils and Leicht beers.

Pilsener

The Pilsener, or "Pils," is a type of lager that is similar in color and texture to the helles style, but slightly more bitter due to the higher amount of hops used for flavoring. Pils is by far the most popular beer in central and northern Germany. In Munich it is less frequently served and is primarily found in special "Pilsbars" that often resemble small, corner neighborhood pubs. The secret of a proper Pils, always with its distinctive whipped-cream head and served in a thin-stemmed wide-mouthed glass, is the time it takes to pour it. The process consists of filling a glass with 90 percent foam and then waiting patiently for the suds to turn to golden beer. Then more foam is poured in, followed by more waiting. Finally, when ready, the beer is served with a small circular paper doily laced around the base. German Pils lovers will tell you it takes a full seven minutes to pour one properly. It's one reason first-time Pils drinkers are certain the bartending crew has gone on break and totally forgotten their order. Pilseners run about 5 percent alcohol by volume. Although Pils is king of beers in other German regions, Münchner-style-beer lovers who venture forth can still have their *helles* and drink it too by ordering an "export." Unfortunately, export in this case has nothing to do with it being available outside the country, but it is essentially the same beer served in Munich.

Dunkeles (dark Münchner)

Dunkeles, or "dark" beer, also comes served in a one-liter glass mug and is a function of taste. It is still basically a lager, bottom-brewed beer, but with a higher concentration of malt. The burnt malt used in the brewing process gives it its dark brown color (it resembles a cola soft drink). Outside the city, it is often referred to as a Münchner. Despite its heavy color, it is relatively weak, running around 4.3 percent alcohol.

Bock Beer

Outside of Germany, "bock" is a term often mistakenly used to refer to any and all dark beers, such as the Münchner style mentioned above. Within the country, especially in Munich, it is the general term for a strong beer, usually pale in color like a helles (there is a dark variety as well), that runs around 6-7 percent alcohol. The name is derived from its city of origin, Einbeck, in Lower Saxony. Since "bock" means billy-goat in German, it is commonly associated in commercial advertising with the symbol of the goat, and the astrological sign of Capricorn. Bock beer is a staple brew during those special highly celebrated festive occasions, such as the March Starkbierzeit and the fall Oktoberfest. Bock beer is strong. Doppelbock is stronger still.

Doppelbock

High-calibered and truly potent, doppelbock beer is the most formidable of Munich's beer arsenal. Approaching a barley wine in its consistency and punch, doppelbock was first brewed by the Paulaner brewery and marketed as its world-famous Salvator brand. The -ator suffix has been adopted by every super-strength beer in Munich (see section on Paulaner Keller). Doppelbock is the liquid fuel for the city's strong beer craziness days. The high alcohol content — a minimum of 7.5 percent and usually more — dominates the taste of this brew. The strongest of the strain is *eisbock,* alluding to the method used in concentrating the alcohol. The beer is reduced in temperature to below freezing. Since alcohol freezes at a lower temperature than water, the liquid that is siphoned off is much higher in alcohol than occurs naturally during the fermentation process. The synthetically high 13 percent alcohol content of eisbock puts it in a league with distilled spirits. A shot of *schnaps* will do essentially the same job.

Diät Pils (Pronounced 'Dee-Ate')

This is a low-salt and low-carbohydrate beer for diabetics. It has little to do with weight reduction. The 6 percent alcohol content of Diät Pils makes it higher in both potency and calories than regular Pils.

Leicht Beers

Taking the lead from marketing successes in fitness-conscious America, several Munich breweries have begun producing *leicht* or "light" versions of their most popular helles beers. Paulaner, Spaten, and Ayinger currently market reduced-alcohol (about 3.5 percent) beers that retain most of the taste but "40 percent less calories and alcohol" than their regular beers. The lower-octane brews are catching on quickly, and the trend will likely lead to all the city's major breweries following suit. Most Munich breweries now sell a still-taste-worthy nonalcoholic (0.5 percent or less) beer that can be drunk as is or mixed with a regular beer as a "spacer" to help deal with the high-volume tendency of Munich's beer-dispensing industry. Weihenstephan, for example, has recently introduced a non-alc beer that's especially tasty.

Top-brewed beers in Munich come in three types, Alt, Kölsch, and Weizen.

Alt

Alt is the German answer to British ale. The name refers to the old-style brewing practice that gives this beer a bitter, hop-accentuated taste. Copper colored and far less carbonated than common lagers, alt, an ale, is not nearly as popular in Munich as it is up north. This brew is an unusual style for Bavaria that appeals to a small but devoted following among the city's beer drinkers. The beer is generally only slightly weaker than lagers, with about a 4.5-5 percent alcohol content.

Kölsch

Kölsch is a Munich import. The characteristic beer of Cologne (Köln in German) from which it derives its name, Kölsch is a lightly carbonated, almost flat, beer that is extremely pale in color. The beer usually runs about 4.6 percent alcohol, and has a mild, lactic taste.

Weizen, Weiss

Weizen, or wheat, beer is the most popular non-lager beer in Munich, probably in Germany. Weizen, often called *Weiss* (white) beer, is a favorite on hot days when it is consumed with a slice of lemon in its special half-liter, tall, vase-shaped glass.

The amber-colored beer is highly carbonated and its wheat base gives it a light, dry quality that makes it especially popular as a summer refreshment. At upward of 6 percent alcohol, its hidden potency will sneak up on the unsuspecting beer drinker. When Weizen beer is mixed half-and-half with lemon-lime soda, it's called *Russiches* and is available at a few of Munich's most populated beer gardens (Chinesischer Turm and Leiberheim, for example).

This 1890s mother and daughter team knew how to deliver when it came to keeping a steady stream of Hofbräuhaus customers fully supplied with one of Munich's most venerable lager beers.

29

Munich's 'Big Six'

The "Big Six" is technically more like the "Big Four." In 1997, Spaten and Löwenbräu merged into one. Belgian brewing giant InBev (formerly Interbrew) swallowed the dual entity in 2003. Along the way, Paulaner bought Hacker-Pschorr Bräu, which itself had been the result of a 1984 merger and hyphenation of two of Munich's best-known beers. Today, Schörghuber Group and Dutch Heineken own the Paulaner and Hacker-Pschorr brands. OK, that's out of the way, because you would hardly know anything had changed at all among Munich's six largest breweries.

And that's just the way new ownership appears to want it. Economies of scale notwithstanding, the mergers and consolidation will certainly add to the corporate bottom line when it comes to associated costs of advertising, distribution, bottling, and even brewing. But most if not all of these corporate transitions are invisible to the consumer, and when you come to Munich and hoist a Maß, that's you. You won't taste the changes. So, we'll continue to talk about the Big Six: Augustiner, Hofbräu, Paulaner, Hacker-Pschorr, Löwenbräu, and Spaten. They still employ some 2,400 people and brew more than 123 million gallons of beer each year. They're so closely intertwined with the history of this town, their stories — which haven't been co-opted by consolidation — are a chronicle of Munich itself.

Augustiner-Bräu

(Augustiner-Bräu Wagner KG)
Landsberger Str. 35
80339 München
Tel: (089) 519940
Fax: (089) 51994111

Augustiner-Bräu got its start like most Munich beers with the same folks who brought you early morning prayers, vows of silence, and selective abstinence. The Augustiner Brothers — not a traveling highwire act — were monks with time on their hands. Busy abstaining from life's more hedonistic temptations, the brothers still had time to quaff a few mugs of suds, once they figured out how to make it.

And break the code they did, because as early as 1328, there is evidence beer was being brewed in the then-cloistered edifice in the Marienplatz where Augustiner Großgaststätte serves Augustiner Edelstoff to this day. The medieval startup had a close call when, that same year, a major fire destroyed fully a third of Munich, but thankfully spared the brothers' brewing works, making Augustiner one of the city's oldest surviving breweries. In 1803 secularization took the brewery out of the hands of the monks and gave it to the state, but the name still remained. The newly privatized brewery moved to a new location in 1817 and in 1829 was purchased by Anton and Therese Wagner, where it remains in their family to this day. The brewery moved again to its current location on Landsberger Straße and was heavily damaged during bombing raids of World War II. Completely rebuilt, the building is a protected historical monument today. Augustiner is renowned as the purveyor of Munich's best beer and its secret may lie nearly 700 feet underground where the brewery draws its water from its own private well. Especially pure and sweet, the water used to make Augustiner beer is at least one reason the beer is so good. The *Reinheitsgebot* is another, but in the case of Augustiner and the other major Munich brands, there is truth to the saying that "there is no such thing as a bad Munich beer."

Hofbräu

(Staatliches Hofbräuhaus in München)
Postfach 81 808
81829 München
Tel: 089/92-105-0
Fax: 089/90-64-26

Everybody knows of the "Haus", but without "Hofbräu" the beer, the Hofbräuhaus would probably be just another walk-up in the middle of Munich. While Augustiner has its religious roots and Hacker-Pschorr its commercial beginnings, Hofbräu has a royal connection. It began with a Duke, Wilhelm V, who founded the Hofbräuhaus and brewery in 1589. The duke wasn't really interested in expansion, only wanting to produce enough for local consumption — a few brewskies for the royal court after a hard day of deer hunting and peasant baiting. And even then, it was to replace the continuing and expensive importation of strong Einbeck beer from Hannover that had proved effective in keeping his royal retinue happy. They remained contented and loyal with the locally brewed variety under their belt, but never quite forgot that wonderful Einbeck beer of yore. So, Hofbräu gave fermented birth to the first "Einbock" strong beer in 1614 and maintained sole production rights for some 200 years. It's popularly called "Maibock" today because it is brewed and sold beginning the month of May. The *Königlisches* (royal) brewery became a state-run operation in 1939, but the logo — with the HB adorned by a crown — still alludes to its regal 16th century beginnings. The brewery had been moved to Innere Wiener Straße (site of today's Hofbräu Keller) in 1896 and later relocated to its current location in Riem. Soon thereafter the HB brand underwent a major consolidation to reduce a confusing 14 different beer varieties to the popular three of today: HB Altmünchener Hellgold (light-colored lager), HB Altmünchener Dunkelgold (dark), and Münchener Kindl Weissbier (wheat). Of course, HB still produces its seasonal beers as well: Maibock, Oktoberfestbier and Weihnachtsfestbier (Christmas brew).

Hacker-Pschorr Bräu

(Hacker-Pschorr Bräu GmbH)
Hoch Str. 75
81541 München
Tel: (089) 51060
Fax: (089) 5106333

Consolidation marches on, and now the Schörghuber Group and Dutch Heineken have bought up the consolidated Paulaner and Hacker-Pschorr Bräu brands, although you won't know it when you taste the brew. Thus far, the brewing processes remain independent and we aren't looking for a Paulaner-Hacker-Pschorr Bräu any time soon.

The first merger — around a couple of decades ago when Hackerbräu and Pschorrbräu consolidated to one — was actually a reenactment of the early history of both brands. The two breweries were actually one and the same in the early 1800s, under the banner of Joseph Pschorr, once considered the king of Munich's brewers. Pschorr's sons later went their separate ways and divided the brewing business into Pschorr and Hacker wings. The Hacker history actually predated Pschorr. That side of the brewing family reaches all the way back to the 14th century. When Joseph Pschorr married into the family in 1793 (see write-up on Altes Hackerhaus) the ambitious and energetic Joseph put the entire family business at the very center of Munich's entrepreneurial map and by 1820 it was considered the premier suds purveyor among Munich's 50 or so brewing houses. Pschorr passed along a veritable brewing empire to his sons Georg and Matthias in 1834. Georg headed Pschorr; Matthias took Hacker. Both did well and both brews prospered.

The two brothers developed what was by most accounts a "friendly competition" between their two businesses. Since Munich was more than happy to make room for both quality brands, this may have well been an affordable luxury. Eventually, Matthias Pschorr took Hacker public in 1881, sold its stock, and remained on the board of directors. He died in 1900 without ever marrying and left no heirs.

Pschorrbräu remained a family enterprise for four generations, and only became a public company in 1922. Of course, the family influence and control remained in both companies.

This was never more apparent than in 1944 when, after a bombing raid shut down Pschorr's brewing works, Hacker allowed the Pschorr family to brew twice a week in its still functioning plant. Blood runs thicker than beer, in a case like that. It was certainly a harbinger of what was to come. The cooperation in hard times led to the two breweries pooling their resources even while business was good.

In 1972, the two companies merged as Hacker-Pschorr Bräu. And a few years ago Paulaner bought the combined brand. Now they're further consolidated under Schörghuber and Heineken.

But Hacker-Pschorr stands alone as one of Munich's six brands that still insists on using wooden kegs in selected pubs and restaurants. The wood containers add a richness to the brew, even after it leaves the brewery. Hacker-Pschorr was also one of the first to begin brewing a light (as in lower calorie and alcohol) *Weizen* or wheat beer.

Löwenbräu
(Löwenbräu AG & Co)
Nymphenburger Str. 7
80335 München
Tel: (089) 52000
Fax: (089) 5200412

At last, a German beer you've heard of. It's good ol' Löwenbräu, that pseudo-German beer that Miller Brewing Company produced under license in the U.S. for decades. The good news is that the Germans have confiscated that license and taken it back. Now when you pick up a six pack, it really will be imported. Maybe next time you should ask for "Ler-vin-broi" because that's the way it's pronounced in Munich. And guess what, it's a good beer — and what Munich beer isn't? — but it's hardly considered to be the cream of the keg by everyday Münchners. The biggest news of all, though, is that Löwenbräu merged with Spaten a few years ago, and in 2003 the Belgian brewing giant InBev (formerly Interbrew) picked up the assets of both companies. Thankfully, the new owners have enough sense not to mess up a good thing. They still leave the brewing of both brands to those German brew masters who know best. Lift a glass of Löwenbräu (or Spaten for that matter) and you won't know the front office has shifted from lederhosen to lace.

New ownership aside, no one can take away this beer's long history. The house at 17 Löwengrube Straße was brewing beer as early as 1324, the first documented connection with the name Löwenbräu. And a pub "Zur Löwen" was serving up brews by 1383. Ursula Lange, a widow of an early Löwenbräu brewer, had Daniel in the Lion's Den painted on her brewery building just after the 30 Years War. Another woman, Maria Theresia Gege became the first known female brew master (Löwenbräuin) working for Löwenbräu in 1747. In 1818, the brewery was given a major boost when Georg Brey, a renowned Munich brewer, took over the reigns of Löwenbräu. He built the brand into what it is today, ubiquitous in every way and an excellent mug of beer, even by Munich's high standards. The key to it all was Brey's decision to move the brewery to its current location on Nymphenburger Straße in 1883. With room to grow and prosper, the company and its product expanded rapidly, eventually overcoming stalwarts like Pschorrbräu and Hackerbräu, at least in terms of customer base. It figured that Löwenbräu would be the one to tap the foreign and overseas markets. The first bottles crossed the Bavarian border around the mid-1800s and by 1900 Americans were enjoying their first imported taste of the "Lion's Brew." Löwenbräu survived heavy bombardment during World War II and rose from the ashes to brew again at the Nymphenburger site. The postwar period ushered in a flourishing export business. Internationally, Löwenbräu is the best-known brand of German beer, with Becks a close second. No matter where you buy your next bottle of Löwenbräu — at the beer garden on Nymphenburger Straße or your local Winn-Dixie back home — expect the real thing. If you're young enough, a license may still be needed to buy it, but there is some satisfaction knowing that a license is no longer being issued to brew it.

Paulanerbräu

(Paulaner-Salvator-
Thomasbräu AG)
Hoch Straße 75
81541 München
Tel: (089) 480050
Fax: (089) 48005409

Certainly a contender for best-tasting beer in Munich is Paulaner. Although a popular brew, Paulanerbräu is often mistaken as three different breweries: Paulaner, Thomasbräu, and Salvator. (Read about "Salvator Starkbier" and the interesting way it got its name in the chapter on Paulaner Keller.) Now you can add Hacker-Pschorr Bräu to the confusion, since Paulaner has taken over control of that brewery and technically the whole enchilada is owned by Schörghuber Group and Dutch Heineken.

But let's keep it simple. Suffice to say that Paulaner, through its Salvator brand, is the premier supplier of one of the world's strongest beers. Paulaner the drink-it-every-day typical Münchner lager, however, is much less potent and very good tasting. They also brew a wheat beer, light, dark and unfiltered and an alcohol-free beer under the Paulaner name. All of it is excellent beer, thanks to several centuries worth of brewing experience.

Paulaner's story, like other Munich breweries, has its beginnings rooted in local lore. In fact, in a city where it sometimes seems more impressive to have been first several centuries ago than first today, Paulaner weighs in with a reputation for brewing the first beer in the Neudeck monastery in 1629. The stronger "Salvator" beers arrived a couple of decades later. The brewing business really took off after secularization and in the case of Paulanerbräu privatization in 1806. An early pioneer in the Munich brewing arts was a Paulaner master named Franz Xavier Zacherl. He was the one who introduced steam-powered production and fashioned large cooling cellars to house vast quantities of brew.

Following Zacherl's era, the Paulaner brewery incorporated as a publicly owned company in 1886 and in 1899 became known formally as the Aktiengesellschaft Paulanerbräu (zum Salvatorkeller). That just about covered it all until Thomasbräu was added to the name (what's another hyphen among friends?) after merging with a smaller brewery in 1928.

The historical footnote Thomasbräu added to the company's history is worth noting. In 1895 the Thomas Brothers produced a light-colored pilsener in what is today the Paulaner Bräuhaus which would become the first Munich-style lager that is served everywhere in Munich today. And that is a major feat that should certainly be remembered by beer drinkers everywhere. Today, Paulaner-Salvator-Thomasbräu is the largest brewery in Bavaria and one of the most modern. The main brewing plant sits across the road from the inviting Paulaner Keller on the "Nockherberg" hill in Munich's "Au" section. This is home to the annual Starkbier celebration which ranks as one of the city's favorites.

Spatenbräu

(Spaten-Franziskaner-Bräu GmbH)
Mars Str. 48
80335 München
Tel: (089) 51220
Fax: (089) 5122401

Blue-collar brewing, that's what Spatenbräu personifies. Although they merged with Löwenbräu and were then absorbed by Interbrew, they're still one of Munich's Big Six brands, for sure. But ask a Münchner to name all six and they'll get five right and then stumble on Spaten. It's not Spatenbräu's fault. They brew a great beer and have been doing so for — you guessed it — a few hundred years. It's just that someone had to be first, and, well, someone had to be Spaten. They're the one you root for, and an underdog if you could consider one of the largest breweries in the world's beer-making capital anything close to an under-achiever.

Their pedigree is without question because Spaten is associated with perhaps the most famous brewing family Munich has ever produced: Gabriel Sedlmayr and his sons Josef and Gabriel II. The Spaten name goes back much further than the Sedlmayrs, to 1397 when records showed the existence of a brewery owned by a Herr Spaeth who was busy producing his Oberspathbräu. The name was modified slightly into the Spaten that exists today. However, the name didn't ensure its fame. That required Gabriel Sedlmayr who beginning in 1807 took it from a run-down brewery that was ranked a lowly 52 on the Munich brewing pecking-order list (amazingly Münchners ac-tually kept track of those things) and built it into the city's third-largest brand (behind Hacker and Pschorr) by the time of his death in 1839. Sedlmayr's sons Gabriel II and Josef built a new facility in the spot where it exists today on Mars Straße. Josef then set off on his own and bought Leistbräu and later the Franziskaner breweries.

Much like the Pschorr brothers, the Sedlmayrs were also able to prosper and expand in a business environment of peaceful coexistence. Josef made local beer history when he introduced the first amber-colored Märzen-style beer in the Schottenhamel tent at the 1872 Oktoberfest. Thus, Oktoberfest beer was born. Gabriel was also busy making his mark. His work is one reason Spaten is associated with the science of beer and brewing. In perhaps his most famous innovation, Gabriel developed a cooling process that aided the bottom-fermenta-tion method that distinguishes lagers from ales and gives Munich beer its distinctive taste and flavor. In 1876 he built the first German brewery that incorporated a va-porization system. After World War I, the two Sedlmayr Brothers combined their massive brewing houses under one cor-porate roof. Finally, in 1972, the trans-formation was complete when the Spaten brewery was incorporated as a publicly owned, family-run business. Maybe least known of the Big Six, but certainly no less appreciated than any one of the city's fine beers, Spaten continues to brew its share of Munich's liquid gold.

Flughafen (Munich Airport)

Exiting customs, you'll find Airbräu in the open Airport Center area, between terminals 1 and 2, just before you reach the entrance to the S-Bahn station. Look for the MAC signs. Arriving from S-Bahn 1, take the escalator up to the MAC and find Airbräu on your left.

Fresh off the plane and fresh out of the Keg: Airbräu brewery, restaurant and beer garden offer something for every visitor arriving in Munich, including house-brewed beers, a full Bavarian menu and even breakfast and a Sunday brunch.

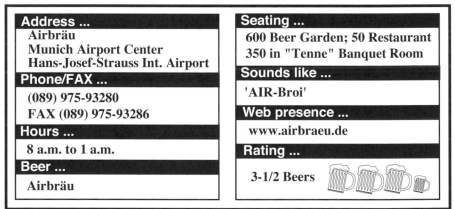

Address ...	Seating ...
Airbräu Munich Airport Center Hans-Josef-Strauss Int. Airport	600 Beer Garden; 50 Restaurant 350 in "Tenne" Banquet Room
Phone/FAX ...	**Sounds like ...**
(089) 975-93280 FAX (089) 975-93286	'AIR-Broi'
Hours ...	**Web presence ...**
8 a.m. to 1 a.m.	www.airbraeu.de
Beer ...	**Rating ...**
Airbräu	3-1/2 Beers

Airbräu

When it comes to Munich beer establishments, we only ask three things: They're convenient, they're good, and, well, they're cheap. We'll usually settle for two out of three, but we get the entire menu when it comes to Airbräu, smack dab in the middle of Munich's airport, Franz-Josef-Strauss International. That last virtue — cheap — is a little hard to believe in an area best known for holding customers captive to € 6 sandwiches and € 7 beers. But there it is, a place serving house-brewed beers for the miserly price of around € 2.10 per half-liter.

Our first indication we had better take a closer look at this place, still in its first decade of service, was the noticeable reverse exodus that seemed underway. More people were flocking to Airbräu from the in-terminal S-bahn 1 line than were leaving to get on with their European vacations. A local *Kneipe* inside an airport is a bit rare, but that's what Airbräu has become.

And why not? There's plenty to attract in- and out-of-towners to keep returning here: Three excellent beers brewed right on the premises, a large and inviting beer garden, a full-service restaurant with plenty of traditional Bavarian fare and then the occasional live music offering to keep everyone entertained.

The on-site brewery is turning out an unfiltered *helles* style lager, called FliegerQuell, running around 5.2 % alcohol, as well as a *hefeweizen* wheat beer, Kumulus, at around 5.4%. They also brew a seasonal brew that could range from a dark *dunkel* to an *Oktoberfest*, to a *doppelbock* they call, naturally, Aviator, that will push nearly 8%.

The restaurant offers a full menu of Bavarian dishes, with most entrees less than € 10. There's also plenty of snack food to go along with that beer, like *Obazda* (traditional, spiced-cheese spread), *Brezen* (pretzels), and cheese and sausage salads. For those on an extreme budget — or diet — there's always the "hangman's lunch" — a glass of tap water, a bread roll and a cigarette for € 0.65. (Obviously these folks don't take themselves too seriously.)

The restaurant and beer garden are in the open concourse area between terminals 1 and 2 called the Munich Airport Center or MAC. If arriving Munich by plane, you should look for MAC signs or those directing you to the S-Bahn terminal. Airbräu is just to the right of the S-Bahn escalator as you depart the terminal. In reverse, if arriving by S-Bahn 1 (last stop, "Flughafen München"), look for the Terminal 1 and 2 sign and take the escalator up, directly to the beer garden.

Airbräu is a great way to start or even end a Munich vacation, but it also adds terrific value to a day trip to the beer gardens in Oberschleißheim, or Freising (Weihenstephan and Plantage). We welcome the idea of an economical beer garden serving fresh beer and reaping in customers instead of ripping them off. Airbräu takes off with 3-1/2 beers.

Altes
Hackerhaus

Hauptbahnhof
U-Bahn 1 or 2 to
Sendlinger Tor.
Sendlinger Tor
Walk up Sendlinger Str. as
shown.

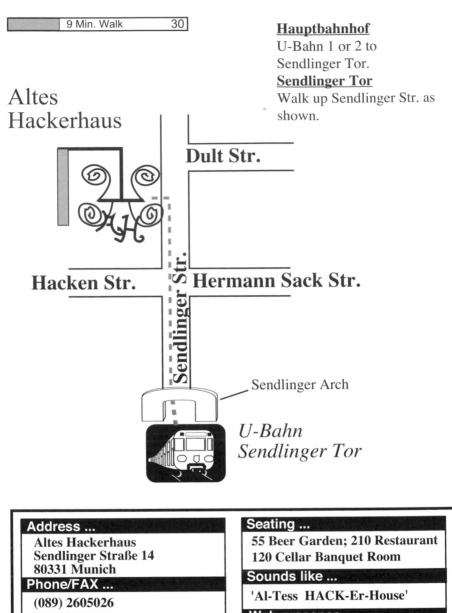

Dult Str.

Hacken Str.   **Sendlinger Str.**   **Hermann Sack Str.**

Sendlinger Arch

U-Bahn
Sendlinger Tor

Address ...	Seating ...
Altes Hackerhaus Sendlinger Straße 14 80331 Munich	55 Beer Garden; 210 Restaurant 120 Cellar Banquet Room
Phone/FAX ...	**Sounds like ...**
(089) 2605026 FAX (089) 2605027	'Al-Tess HACK-Er-House'
Hours ...	**Web presence ...**
9 a.m. to 12 midnight	www.hackerhaus.de
Beer ...	**Rating ...**
Hacker-Pschorr Bräu	3 Beers

Altes Hackerhaus

The "altes" or "old" in its name indicates a deep appreciation of its past, and Altes Hackerhaus certainly has that. In fact, a room of this ancient edifice is dedicated to the memory, the life and times of one of the city's oldest brewing families, Hacker-Pschorr. An entire wall is taken up with a mural depicting the historic family tree. There's hardly room to depict the full story of this traditional Bavarian restaurant and beer garden. It must have been a welcome sight to thirsty travelers arriving at Munich's back door in 1738 when Brewer Simon Hacker (thus "Hacker-Bräu") decided to post his menu. Just inside Munich's southern gate, Sendlinger Tor, the offering included fresh beer brewed on the premises, and a growing list of late-Renaissance munchies that would have oiled the sandals of any wayfaring stranger.

Josef Pschorr

A Hacker daughter, Therese, expanded the family business by marrying one Josef Pschorr in 1793 (thus "Hacker-Pschorr-Bräu"). The ancestral digs handed down among the Hackers and Pschorrs, father to son, uncle to nephew, blossomed and the centralized beer outlet remained a Munich fixture for another quarter century. In 1825, the brewery portion burnt to the ground, but the family living quarters survived, though badly damaged. By 1831, the house was completely rebuilt. Beer was brewed elsewhere, and the *brauhaus* continued operation, in much the same manner as today.

Altes Hackerhaus is on Sendlinger Straße, about midway between Sendlinger Tor and the Neues Rathaus (the one with the Glockenspiel). Munich's own version of Fleet Street, the Sendlinger Straße also houses the editorial headquarters of most of the city's major newspapers. Inside the restaurant's vaulted-arch corridors, journalists rub elbows and exchange *Prosits* (toasts) with well-heeled Münchners who frequent the district's nearby jewelry shops and expensive chic haberdasheries.

A local refuge of sorts, it's filled with old-timey atmosphere and ancient memorabilia adorning the walls. Reasonable prices and a small but comfortable courtyard beer garden round out this establishment. Worth mentioning is the retractable roof that guarantees a dry beer garden regardless of the weather. It's a place to relax and enjoy a good meal, in a convenient location that is just around the corner from the Marienplatz and Munich's main pedestrian zone. Wirt and proprietor Paul Pongratz maintains authenticity throughout the restaurant. It shows on the menu with traditional Bavarian dishes served in a quiet setting amid the hubbub of one of the town's busier commercial areas. Maybe not a full day venue, but definitely worth a visit, especially during a leisurely walk through Munich's historic quarter. It gets a respectable 3 beers.

Hauptbahnhof
U-Bahn 4 or 5 to Heimeranplatz
Heimeranplatz
Exit to Bus 133(to "Forstenrieder Allee"); Take Bus 133 to Siegenburger Str.
Siegenburger Str.
From bus stop, walk down stairs to Siegenburger Str., past sports arena to beer garden.

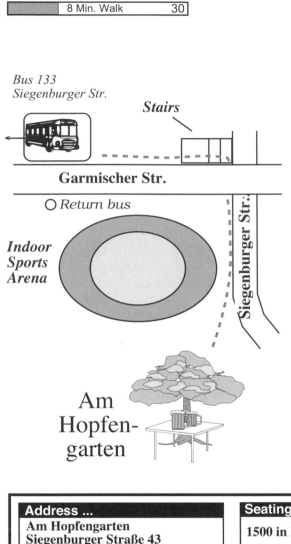

*Bus 133
Siegenburger Str.*

Stairs

Garmischer Str.

○ *Return bus*

Siegenburger Str.

*Indoor
Sports
Arena*

Am
Hopfen-
garten

Address ...	Seating ...
Am Hopfengarten **Siegenburger Straße 43** **81373 Munich**	**1500 in Beer Garden**
Phone/FAX ...	**Sounds like ...**
(089) 7608846 **FAX (089) 76991624**	**'Ahm-HOPE-Fin-Gart-In'**
Hours ...	**Web presence ...**
10 a.m. to 10:30 p.m.	**www.hopfen-garten.de**
Beer ...	**Rating ...**
Löwenbräu	**3-1/2 Beers**

Am Hopfengarten

Remember that teenage girl next door with the freckles and the braces on her teeth? Well, look at her now, she's all grown up and queen of the prom. Am Hopfengarten, in West Park's eastern fringe, is yet another reminder that good things come to those who wait. Patience and more than two decades of maturity have brought plenty of improvements. The chestnut trees, barely providing a place to hang your hat when Am Hopfengarten was first listed in the Beer Drinker's Guide's first edition, are now grown and their foliage spread over the entire beer garden like a giant green umbrella. The beer garden fits rather well in the neatly manicured setting of rolling hillocks and man-made lakes.

Shade is no longer in short supply as it once was in the first few years after the West Park was developed for the International Botanical Exhibit of 1983. One of the best things Am Hopfengarten has going for it is its association with one of Munich's most renowned Gasthaus families, Haberl. As expected the quality standard is relatively high here. Thomas Weigert ably runs the beer garden today and has added a wooden dance floor along with live music every Thursday and Sunday, 6 p.m. and 4 p.m., respectively. Am Hopfengarten sports a self-service fast-food (*schmankerl*) stand completely rebuilt a few years ago whose speciality — in addition to good Löwenbräu beer — is some of the meatiest spareribs this side of a Texas barbecue. The chef isn't afraid to experiment either, and tasty brew fare like chicken wings, chili, and even crab cocktails are found on the *Tageskarte* (daily specials).

The beer garden includes a large children's play area that should keep the kiddies entertained for hours. All the more lucrative for the grown-ups to enjoy a relaxing day with a cold *Maß* (liter mug) of Munich's most prolific beer and some of the best (and cheapest!) take-out food in town.

With a little help from nature and nurture, Am Hopfengarten is constantly improving to meet Munich's high standards for such beer-dispensing emporia. It's certainly worth checking out and has earned an upgraded 3-1/2 beers in this sixth edition.

Am Hopfengarten has grown an abundance of shade to go along with its excellent reputation.

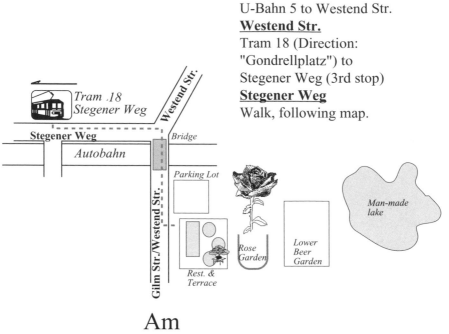

Hauptbahnhof
U-Bahn 5 to Westend Str.
Westend Str.
Tram 18 (Direction:
"Gondrellplatz") to
Stegener Weg (3rd stop)
Stegener Weg
Walk, following map.

Am Rosengarten

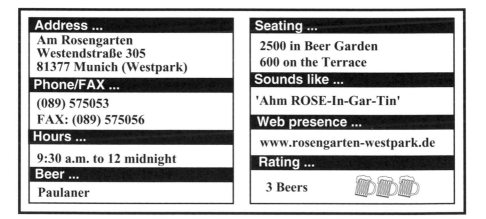

Address ...	Seating ...
Am Rosengarten Westendstraße 305 81377 Munich (Westpark)	2500 in Beer Garden 600 on the Terrace
Phone/FAX ...	**Sounds like ...**
(089) 575053 FAX: (089) 575056	'Ahm ROSE-In-Gar-Tin'
Hours ...	**Web presence ...**
9:30 a.m. to 12 midnight	www.rosengarten-westpark.de
Beer ...	**Rating ...**
Paulaner	3 Beers

Am Rosengarten

A m Rosengarten has always had this split personality: never quite sure whether to cater to Munich's upper crust or the blue-collar, brew-in-the-afternoon crowd . It may all have been the result of the 1983 International Botanical Exhibition, which really gave this place its start. One can imagine a convention of thirsty horticultural designers descending on Munich's spacious West Park with a truckload of bulbs and several kegs of beer. "OK, let's put the rose garden here, right next to the lake," must have been the plan. "Now, where to put the beer?"

The welcome answer became Am Rosengarten, a two-tiered beer garden with a little something for everybody. The upper restaurant has a terrace designed in triangular red brick. Lots of umbrellas provide the shade over a series of bedecked tables serviced by bow-tied waiters. The glass-enclosed restaurant itself is decorated in a modern, somewhat sterile varnished wood style. The food is

The portal to Am Rosengarten's upper-crust eatery.

hearty, although a little expensive, and the ambience invites more the "Kaffee and Küchen Klatch" folks than the down-and-dirty suds for lunch bunch.

No matter. Just below the terraced haute cuisine centrum, and a (no foolin') rose garden with a reported 100 varieties of living corsages, is a neat, clean and exceedingly welcome beer garden in the traditional mode (even a May pole). Benches and tables under the mandatory stand of chestnut trees mark this analgesic annex. There's a beer and *schmankerl* outlet, manned by folks wearing Levis, where you can help yourself to brew by the liter, smoked fish on a stick, and Bavarian delicacies by the paper-plateload. Predictably, the prices are more conventional and the gastronomic fare no less filling.

With more than 25 years behind it now, Am Rosengarten is showing promise in terms of its natural shade-bearing flora. A few more rough edges and a few less gardeners would help. The well-manicured look is fine for the local arboretum, but beer gardens deserve more grass and less class. Still, Am Rosengarten is a fine place to while away the afternoon and a chance to enthrall your date with your adroit handling of the terrace wine list, then retire to the more sympathetic beer garden for some real fun.

Freedom of choice is worth something. The dual-faceted Am Rosengarten earns 3 beers.

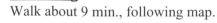

Aubinger Einkehr

Hauptbahnhof
S-Bahn 5 to Neuaubing.
Neuaubing
Walk about 9 min., following map.

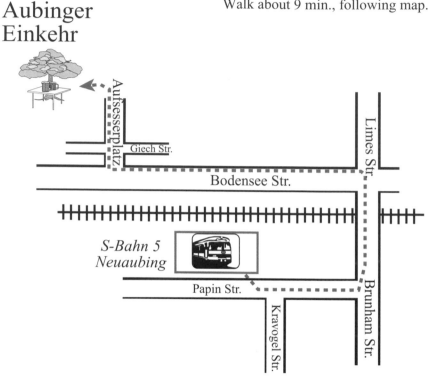

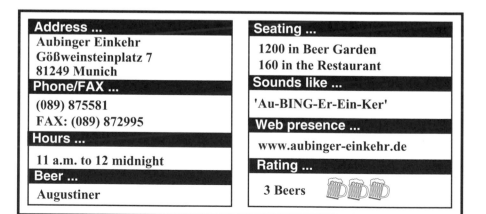

Address ...	Seating ...
Aubinger Einkehr Gößweinsteinplatz 7 81249 Munich	1200 in Beer Garden 160 in the Restaurant
Phone/FAX ...	**Sounds like ...**
(089) 875581 FAX: (089) 872995	'Au-BING-Er-Ein-Ker'
Hours ...	**Web presence ...**
11 a.m. to 12 midnight	www.aubinger-einkehr.de
Beer ...	**Rating ...**
Augustiner	3 Beers

Aubinger Einkehr

Where has Aubinger Einkehr been hiding all these years? This blue-collar suds emporium opened its doors some 70 years ago and has managed anonymity ever since. A neighborhood beer garden to be sure, but still you would think someone farther afield would take notice. OK, maybe that someone is us. With 1200 seats in the beer garden — almost all with self-service — Aubinger Einkehr is more than just locally appealing. The new wirt, Detlef Trippner, took over about a year ago and has given the business new life. He added renovations to spruce up the structural underpinnings, an improved menu with cheap luncheon specials, occasional live entertainment and most importantly an *ausschank* featuring Munich's best liquid offering,

Augustiner beer. As one would expect from a neighborhood establishment, the prices are more in line with a growing business interested in attracting a returning clientele. A *maß* of Augustiner goes for just over € 5 (Augustiner Edelstoff premium lager costs slightly more). Daily lunch and dinner specials are relatively cheap. That epicurean beer garden benchmark — barbecue spareribs — is less than € 8, self-service. The beer garden is easy to get to using public transport, although without a map this place would be easier to miss. A ride with S-Bahn 5 to Neuaubing is followed by about a nine-minute walk. The stroll along Bodensee Str. winds through an upper-crust residential area and a courtyard colonnade, where a stand of tall chestnut trees envelops the beer garden.

Herr Trippner will tell you this is still a work in progress, despite the major innovations to date. When he's not busy tooling around in his classic 1955 "Weltkugel" Ford Taunus, he's thinking up even more improvements to the gasthaus and beer garden. That augers well for the future of what is already a worthy venue today. Aubinger Einkehr checks in with an inaugural 3 beers.

Entrance to Aubinger Einkehr.

Hauptbahnhof
S-Bahn 1-8 to Hackerbrücke
Hackerbrücke
Walk over the bridge from the
S-Bahn platform and follow
the map to the beer hall, a
short walk.

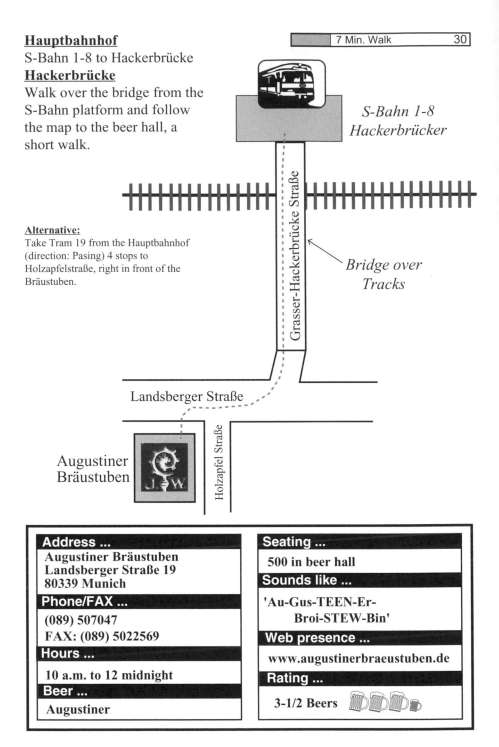

S-Bahn 1-8
Hackerbrücker

Alternative:
Take Tram 19 from the Hauptbahnhof
(direction: Pasing) 4 stops to
Holzapfelstraße, right in front of the
Bräustuben.

Grasser-Hackerbrücke Straße

Bridge over
Tracks

Landsberger Straße

Augustiner
Bräustuben

Holzapfel Straße

Address ...	Seating ...
Augustiner Bräustuben **Landsberger Straße 19** **80339 Munich**	**500 in beer hall**
	Sounds like ...
Phone/FAX ...	**'Au-Gus-TEEN-Er-** **Broi-STEW-Bin'**
(089) 507047 **FAX: (089) 5022569**	**Web presence ...**
Hours ...	**www.augustinerbraeustuben.de**
10 a.m. to 12 midnight	**Rating ...**
Beer ...	**3-1/2 Beers**
Augustiner	

Augustiner Bräustuben

Ever wonder where they keep those huge Clydesdales that pull Munich's beer wagons during the annual Oktoberfest kickoff parades? Of course not, why would you.

But, in the case of Augustinerbräu the answer is a stable on Landsberger Straße, just down the street from the brewery itself. The 10 horses that make up the Augustiner equestrian team were housed here for many years. In the early 1990s the horses were moved out and the place went from barn to beer hall. Sounds like a fair enough trade to us.

A little renovation and a few additions here and there — a kitchen, beer-serving area, tables and benches where stalls used to be — and in 1994 Augustiner Bräustuben was open for business. Besides serving several versions of Munich's most beloved beer, Augustiner, this beer-hall-sans-garden is now one of the city's most visited indoor lokals. (Management is working up plans to build a small beer garden on the roof!) In fact, Augustiner Bräustuben does its best business No-vember to March, when the beer gardens are still covered in ice and snow.

Manfred Vollmer, the accomplished wirt who runs Augustiner's tent at the Oktoberfest and the Augustiner Großgaststätte near the Marienplatz, is also in charge of the Bräustuben. His menu is extensive, filled with traditional Bavarian specialities like Jägerschnitzel (pork chops smothered in mushrooms) and lots of onion roasts and fried pota-toes. The Augustiner beer comes in sev-eral styles, from the basic *Helles* to the more premium Edelstoff. The price is right: a liter of Edelstoff costs barely more than € 5.

The beer hall is long and narrow, with a row of center posts the only reminder of the Bräustuben as the former OK Corral. For an idea how this watering hole looked when still a barn, the proprietors have recreated a typical stall, complete with straw and hanging horse rigging, seen through a glass window just beyond the copper-covered beer dispenser. In ad-vance of the annual Oktoberfest parade, team horses are still briefly stabled here.

Augustiner Bräustuben is a busy addi-tion to the Munich beer scene, and with only about 500 seats available it can get crowded. It's well worth the effort to find a spot anyway. The atmosphere is smoky, loud and rowdy, just the way we love it. Augustiner Bräustuben rides in with a solid recommendation and 3-1/2 beers.

Augustiner Edelstoff on delivery.

Hauptbahnhof
Take one of several S- or U-Bahns one
stop to Karlsplatz (Stachus). There are a
number of possible exits, choose the
exit to Neuhauser Str.
Karslplatz (Stachus)
Short walk — just a few feet — to the
Beer Hall.

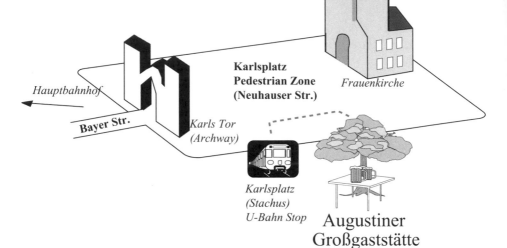

Augustiner
Großgaststätte

Address ...	Seating ...
Augustiner Großgaststätte **Neuhauserstraße 16** **80331 Munich**	**250 in Beer Garden** **1500 in Restaurant and Beer Hall**
Phone/FAX ...	**Sounds like ...**
(089) 2604106 **FAX: (089) 2605379**	**Ah-Gus-TEEN-Er** **GROSS-Gast-State-Uh**
	Web presence ...
Hours ...	**www.augustiner-restaurant.com**
9 a.m. to 12 midnight	**Rating ...**
Beer ...	**4 Beers**
Augustiner Bräu	

Augustiner
Großgaststätte

You'll fall in love with this place faster than you can say Augustiner Großgaststätte (Ah-Gus-Teener Gross-Gast-State-uh). Munich beer halls aren't big on easy name recognition. Not that it mattered much when this establishment was founded in 1328. The Augustin Brothers were not exactly dealing in heavy intellectual challenges back then. Their mental gymnastics were limited to the opening stanza of early morning prayers and remembering the four main ingredients — hops, barley, yeast and water — of the beer they brewed. Eventually, secular entrepreneurship won out over clerical enterprise, and the State of Bavaria took over the brewing art from the heavenly brethren. (Anything you can brew, we can brew better!) Up until 1885, the beer that many still consider the best in Munich was produced on site. The brewery was later moved to its current location on Landsberger Straße (check out Augustiner Bräustuben), but the *Gasthaus* remained.

Augustiner Großgaststätte, essentially a traditional beer hall with a small beer garden, is today a veritable in-door beer oasis, smack dab in the middle of Munich's pedestrian zone. The Gothic-arched ceilings and fresco-painted walls

A Kellnerin delivers a meal in Augustiner's beer hall.

promote a medieval, "cloistered" environment. The scenes portray the brethren at their best, totally immersed in a centuries-old quest for the quintessential brew. One side of the establishment is primarily restaurant and food service; the other knock-it-down-and-order-another beer hall. The interior is reminiscent of the better-known Hofbräuhaus without the raucous atmosphere, for better or worse, depending on the mood of the moment.

The restaurant and beer hall serve up excellent food, with roasted pork knuckles and white sausages as menu mainstays. Still, the sweet, aromatic and liberally dispensed Augustiner beer is the liquid hallmark of this establishment. Half-liters are readily available, thus eliminating the usual investment in time and saturability demanded by nearby competitors. The relatively small, courtyard beer garden, more a filtered place in the sun, is refuge from the smoke-filled cavernous rooms of the beer hall. Yet, its Italian rococo styling and historic value as the original cloister garden make it a favorite among beer aficionados who know their way around Munich.

Augustiner Großgaststätte is a lot of the old world with a bit of the new. There is no more traditional a beer hall in all of Munich. The *gemütlichkeit* index is high, garnering this living historical monument a rating of four full and frothy beers.

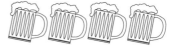

Augustiner Großgaststätte around 1890. A liter of beer cost 26 pfennigs.

50

Summertime crowds enjoy outside dining at Augustiner Großgaststätte.

Augustiner Keller

Hauptbahnhof
Exit to front of main train station on Bahnhof Platz. Take Tram 17 in direction "Amalienburg Str." Get off at Hopfenstraße. Walk a half block to the beer garden.

Herbst Str. **Hopfen Str.** **Seidl Str.**

Arnulf Str.

Tram 17 stop at Hopfenstraße

Bahnhof Platz

Tram 17

Marienplatz

Hauptbahnhof

Bayer Str.

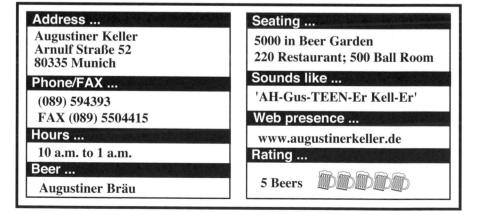

Address ...	Seating ...
Augustiner Keller **Arnulf Straße 52** **80335 Munich**	**5000 in Beer Garden** **220 Restaurant; 500 Ball Room**
Phone/FAX ...	**Sounds like ...**
(089) 594393 FAX (089) 5504415	'AH-Gus-TEEN-Er Kell-Er'
Hours ...	**Web presence ...**
10 a.m. to 1 a.m.	www.augustinerkeller.de
Beer ...	**Rating ...**
Augustiner Bräu	5 Beers

Augustiner Keller

Now a chance to partake of Munich's best-tasting beer in one of its most famous, historic and attractive beer gardens is just a short streetcar ride away. You don't even have to walk any more to Augustiner Keller, not far from the Hauptbahnhof on Arnulf Straße. Tram 17, an important addition to the city's transit system will take you literally to Augustiner's front door. No one should visit Munich, even for a day, and miss this wonderful beer garden experience. Augustiner is a spacious setting, amid centuries-old chestnut trees, seemingly spread over several country acres. On a warm summer day 5,000 seats are hardly enough to accommodate the hordes of Germans who congregate here. The *stammtisches* are often filled with high-ranking political figures and the most famous names of Germany's entertainment industry (Bavarian Radio and TV network headquarters nearby). There's still plenty of room for "common folk," though, and Augustiner is a great equalizer among the classes of this Bavarian capital, where blue, white and embroidered native garb collars match beer for

Five thousands seats are barely enough to handle the large crowds of thirsty Münchners frequenting Augustiner Keller on warm summer afternoons.

beer, elbow to elbow. Unlike other beer gardens which tend to empty out soon after dark, Augustiner maintains its high level late into the evening. The final table of customers will grudgingly depart only after "last call," fast on the heels of midnight.

˘ The "keller" alludes to decades past, before refrigeration, when wooden kegs of brew were kept in the cellar to retain the freshness and cool temperature of their liquid contents. Aptly named "beer oxen" were employed to turn the wheel of a leveraged pulley system that would raise the casks from their subterranean storage to allow gravity-fed distribution of the beer to thirsty customers in the Augustiner garden. The last bovine beer caddy was given his retirement papers in 1891, replaced by a more efficient *deus ex machina* born of the Industrial Revolution.

Previously, the business had been in the hands of a family of book publishers, thus the name Büchlbräukeller until 1848 when it was sold to Gabriel Sedlmayr, patriarch of the Spaten brewing chain. Ol' Gabe didn't hold onto it long, though, and in 1862, Augustiner Brewery under the proprietorship of Joseph Wagner took over. It has remained a purveyor of the label ever since. Wagner was instrumental in expanding the garden portion of the property by incorporating a nearby meadow.

Augustiner Keller's reputation as foremost among Munich's beer establishments is well deserved. The mix of table- and self-service beer and food stands offers its diverse group of customers a choice of fare. The service is polite and efficient, probably owing to the relative high-brow clientele ("was that the Bavarian interior minister I just spilled a Maß of beer on!") and the paucity of transient trade. People who come to Augustiner, come back for refills.

Augustiner Keller actually lives up to its name, since a large, cavernous 250-seat cellar beer hall is tucked away behind a wrought-iron gate inside the restaurant. A steep stairway will lead you to the beer hall, usually open only in winter and when heavy summer downpours manage to scatter the clientele from the beer garden.

The restaurant, although dwarfed by the sheer magnitude of the beer garden,

A *Kellnerin* totes a double-fisted ration of Augustiner Edelstoff, the people's choice among Munich's premium beers.

54

could easily stand on its own. It offers full meals in the best Bavarian culinary tradition. On special occasions such as Fasching and Starkbier fests, the interior *Große Festsaal* is employed to host industrial-strength beer bashes. There is even a large children's play area in one section of the beer garden, slightly elevated and blessedly removed from the mainstream of activity.

If there is any negative aspect, it is due to the popularity of this remarkable beer garden: when the weather is good, the seats are as hard to find as a downtown Munich parking place. Worth the gamble, though. Augustiner Keller is a full keg of enjoyment, with a maximum 5 beer rating.

The Beer Gardens of Tram 17

The same tramline that dropped you off at Augustiner Keller also delivered new travel options for exploring Munich. Tram (Straßenbahn) 17, which leaves directly in front of the Hauptbahnhof, was established a few years ago. It opened up new travel modes to reach several beer gardens and alternatives for others. Here is an ideal itinerary using Tram 17 that works very well in visiting four of Munich's best, and in two instances, from a different direction than we've mapped out in their individual write-ups.

You can do this trip forward or reverse, as it works well either way. We recommend reverse which goes like this:

1. Fasanerie. Take Tram 17 to the end of the line at Amalienburg Str. and follow the map from the section on Fasanerie.

2. Zur Schwaige. Get back on Tram 17 and head back toward the Hauptbahnhof, exiting to your right on Romanplatz. Walk down Roman Straße to the side door for Zur Schwaige (you can't miss it).

3. Hirschgarten. Have a quick beer at Zur Schwaige then take a walk down Hirschgartenallee, past Woton Str. and Kriemhilden Str. to Königbau Str. Turn right to the entrance to Hirschgarten. Enjoy the afternoon here and then retrace your steps to Kriemhilden Str. Turn right and take a short-cut to Tram 17.

4. Augustiner Keller. From Kriemhilden Str., take Tram 17 (continuing your way toward the Hauptbahnhof) to the stop at Hopfen Straße. Across the street (Arnulf Str.) is Augustiner Keller. Kill what's left of the day or night here and then return trip back to the Hauptbahnhof and home.

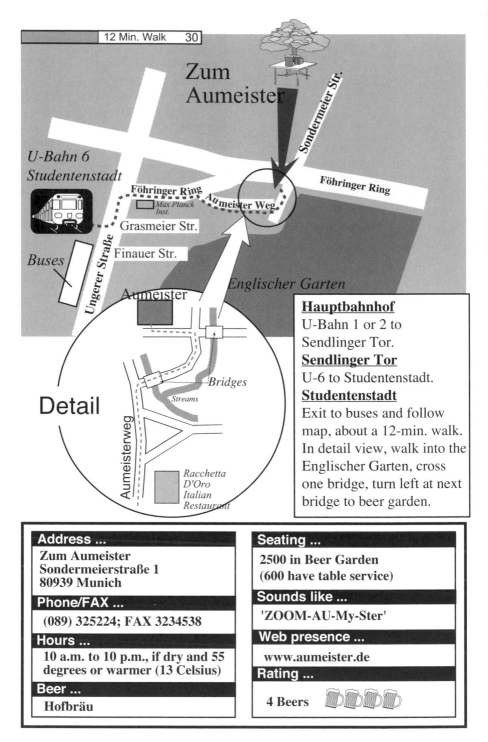

Zum Aumeister

U-Bahn 6
Studentenstadt

Föhringer Ring

Sondermeier Str.

Aumeister Weg

Föhringer Ring

Max Planck Inst.

Grasmeier Str.

Buses

Ungerer Straße

Finauer Str.

Aumeister

Englischer Garten

Detail

Bridges

Streams

Aumeisterweg

Racchetta
D'Oro
Italian
Restaurant

Hauptbahnhof
U-Bahn 1 or 2 to
Sendlinger Tor.
Sendlinger Tor
U-6 to Studentenstadt.
Studentenstadt
Exit to buses and follow
map, about a 12-min. walk.
In detail view, walk into the
Englischer Garten, cross
one bridge, turn left at next
bridge to beer garden.

Address ...
Zum Aumeister
Sondermeierstraße 1
80939 Munich

Phone/FAX ...
(089) 325224; FAX 3234538

Hours ...
10 a.m. to 10 p.m., if dry and 55
degrees or warmer (13 Celsius)

Beer ...
Hofbräu

Seating ...
2500 in Beer Garden
(600 have table service)

Sounds like ...
'ZOOM-AU-My-Ster'

Web presence ...
www.aumeister.de

Rating ...
4 Beers

Aumeister

At the outer edge of the Englischer Garten is Zum Aumeister, never lagging in the hearts of Munich's beer garden fans. The old Munich tradition and atmosphere of a hospitable country inn is in evidence here today. The Aumeister dates back to 1810, when it was the region's primary hunting lodge and staging area for the duke's frequent hunts. As time went on, and the huntsmen began outnumbering the game, the lokal expanded its charter. The chase finally gave way to the dispensing of beer, and in 1914 the local hunting club was replaced with a full-time restaurant and beer garden. In 1959, the restaurant was completely rebuilt and a terrace garden was added.

The Aumeister, with its sizeable beer garden (2500 seats) and well-stocked self-service food stand (home-baked soft pretzels), deserves its reputation as one of the best-known and traditional beer gardens in all of Munich. The atmosphere is comfortable and serene, with excellent shade from mature chestnut trees. Thomas and Katrin König, the same wirts who run Leiberheim, now operate Aumeister. In a fit of common sense, they established beer garden operating hours thusly: open daily — so long as it's not raining and the temperature reaches at least 55 degrees (13 celsius) by 10 a.m. The restaurant offers a list of Mediterranean specialities and traditional seasonal dishes, including white *spargel* (asparagus), forest-grown mushrooms, and wild game. Unique to Aumeister is a self-contained children's play area with tables and benches for adults as well as the usual slides, swings and other play structures for the kids. Like a "crying room" for beer gardens, it sits blessedly across the path and removed from the main seating area.

Although technically within the boundaries of the Englischer Garten, Aumeister draws patrons from a wider area of Munich and is a favored haunt of many northern city dwellers. If you really want to make a hike of it, you could walk a couple of miles from Seehaus to get here, but better to take a U-bahn to Studentenstadt and a short, 12-minute walk to the beer garden.

This is a place for relaxation and convivial conversation. Although an institution among Munich's knowledgeable beer-drinking throngs, Aumeister is almost unknown to the city's foreign visitors. That is, until now. It draws a solid 4 beers and a high recommendation for a visit to one of Munich's more traditional beer gardens.

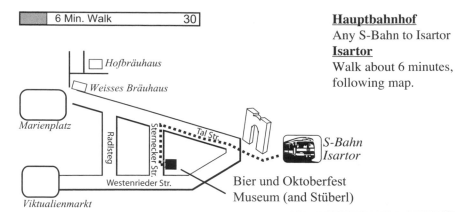

☐ *Hofbräuhaus*

☐ *Weisses Bräuhaus*

Marienplatz

Radlsteg

Sternecker Str.

Tal Str.

Westenrieder Str.

Viktualienmarkt

S-Bahn
Isartor

Bier und Oktoberfest
Museum (and Stüberl)

Hauptbahnhof
Any S-Bahn to Isartor
Isartor
Walk about 6 minutes,
following map.

**Museum Director
Lukas Bulka with the
"Brewers Ark," a
highly revered icon to
Munich's aspiring
master brewers.**

Note: Tickets for the Museum are € 4 for
adults and € 2.50 for children; a family
pass is € 6 and groups of more than 6
persons get in for € 3 each.

Address ...	**Beer ...**
Bier und Oktoberfest Museum Sternecker Str. 2 80331 Munich	From six Munich breweries
Phone/FAX ...	**Seating ...**
(089) 24231607/ (089) 24231608; Stüberl: 24243941 (for reservations)	50 in Museum Stüberl
Hours ...	**Web presence ...**
Museum: 1 - 5 p.m. Stüberl: 5 p.m. - Midnight Closed Monday and Sunday	Bier-und-Oktoberfestmuseum.de
	Rating ...
	3-1/2 Beers

Bier und Oktoberfest Museum (and Stüberl)

Who says there are no churches or museums in The Beer Drinker's Guide to Munich? Witness Kloster Andechs, Weihenstephan and Augustiner Salzburg, just for starters on the ecclesiastical side. And now, of course, there's the Bier und Oktoberfest Museum. Opened in 2005, the museum tells the story of Munich's beers as well as its most famous excuse to imbibe them — Oktoberfest.

Appropriately, the museum is on Sternecker Straße*, between the Isar Tor and the Marienplatz, in Munich's oldest residential building, dating back to 1340. What sets this museum apart from all those not listed in The BDG2M besides its theme is its stüberl restaurant and beer cafe. A chance to learn all about Munich's "Big Six" and then sample their brews is too good to miss. Lukas Bulka, the museum's head curator, stresses the ecumenical point that all of Munich's top breweries are represented and available here, well, at least in bottled form. We want to stress the more discerning point that the beer on tap is Augustiner. That's not totally coincidental, since the Edith Haberland-Wagner Foundation supports the museum. That's the same Wagner family that has owned Augustiner Brewery since 1829. (Augustiner logo: the "J.W." stands for Jens Wagner.)

The museum is on several levels, serviced by a steep wooden staircase. Each level is themed to cover the history of beer in general and in Munich specifically. Subsequent floors tell the story of the Oktoberfest, complete with a collection of commemorative *Krüge* or mugs dating back to the first issue in 1978. Visitors are also invited to view a 12-minute film that bridges any information gaps left in the displays, most of which include English translations.

The prize artifact is the historical "brewers ark" which holds near mystical relevance to those who covet and earn master brewer status. Each year, the ark is temporarily removed from its honored place in the museum and taken to the site of the ceremony anointing new brewers in Munich. The museum is a must-see, to be sure. But the stüberl is fast-becoming a popular *Stammtisch* attracting regulars from around Munich.

Wolfgang Schad, Munich beer drinker extraordinaire, is one such. Wolfgang, who graced the covers of the third through fifth editions of The BDG2M now shares time here with friends from other prominent watering holes, such as Viktualienmarkt and the Hofbräuhaus.

At long last, a museum to hold our attention and a chance to do more than just play with the exhibits. We welcome the Bier und Oktoberfest Museum with an informative 3-1/2 beers.

*If Sternecker Straße sounds historically familiar, it should. Out a window of the museum can still be seen a next-door building that once housed the headquarters for the Brown Shirts, the Nazi party, and what was once Sterneckerbräu beer hall.

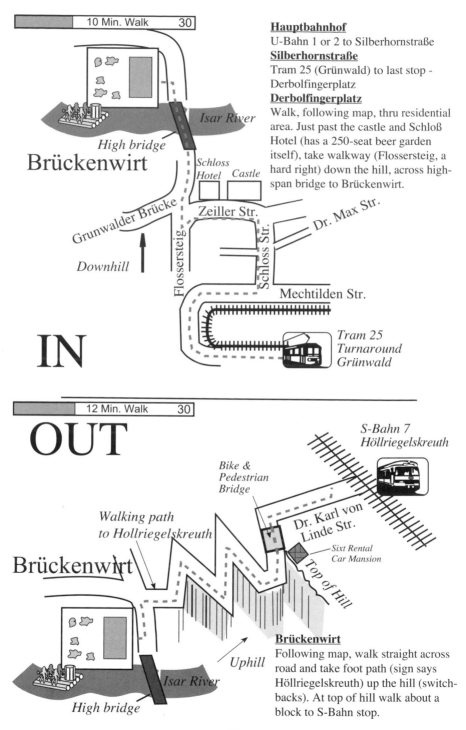

Hauptbahnhof
U-Bahn 1 or 2 to Silberhornstraße
Silberhornstraße
Tram 25 (Grünwald) to last stop - Derbolfingerplatz
Derbolfingerplatz
Walk, following map, thru residential area. Just past the castle and Schloß Hotel (has a 250-seat beer garden itself), take walkway (Flossersteig, a hard right) down the hill, across high-span bridge to Brückenwirt.

10 Min. Walk 30

Isar River

High bridge

Brückenwirt

Schloss Hotel   Castle

Grunwalder Brücke

Zeiller Str.

Dr. Max Str.

Flossersteig

Schloss Str.

Downhill

Mechtilden Str.

IN

Tram 25
Turnaround
Grünwald

12 Min. Walk 30

OUT

S-Bahn 7
Höllriegelskreuth

Bike & Pedestrian Bridge

Walking path to Hollriegelskreuth

Dr. Karl von Linde Str.

Brückenwirt

Sixt Rental Car Mansion

Top of Hill

Uphill

Isar River

High bridge

Brückenwirt
Following map, walk straight across road and take foot path (sign says Höllriegelskreuth) up the hill (switchbacks). At top of hill walk about a block to S-Bahn stop.

60

Brückenwirt

We're going on a field trip, boys and girls. Just a little *ausflug* in the country. And, we'll not retrace our steps along the way. The proprietors of Brückenwirt, literally an anchoring end of the high-span Grünwalder Bridge over the Isar River, are quick to note the variety of means its customers employ to get there. Boat, raft, canoe, swim. (Yeah, you can actually take a dip at this upstream, clear-water point.) On the other hand, you can also take a tram or an S-bahn, and the maps on the opposite page portray two routes, in and out. The in route, arriving by tram, winds by a medieval castle (complete with moat) and then down the hill and across the bridge to the restaurant and beer garden.

The out alternative is a route that winds uphill through a forested area, leading to an S-bahn stop with a direct connection back to the city center. Getting to and fro in this case is literally half the fun.

The trip is longer than most, and about a 10-minute walk each way. But the destination is well worth it, along with an outstanding menu and the usual Maß of beer in the garden. Brückenwirt offers our fieldtrip class a chance to learn about the uniquely Bavarian art of *Floß* (pronounced "flohes," not "flob"), or party rafting.

Now, Bavarians are well-known for their ability to mix business with pleasure. Such was the case a couple centuries ago when loggers in the upper reaches of the Isar would cut their lumber and float it down the river in make-shift rafts to the inhabited regions below. After a hard day on the wooded slopes, the *lederhosen*-clad lumberjacks would see their product safely to market accompanied by a little celebration, a round of song and a great deal of beer. The cruise down the slow-flowing Isar took four to six hours to the nearest waiting mills. That left plenty of time for song and brew, and a tradition was born. Eventually, the lumber was more efficiently hauled by truck. So much for the work, but why give up the fun?

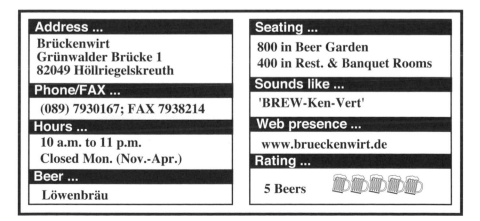

Address ...	Seating ...
Brückenwirt Grünwalder Brücke 1 82049 Höllriegelskreuth	800 in Beer Garden 400 in Rest. & Banquet Rooms
Phone/FAX ...	**Sounds like ...**
(089) 7930167; FAX 7938214	'BREW-Ken-Vert'
Hours ...	**Web presence ...**
10 a.m. to 11 p.m. Closed Mon. (Nov.-Apr.)	www.brueckenwirt.de
Beer ...	**Rating ...**
Löwenbräu	5 Beers

Floß is alive and well. Seated in the riverside beer garden at Brückenwirt, one can gain a first-hand glimpse of this venerable local custom. The first clue is the distant sound of an "oompah band" playing traditional Bavarian *Blasmusik*. Eventually a fully laden party raft floats into view, with about 60 revelers, each with a raised mug of foamy beer poised in full *prosit*. Toasts are exchanged with the envious observers along the shore, and as quickly as it came it has floated by. That is, until the next raft 10 minutes later. Brückenwirt is one of the rare locations to view and enjoy this festive scene. (See Gasthof Hinterbrühl, another.) A boat landing is adjacent to the beer garden, so you may find yourself sharing table space with several hundred disembarking celebrants as each raft pulls into dock.

Brückenwirt is probably the most rural lokal and beer garden presented here. Yet, it is relatively easy to get to. The scenic mix of pine and chestnut trees gives one the feeling of being literally out in the woods. For those who enjoy a walk in the outback, a network of hiking trails — mostly running along the river — is nearby. The Wirts, Helga and Erich Müller, have upgraded the restaurant and the beer garden to a level that places Brückenwirt among Munich's finest.

Brückenwirt is a combination of scenic enjoyment, fine food and beer, and the opportunity to experience an unusual and invigorating local ritual. Added together, they give this fieldtrip destination a top 5-beer rating. We're happy to have Brückenwirt in the Prosit! free-beer offering as well. (See coupon pages in the back.)

Want to go rafting?

The Floß season runs generally from the first of May through the middle of September, primarily on weekends. Those tempted to jump in and swim out to where the fun is can stay dry and book passage on a Floß through several companies who provide the service:

Michael Angermeier Tel. (08042)-1220/ FAX (08042)-3724

IPS München Events Tel. (089)-8712399 www.isarflossfahrt.de

DER-Reisebüro Tel. (089)-1204236 (Cost for the full day — including a lunch in a local Gasthaus during the float trip, beer, soda and snacks on the raft — is around € 130 per person through the DER travel bureau, with bus pickup and return from the Hauptbahnhof.)

The float trip is nearly 30 kilometers (about 18 miles) from Wolfratshausen to Thalkirchen in the vicinity of Hinterbrühl beer garden. The trip takes 5-6 hours and will usually begin around 9 a.m. and end at 3-4 p.m. There is usually a one-hour stop for lunch. The 22-ton raft will hold up to 60 people, along with an Oompah band and plenty of beer. (And there is a covered unisex — knock first — porta potty at one corner of the raft.)

Brückenwirt, on the banks of the Isar.

A woodcut from 1885 portrays the centuries-old tradition of Floß.

| 5 Min. Walk | 30 |

*Tram 20 or 21
Olympia Park
West*

Olympic
Stadium

Dachauer Str.

Landshuter Allee

*Aral
Gas
Station*

Concordia
Park

Hauptbahnhof
Front of Hauptbahnhof on Bahnhofplatz, cross street to Post Office side. Take Tram 20 (direction "Moosach") or Tram 21(direction "Westfriedhof") eight stops to Olympiapark West.

Olympiapark West
Cross the street, follow map along Landshuter Allee and turn right at Aral Gas Station. Walk straight to beer garden. It's only a 5-min. walk.

Note: Taxisgarten is just around the corner. Return to Landshuter Allee and turn right at the Aral gas station along Landshuter Allee to Haneberg Str. Right on Haneberg Str. to Taxis Str. Right again about 100 yards to Taxisgarten. 10-minute walk.

Address ...
**Concordia Park
Landshuter Alee 165
80637 Munich**

Phone/FAX ...
(089) 155241; FAX (089) 15970804

Hours ...
**10 a.m.-10:30 p.m. Closed
Mondays in winter**

Beer ...
Löwenbräu

Seating ...
900 in Beer Garden

Sounds like ...
'Kon-KOR-Dee-Ah Park'

Web presence ...
None

Rating ...
3-1/2 Beers

Concordia Park

Will sing for beer! Now that is a placard you might expect to see someone wear at Concordia Park beer garden. This establishment was named after the Concordia Men's Choir (Männergesangverein) that got its start more than a century ago and is still in good voice. The choir meets several times weekly and practices Tuesday evenings around 7:30 p.m. in the beer garden. The small restaurant and beer garden are sort of a club house for the choir, who first obtained leased title to the land in 1913. Singing is thirsty work, and less than a year later the first beer stand was erected. In 1924 a restaurant was added and all was opened to the public. The structure was damaged during a 1943 bombing raid and completely rebuilt by choir members a decade later.

A close call came in 1968 when Concordia Park was scheduled for the wrecking ball to make way for the impending 1972 Munich Summer Olympics. But, local residents, as much fans of their neighborhood beer garden as they are of the musical arts, protested and saved it. So today Concordia Park is several blocks away from the imposing Olympic Stadium, not buried by it.

The business changed hands in 2007, and the Gaitanidis family has spiced up the menu with Greek dishes like gyros, souvlaki, and calamaris, to name a few. At the same time, the new owners have kept the lid on prices and a Maß of beer can still be had for € 5.50.

Concordia Park is a peaceful setting with abundant shade, surrounded by a string of carefully cultivated private garden plots. The weekend gardener syndrome is played out somewhat differently in Germany. Land is at such a premium that the backyard garden is often by necessity several miles from the house. Very near to Concordia Park, in this case. So be ready to talk fertilizers and hybrid chrysanthemums as well as beer selections with your table mates.

Concordia Park, with its cheap prices, excellent food and invigorating atmosphere, gets 3-1/2 beers.

A memorial plaque at the entrance to the beer garden pays tribute to fallen heroes from the original men's choir.

Hauptbahnhof
S-Bahn 4 to Lochhausen
Lochhausen
For **Deutsche Eiche**: The restaurant and beer garden can be seen across the street from the station.
For **Waldgaststätte Bienenheim**: Exit station to left on Henschel Str. Take Bus 161 in direction Eichelhäher Str. (bus stop is same side of the street as S-Bahn station). Take Bus 161 two stops to Federsee Str. Walk short distance, following map.

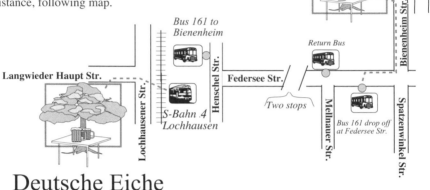

Address ...	**Seating ...**
Deutsche Eiche **Ranertstraße 1** **81249 Munich**	**650 in Beer Garden** **200 in Restaurant**
Phone/FAX ...	**Sounds like ...**
(089) 8649000 FAX (089) 86490098	'DOY-Cher Eye-Ka'
Hours ...	**Web presence ...**
7 a.m. to 12 a.m., Closed Tues.	www.deutsche-eiche-mendel.de
Beer ...	**Rating ...**
Augustinerbräu	**4 Beers**

Deutsche Eiche

(and Waldgaststätte Bienenheim)

When we first discovered Deutsche Eiche about 25 years ago, we were certain this beer garden was the lone jewel of Munich's rural Lochhausen district. Then the Conrad-Mendel family who own and operate Deutsche Eiche opened a "sister" beer garden in nearby Bienenheim. The two together — just a short bus-ride distance from each other — made this trip to Munich's suburbs even more worthwhile. The Bienenheim outlet has changed hands again and now belongs to the Hajnal family, but the incentive to visit the tandem remains. They are close to the Lochhausen S-Bahn stop, and easily accessed with local transportation. A short walk across the tracks and a brief bus ride are all it takes to enjoy two outstanding Munich beer gardens.

We recommend beginning with **Deutsche Eiche**, directly adjacent to the train station. This traditional watering hole is an impression of old Munich, when the local restaurant and beer garden

Rural Lochhausen, shown here in 1922, remains a tranquil Munich suburb with two great beer garden retreats.

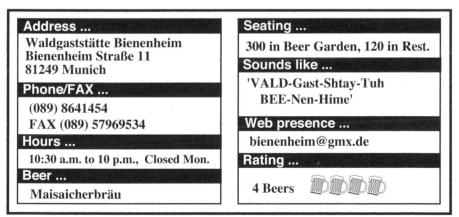

Address ...
Waldgaststätte Bienenheim
Bienenheim Straße 11
81249 Munich

Phone/FAX ...
(089) 8641454
FAX (089) 57969534

Hours ...
10:30 a.m. to 10 p.m., Closed Mon.

Beer ...
Maisaicherbräu

Seating ...
300 in Beer Garden, 120 in Rest.

Sounds like ...
'VALD-Gast-Shtay-Tuh
BEE-Nen-Hime'

Web presence ...
bienenheim@gmx.de

Rating ...
4 Beers

were an institution alongside the country church and corner train station. This was a place to meet and while away a quiet Sunday afternoon among friends and family. Cares were few, worries better left to those city dwellers down the road.

Life was simple in 1899 when the house on Lochhausen's Ranertstrasse opened its doors and began trading in the gastronomical arts. Deutsche Eiche retains much of that old country charm. The story of this traditional farmhouse turned beer garden revolves around the Mahl and Reisländer families who have managed the business since its inception. Martin and Theresa Mahl were first on the scene at the turn of the century, offering home-cooked meals and cellar-chilled brew. They built a loyal patronage over the next two decades. In 1923, the child-less couple turned the business over to their niece Rosa, who had recently married Johann Reisländer upon his return from serving in the Kaiser's Imperial Guard in World War I. The Reisländers and their married daughters have carried forward the family tradition until today, to include the Conrads and Mendels who now operate the restaurant and beer garden.

At a time when large, faceless corporations are snapping up beer gardens by the case, Deutsche Eiche is a rare and pleasant anachronism, a nostalgic hold-over from a bygone era. Pride and quality remain trademarks of this establishment. The service is excellent, the food outstanding and now the beer served is Augustinerbräu. Lochhausen, a rural farm village when Deutsche Eiche got its start, is today a thriving Munich suburb. Yet, the annexation is in name only. The village — it remains that — is a world apart from the bustle of the busy Munich metro-center. Deutsche Eiche is in close harmony with this slower-paced way of life. The relaxed atmosphere and unruffled setting is a soothing time-out from the more exciting alternatives offered in the inner city.

In 1923, Johann and Rosa Reisländer (inset) turned 'the house on Ranert Straße' into a family-led business. Deutsche Eiche's restaurant and beer garden staff take special pride in serving their customers.

It's a family affair, and a lot like being invited home for dinner. **Waldgaststätte Bienenheim** is the other half of this equation. It's slightly smaller than the beer garden across the tracks, but no less enjoyable. The also family-owned-and-run establishment may be a little quieter, too. Maybe nobody wants to upset the many colonies of bees that swarm this place. Somewhere just beyond the cluster of shade trees that rims the beer garden are working apiaries — bee hives — that give Bienenheim its name (literally "bees' home"). The collecting of honey is a cottage industry in Bienenheim and the restaurant sells its own. The other name, Waldgaststätte, is also based in fact. The *wald*, or forest, surrounds the beer garden adding to its isolated setting. The food and beer are cheap here. An unexpected well-accoutered menu contains a long list of traditional Bavarian dishes, from rollbraten to Münchner Zwiebelfleisch (beef smothered in stewed onions). A daily *Tageskarte* adds even more value to the food offerings, and with the new management comes expanded culinary possibilities, including Hungarian and spicy east European dishes.

The beer garden is small but adequate, with a sun terrace running along side the restaurant. Although this no longer belongs in the Deutsche Eiche stable, the current owners have maintained the high quality and tradition that first brought this place to our attention. As with other outback venues Waldgaststätte Bienenheim is a tranquil, easy-to-take atmosphere, heavy on relaxation and leisurely beer drinking. With Deutsche Eiche just down the road, they add up to good medicine for anything that might ail you. Take them both together, they will go down easy that way. Waldgaststätte Bienenheim and Deutsche Eiche get four beers and a recommendation to take an S-Bahn ride for an enjoyable day in Munich's countryside.

The buzz at Waldgaststätte Bienenheim is more than just the bees. This a honey of a beer garden.

Hauptbahnhof
Any S-Bahn to Marienplatz.
Marienplatz
Refer to map: Donisl is at left edge of the Rathaus (looking directly at the Glock-enspiel), Andechser am Dom, just around the corner on Filserbräu Gaße.

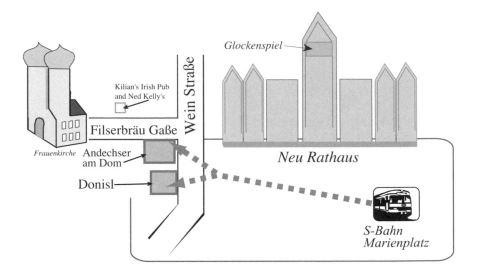

Address ...	Seating ...
Donisl	300 in Restaurant and Stüben
Wein Straße 1	
80333 Munich	**Sounds like ...**
Phone/FAX ...	'DOEN-Ee-Sell'
(089) 29084124;	
FAX (089) 2285884	**Web presence ...**
	www.bayerischer-donisl.de
Hours ...	
9 a.m.- Midnight	**Rating ...**
Beer ...	3-1/2 Beers 🍺🍺🍺🍺
Hacker-Pschorr Bräu	

Donisl and Andechser am Dom

Two Munich establishments tucked between two of the city's most visible monuments — the New City Hall (Rathaus) on the Marienplatz (with Glockenspiel) and the Frauenkirche or "Dom" as many refer to it — deserve mention for their popularity among Munich's indoor beer drinkers. Donisl, is one of Munich's oldest inns. Andechser am Dom is more recent, but with an ancient pedigree. The two, which practically share each other's back porch, are worthy of a convenient visit by even the most discerning beer aficionados.

Donisl

Donisl got its start in 1715 when it was opened as a beer hall in a section of town best known for dispensing wine. Thus, "Weinstraße" where Donisl sits today is not without meaning, but if the fruit of the vine had not been so expensive back then, local businessman Max List might not have felt compelled to promote the suds in place of the wine. It opened originally as "Zur alten Hauptwache" — a subordinate name the establishment retains to this day. The "Donisl" monicker came later and in honor of Dionysius Haertl. Dionysius was the wirt here from 1760-75 and so successful in taking care of a growing crop of customers, they began referring to his place by referring to him, of course with the usual Bavarian dialectic that somehow massages Dionysius into Donisl.

Today, Donisl is more the restaurant and courtyard beer garden than beer hall of yesteryear. The menu and quality of food service are among the very best Munich has to offer, and at a very reasonable price. The menu lists plenty of traditional Bavarian fare, with no main course over € 8. Although primarily indoors, the windowed

Atrium entrance to Donisl on the Marienplatz.

ceilings give the entire place an arboretum effect, letting in plenty of sun and no precipitation. The Wildmoser family, which also operates Gasthaus Hinterbrühl, does an excellent job here in making customers feel welcome in a manner even Dionys . . er, Donisl would have approved.

Donisl is a great place to start the day, and Andechser am Dom, waiting literally just around the corner, an even better place to end it.

Andechser am Dom

Andechser am Dom, as its name suggests, is quite close to the Frauenkirche, but even more so to the left rear corner of the Rathaus on the Marienplatz. In fact, walk out the door of Donisl, turn left, and left again on Filserbräu Gaße. You're there in less than a minute.

Sepp Krätz (Waldwirtschaft Großhesselohe) owns this place, so you know it's good, packed, and filled with local luminaria. Candid photos on the wall attest to celebrity visits running the gamut from pro golfer John Daly to German Chancellor Angela Merkal.

After extensive restoration of a centuries-old historical building that once housed cloistered monks, Sepp has transformed a onetime pious sanctuary into a pulsating *Kneipe* that's fast becoming one of Munich's most popular. Lots of ancient wood paneling is left over from a bygone era. A noteworthy local artist, Rainer Maria Latzke, was commissioned to produce ornate ceiling frescos that harken back to an earlier time before religious meditation over morning prayers was replaced by brisk conversation over afternoon beers.

Within Andechser's somewhat cramped interior, small groups convene around wooden tables and benches. The air is thick with cigarette smoke in this restaurant area, but an adjacent covered exterior patio and small beer garden provide an escape to cleaner breathing room, but no less crowded conditions, albeit mostly around standing room only tables.

The menu here is traditional Bavarian, but the real prize is Andechser beer. The monastery brew that flows freely along the banks of Ammersee at Kloster Andechs is available here. That includes a *helles*, *weizen* and a high-octain Andechser dark *doppelbock*. Think about it, not having to wait until *Starkbierzeit* to enjoy one of Munich's most potent and tasty libations.

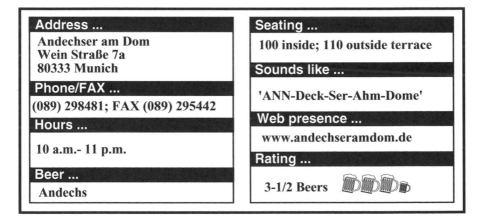

Address ...	Seating ...
Andechser am Dom **Wein Straße 7a** **80333 Munich**	**100 inside; 110 outside terrace**
Phone/FAX ...	**Sounds like ...**
(089) 298481; FAX (089) 295442	**'ANN-Deck-Ser-Ahm-Dome'**
Hours ...	**Web presence ...**
10 a.m.- 11 p.m.	**www.andechseramdom.de**
Beer ...	**Rating ...**
Andechs	**3-1/2 Beers**

Respectively, Donisl and Andechser am Dom work well in tandem to offer appealing dining and beer-drinking experiences to Munich visitors, and in a small area at one end of the Marienplatz. We should also note that just beyond Andechser am Dom is Kilian's Irish Pub and Ned Kelly's Australian Bar (late night) in case you felt there wasn't enough to stay busy. Quite a bit happening in this small corner of the world, and we give it 3-1/2 beers in welcoming these establishments to the 6th edition of the BDG2M.

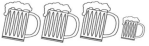

Andechser am Dom offers cloister-brewed beers in the heart of Munich.

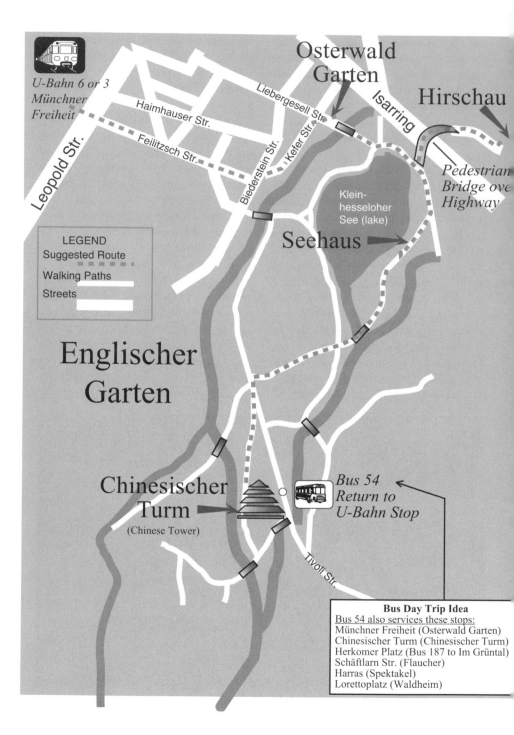

U-Bahn 6 or 3
Münchner
Freiheit

Leopold Str.

Haimhauser Str.

Feilitzsch Str.

Liebergesell Str.

Biederstein Str.

Kefer Str.

Isarring

Osterwald
Garten

Hirschau

Pedestrian
Bridge over
Highway

Klein-
hesseloher
See (lake)

Seehaus

LEGEND

Suggested Route

Walking Paths

Streets

Englischer
Garten

Chinesischer
Turm
(Chinese Tower)

Bus 54
Return to
U-Bahn Stop

Tivoli Str.

Bus Day Trip Idea
Bus 54 also services these stops:
Münchner Freiheit (Osterwald Garten)
Chinesischer Turm (Chinesischer Turm)
Herkomer Platz (Bus 187 to Im Grüntal)
Schäftlarn Str. (Flaucher)
Harras (Spektakel)
Lorettoplatz (Waldheim)

Englischer Garten
A Day in the Park

Thanks to a transplanted American count, Münchners today enjoy one of the most pleasing central parks in any metropolitan area in the world. The Englischer Garten is a haven for the young and the young at heart. It's a place where strollers mingle unabashedly with nude sunbathers, bicyclists cruise along lakes where non-powered boaters ply their oars through crystal clear waters. Families pack their lunches and spread blankets over lush green lawns amid rolling hills and dales. And, when the weather is best, they all congregate together in one of Englischer Garten's beer gardens: Osterwald Garten, Seehaus, Hirschau, and Chinesicher Turm (Chinese Tower).* (See footnote, next page.) The four are excellent beer gardens, and one (Seehaus) is in our five-beer club and participating in the free beer offer. They are presented here in logical order, like a walk in the park. First, though, some history on the Englischer Garten. The park began as a compromise, a royal bribe from Karl Theodor to a rebellious Munich populace. Due to gross mismanagement on his part, the Wittelsbach monarch was faced with a poor wheat harvest and subsequent widespread starvation that threatened his overthrow in 1789. Seeking to avoid the fate of a contemporary royal peer, King Louis XVI, forced to flee his palace that same year during the bloody French Revolution, Karl Theodor relied on the aid of a foreigner, Benjamin Thompson. Thompson was an American without portfolio who sided with the British during his own country's revolution of a decade earlier. Despite questionable loyalties, he was nevertheless awarded the title Count von Rumford and commissioned to do something, anything that might quiet the tumultuous Bavarians.

Trip Plan - Refer to map, opposite page.

Hauptbahnhof
U-Bahn 1 or 2 to Sendlinger Tor.
Sendlinger Tor
U-6 or U-3 to Münchner Freiheit.
Münchner Freiheit
Exit on Feilitzsch Str., follow map to Osterwald beer garden. At the fourth beer garden, Chinesischer Turm, there is a bus stop to take you back to a U-Bahn stop, either Münchner Freiheit or Prinzregentenplatz (U-Bahn 4 line), take your pick.
Note: If you want to do beer gardens in reverse order, from Münchner Freiheit U-Bahn stop, take Bus 54 directly to Chinesischer Turm and then walk back, following this map.

Demonstrating some of that Yankee ingenuity that had served him well in avoiding being hanged as a traitor in Concord, New Hampshire, Rumford set up soup kitchens and welfare programs that muted the aspiring expectations of the local populace, at least temporarily. As a culminating gesture, he convinced Karl Theodor to set aside a large chunk of his game preserves and a swamp along the Isar on the outskirts of Munich. The whole real estate package was to be developed into a huge public park. The land was drained in order to support something more than water sports, and the park was laid out in the natural English style, rather than the French neatly manicured mode (anything to avoid inviting comparisons to the revolutionary turmoil going on in Paris at the time).

Englischer Garten was officially dedicated in 1792 and Rumford and his park were an immediate success. They even named a potato and barley soup after him (cleverly, *Rumfordsuppe*). Still, one is left to only wonder, had Rumford backed a winning horse, would it not be the Amerikanischer Garten today.

The park is three miles long, and a little over a half-mile wide in parts. In addition to being bordered on one side by the Isar River, it has three streams flowing through it. At one edge of the Englischer Garten, where the residential area abuts the park itself, is Osterwald Garten, an excellent entrée to the greenbelt beyond. There is a Japanese Teahouse in the southern section. In the central region of the park is a Chinese Pagoda, dating from 1790, which serves as a backdrop to Chinesischer Turm beer garden. Nearby is Kleinhesselohe Lake, a venue for paddle boating and also the setting for Seehaus restaurant and beer garden. Near to

Seehaus is a pedestrian bridge over the busy Isarring highway that bisects the park. At the base of the bridge on the other side is a path leading off to the right and to Hirschau beer garden. Hirschau has returned to The BDG2M, now that new management has placed it back among the living.

As the map shows, our recommendation is to begin at Osterwald Garten, walk from there through the park directly to Seehaus, and then a quick side trip over the bridge to Hirschau and back. Finally, finish up with a visit to Chinesischer Turm, where there is available public transportation to return you home. Better plan, though, to make a day of it and take a stroll through this naturalist's paradise, pausing for a cool one at each stop along the way.

---

*Readers of earlier editions of the BDG2M will note a number of variations in the inclusion or omission of **Hirschau** and **Aumeister** from this Englischer Garten section. Hirschau had fallen on hard times and we dropped it from the fourth edition. However, a complete makeover of the restaurant and beer garden was completed in 2002 and Hirschau was back for the fifth edition. Aumeister, at the extreme northern edge of the park, has always been a high-quality beer garden that we listed in the Englischer Garten section of the first and second editions of the BDG2M. But the walk from **Seehaus** to Aumeister is quite a stroll of some 3 miles or so, although we admit to not making much of this fact when we were a bit younger. Still, time is always limited and we felt it more appropriate to list Aumeister separately and now recommend a faster MVV public transportation method to get there. **Osterwald Garten**, on the other hand, after major improvements documented in previous editions, is strategically situated at the starting point of a very logical and certainly more convenient route to visit all four Englischer Garten beer meccas — especially with a viable mode of public transportation (Bus 54) waiting at Chinesischer Turm. The net result is a much more rewarding day in the Englischer Garten and a lot less mandatory walking that might detract from the time needed to enjoy several of the best beer gardens Munich has to offer.

76

Osterwald Garten

Osterwald Garten is a great way to begin a trip to the Englischer Garten. Its proximity to the major Münchner central park and occasional nudist colony makes it an ideal entryway to the vast public green and its two best watering holes: Seehaus and Chinesischer Turm.

But before we give Osterwald Garten some sort of complex, the fact is this restaurant and beer garden has made some tremendous strides over the past decade. Major renovations have brought the quality and atmosphere to much higher levels than before. The entire restaurant was gutted and expanded to better serve both the beer garden and those dining in for the day. Also, the outstanding list of menu items and the lively clientele add more zest to this urban beer outlet. Osterwald Garten is as near to the Munich student quarter of Schwabing as it is to Englischer Garten and is frequented by a young and enthusiastic crowd who still know how to order 'no a Maß 'of Spaten beer before heading off for class.

Five large chestnut trees provide the shade, and a row of private booths provide the seclusion to hold forth with impromptu seminars on why Germany makes the best beer and the worst paci-

The tradition of a neighborhood beer garden is seen in the faces of the modest staff that served Englischer Garten visitors to Osterwald Garten in 1912, just as it is today.

77

fists. The table service is adequate and the menu is filled with traditional Bavarian meals and specialty salad and vegetarian dishes as well. Chalkboard specials are worth considering and the beer can be had in small, regular, and super thirst-quencher (1 Maß) sizes.

Sunday morning *Frühschoppen*, when husbands talk politics and drink beer while their wives and children are in church, are sometimes accompanied by jazz bands at Osterwald Garten. The label "neighborhood beer garden" is used sparingly because most establishments seem bent on attracting huge crowds of tran-

sient beer drinkers in lieu of a smaller, familiar band of thirsty regulars. Osterwald Garten, however, fits the profile in every way and just happens to be in a great section of town as well.

Osterwald Garten is strategically positioned for an assault on Englischer Garten's legion of beer bastions, so stop by for a beer and get off to the perfect start. For openers, Osterwald Garten gets a steady 3 beers.

A couple of *Stammgäste* (regulars) take a break for a beer and a story or two at Osterwald Garten.

Address ...	Seating ...
Osterwald Garten Kefer Straße 12 80802 Munich	350 in Beer Garden 120 in Restaurant
Phone/FAX ...	**Sounds like ...**
(089) 38405040 FAX (089) 38405035	'OHST-Er-Vald-Gar-Tin'
Hours ...	**Web presence ...**
10 a.m. to 1 a.m.	www.osterwaldgarten.de
Beer ...	**Rating ...**
Spatenbräu	3 Beers

Lakeside seating is a special attraction of Seehaus, in Englischer Garten. One of Munich's best-tasting beers, Paulaner, is another.

Seehaus

in Englischer Garten

A surprising number of visitors to Englischer Garten overlook what one local scribe has termed "the most beautiful interlude in Munich." Seehaus is certainly that, and to stop short of this marvelous, lush green lakeside gem is to forego a rare opportunity to savor mouth watering traditional Bavarian fare along with liters of a top variety local brew, Paulaner. It's all available in an idyllic setting of abundant shade-bearing chestnut trees that ring the beer garden, right up to the water's edge.

Alas, the nearby Chinesischer Turm is to blame. An ample experience in itself, the better-known Chinese Pagoda and beer garden often steal the limelight from Seehaus. Too many would-be seasoned beer drinkers fail to venture the several hundred yards farther to Seehaus. They should realize that, when it comes to the Englischer Garten, good things really do come in bunches, four in this case since Osterwald Garden and Hirschau are included in this group.

The modernity of Seehaus' Medeterranean-style cafe-restaurant belies the 200-year history behind this establishment. It began as a converted wood building left over from a nearby dairy

Seehaus beer garden on the banks of Kleinhesselohe See.

80

farm in 1791. Pressed into service as an inn, the building housed the first beer-dispensing outlet in 1811 and served local patrons well for most of the next century. In 1882-83 the local architect Gabriel von Seidl built the nearby boathouse on Kleinhesselohe Lake — in use today — and the restaurant was reconstructed in 1935. The existing facility was built in 1985.

Today, Seehaus caters to a middle- to upper-class crowd, even offering the ultimate warm afternoon treat, a frozen yogurt stand! Adjacent boat rentals allow one to work up an appetite along with a mammoth thirst, all easily satisfied by the sustenance Seehaus has to offer.

The restaurant is a bit pricey, in contrast to the self-service food stand that appeals to a more pedestrian pocketbook. Paulaner beer, a choice brew, is the beer of choice at this establishment. For those who must, a kiosk selling wine is now available at one corner of the beer garden. Stephan Kuffler, scion of one of Munich's most prominent families in the hospitality trade, runs the Seehaus and has built it into the premier beer outlet it is today.

If one were limited to visit only one beer garden in Munich — a depressing thought — this would be at the very top of the list. When the weather is warm and the throat dry, there is no better alternative than Seehaus. It's the best of the Englischer Garten. Five beers and a helping of O'batzer on the side! (Seehaus is a participant in the Prosit! beer offer. Check coupon page.)

Address ...	Seating ...
Seehaus Kleinhesselohe 3 80802 Munich	2500 in Beer Garden 320 in Cafe-Restaurant
Phone/FAX ...	**Sounds like ...**
(089) 3816130 FAX (089) 341803	'SAY-House'
Hours ...	**Web presence ...**
9 a.m. to 1 a.m.	www.kuffler-gastronomie.de
Beer ...	**Rating ...**
Paulaner	5 Beers

Hirschau

in Englischer Garten

Hirschau, our third stop in the Englischer Garten, is accessed by a pedestrian bridge next to Seehaus that crosses over Isarring, one of Munich's major highways. This excellent restaurant and beer garden has a long history, reaching back 150 years to a time when the area was part of the royal game preserve. Hirschau was one of Munich's most traditional and celebrated beer gardens for many years. On summer weekends, the place was packed and seats were hard to find. We gave it a well-deserved four-beer rating in the 3rd edition of The Beer Drinker's Guide. But things

changed. Disinterested management let the place deteriorate and benign neglect took over from there. By the late 1990s, its many loyal customers had thrown in the towel. We did too, dropping Hirschau completely from the 4th edition.

That might have been the sad end to it, but along came the Schottenhamel family. The Schottenhamels have a near-legendary background in the festive arts, most publicly represented by the wild-and-crazy tent with their name they host each year at the Oktoberfest. If these folks know anything, it's how to throw a party for thousands of guests enjoying

Practically defunct just a few years ago, Hirschau is today making its way back into the hearts and minds of Munich's *Biergärtler*.

themselves to the limit. So maybe it was a natural that Franziska and Peter Schottenhamel would buy what was left of the restaurant and beer garden and turn it into something unrecognizable. In this case, that was a good thing.

They gutted the restaurant and started over. They expanded the beer garden from the old 1500 to just about 2,000 seats today. They tossed the falling-down plastic furniture and brought in hundreds of new benches and tables to resurrect a traditional Bavarian beer garden once again. With a nod to tradition, they set aside a large portion of the expanded beer garden seating for *selbst bedienung* or self-service where you could bring in your own food if you wish.

Reopened in 2002, the business worked at winning back those customers who had fled over the past decade to more amenable parts of the Englischer Garten. The food service team began offering top-notch traditional Bavarian dishes once again. Weekday promotions and after-noon entertainment began drawing the after-work crowd. Jazz bands to rival Wa-Wi (Waldwirtschaft Großhesselohe) have become a regular attraction in the beer garden to attract families and week-end park visitors. Even the kids have something to look forward to when they climb aboard an apparently seaworthy pirate ship in the children's sandbox play area.

Two new wirts — Christian Hoyer and Thomas Böhm — have taken a hand-off from the Schottenhamels and continue to improve the place. All in all, they've put Humpty Dumpty back together again and handed him a beer. If you've been there before, you haven't been there yet. It's that different and that much improved. So now there are four beer gardens to try to cram into a visit to Englischer Garten. What agony we must endure to walk in the footsteps of beer drinkers in Munich. But we try.

Hirschau still has a way to go before it meets the standards of old, or even those of its competition right there in the park. But it's back in business and on its way. We think it will get better over time, but right now it gets 3-1/2 beers.

Note — Live jazz bands are scheduled regularly in the beer garden: Wed. and Fri. at 5 p.m; Sat. 3 p.m., Sun. 2 p.m.

Address ...	Seating ...
Hirschau Gyßling Straße 15 80805 Munich	2000 in Beer Garden 310 in Rest., Banquet Rooms
Phone/FAX ...	**Sounds like ...**
(089) 3221080 FAX (089) 32210819	'HEER-Shau'
Hours ...	**Web presence ...**
10 a.m. to 1 a.m.	www.hirschau-muenchen.de
Beer ...	**Rating ...**
Spatenbräu	3-1/2 Beers

Chinesischer Turm

in Englischer Garten

W ild and crazy people show up at the Chinesischer Turm. "Normal" folk too. Fire-red spiked punk hairdos compete with the Yuppie clean-cut brief-cased look at this massive beer garden (7,000 seats), second only to the Hirschgarten as Munich's largest. Anything and everything is in season. The atmosphere is about as informal as a Saturday morning laundromat, with shorts, tank-tops, barefoot or sandals as the preferred apparel. In fact, a few local patrons may seem to have left their clothes still in the dryer. Nude bathing "beaches" are just a couple hundred yards away.

Chinesischer Turm is the watering hole of choice for most of Munich's student crowd, but by no means their sole mo-

Chinesischer Turm beer garden in the English Garden.

nopoly. The democratic beer garden caters to all walks, all ages, and all circumstances. Everyone is welcome here. The whole affair fronts on a very real looking multi-tiered Chinese wooden pagoda (the stage for Bavarian brass bands on Saturday and Sunday afternoons). The structure's incongruity with the popular image of the traditional Munich beer garden dissipates quickly with a casual review of the attending clientele. As though it really mattered. The place is fun.

The restaurant next door is run by the same folks who operate the beer garden. It offers a decent in-door selection of traditional Bavarian meals and blue-plate specials. Thus it augments the outside fast-pour beer outlet that serves *radlers* (half beer, half lemon-lime soda), *helles*, and *Russiches* beers by the Maß-ful. Take-out, fast food stands offer tasty and economical fare. Russiches, by the way, is a *weiß* or wheat beer, that is also mixed half-and-half with lemon lime soda. Just as accessible are tall glass liter mugs of

the more familiar Hofbräu brew. It was front-page news in Munich several years ago when after many years, Chinesischer Turm switched from Löwenbräu to Hofbräu. Generally, you'd have to say customers are glad they did.

The crowds are unusually large here, attracted by all that the beer garden has to offer coupled with its central location in Munich's largest public park. There's a carousel just for the kids. Also, it is the only interior Englischer Garten beer bazaar readily adjacent to public transportation (bus stop just behind the beer garden). Chinesischer Turm is a marvelous place for people watching, where the beer is bountiful and the well-shaded setting could hardly stand improvement.

We think Chinesischer Turm runs a close second to Seehaus when it comes to honors for best Englischer Garten beer emporium. That's not bad, it's just not perfect. Still, Chinesischer Turm gets a can't-be-missed recommendation and a 4-1/2 beer rating.

Address ...	Seating ...
Chinesischer Turm Englischer Garten 3 80805 Munich	7000 in Beer Garden
Phone/FAX ...	**Sounds like ...**
(089) 383870 FAX (089) 38387373	'Chin-NEZ-Ish-Er-Term'
Hours ...	**Web presence ...**
10 a.m. to 1 a.m.	www.chinaturm.de
Beer ...	**Rating ...**
Hofbräu	4-1/2 Beers

85

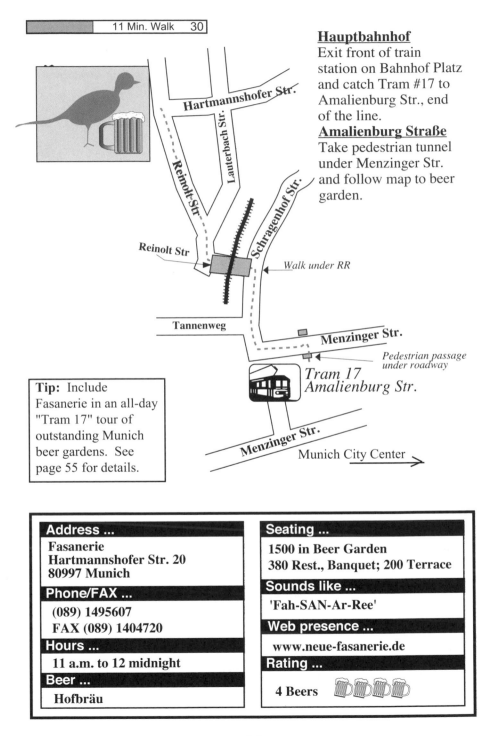

Hauptbahnhof
Exit front of train station on Bahnhof Platz and catch Tram #17 to Amalienburg Str., end of the line.
Amalienburg Straße
Take pedestrian tunnel under Menzinger Str. and follow map to beer garden.

Hartmannshofer Str.

Lauterbach Str.

Reinolt Str

Reinolt Str

Schragenhof Str.

Walk under RR

Tannenweg

Menzinger Str.

Pedestrian passage under roadway

Tram 17 Amalienburg Str.

Tip: Include Fasanerie in an all-day "Tram 17" tour of outstanding Munich beer gardens. See page 55 for details.

Menzinger Str.

Munich City Center

Address ...	Seating ...
Fasanerie Hartmannshofer Str. 20 80997 Munich	1500 in Beer Garden 380 Rest., Banquet; 200 Terrace
Phone/FAX ...	**Sounds like ...**
(089) 1495607 FAX (089) 1404720	'Fah-SAN-Ar-Ree'
Hours ...	**Web presence ...**
11 a.m. to 12 midnight	www.neue-fasanerie.de
Beer ...	**Rating ...**
Hofbräu	4 Beers

86

Fasanerie

Pheasants. That's where the name Fasanerie comes from. This restaurant and beer garden is in a pleasant country setting, but no pheasants to be found. No doubt anxious German hunters weeded them out years ago and they've long since disappeared from everything, including the restaurant's menu.

Fine, who needs them? Chicken tastes better anyway. And so do all the other gastronomic treats Fasaneric has to offer. Plenty of grilled meats, chilled salads and aged cheeses dominate the menu along with refreshing Hofbräu Beer. Fasanerie is in the middle of a parklike setting, not far from the New Botanical Garden (the "old" version is near the Hauptbahnhof, where Park Cafe beer garden is located). Also close by is the Nymphenburg Palace. The historical connection with game fowl reaches back to the latter half of the 17th century. Evidently, at the close of the 30 Years War, local monarchs had time on their hands so they took to establishing pheasant hatcheries, or Fasaneries, to up their odds during their hunting expeditions. Bavarian Duke Max Emanuel built the first Fasaneries in nearby Nymphenburg, Moosach, Schleißheim, and the site where the beer garden is today. Somewhere in his biographical notes is a ledger indicating the king bagged 39,665 hunting trophies, of which 2,351 were pheasants. One would think that he would have bagged even more. Also worth noting is the fact that the Fasanerie was valued enough to have been "plundered" in 1742 during the War of Austrian Succession, burnt to the ground in 1797 by the French, and rebuilt by the Bavarians in 1806. By the end of the First World War, the Fasanerie was no longer hatching birds, but looking for other more lucrative endeavors. In 1920 a hunter named Engelbert Brieschenk managed a restaurant and lodge on the site. That business grew to what it is today. When the business changed hands a few years ago, the new team began referring to the "Neue" Fasanerie. What's new are the occasional weekend bands geared to a younger audience with predictably later closing hours.

Still, Fasanerie is a beer garden you would not even know existed without prior knowledge and a map to go with it. With some 1500 seats in the expanded beer garden and another 200 on the umbrella-covered terrace, there is ample room to handle the crowd. Prices here are a little higher than elsewhere, but the atmosphere and high-quality of fare and service help balance out the value. Also, a self service beer *ausschank* at one end of the beer garden is available to do-it-yourselfers who hate to pay retail. Techie alert: the entire beer garden is a wireless hotspot, so you can boot up your laptop and surf the net while sampling the suds. In all, Fasanerie is a worthy venue, in a tranquil setting, with a little more shine on the flatware than some other Munich beer gardens. With or without pheasants, it gets four beers.

Hauptbahnhof
S- or U-Bahn to Marienplatz.
Marienplatz
U-Bahn 3 to Brudermühle Str.
Brudermühle Str.
Bus 54 (direction: "Scheidplatz") one stop to Schäftlarn Str.
Shäftlarn Str.
Walk, following map, across bridge then down pathway along the river. (Note: if you prefer, walk from Brudermühle Str. U-Bahn stop. Only adds a few minutes to walk.)

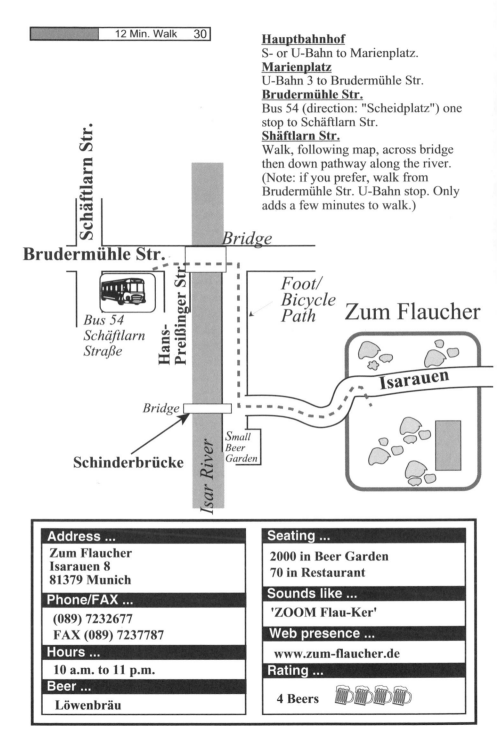

Address ...	Seating ...
Zum Flaucher Isarauen 8 81379 Munich	2000 in Beer Garden 70 in Restaurant
Phone/FAX ...	**Sounds like ...**
(089) 7232677 FAX (089) 7237787	'ZOOM Flau-Ker'
Hours ...	**Web presence ...**
10 a.m. to 11 p.m.	www.zum-flaucher.de
Beer ...	**Rating ...**
Löwenbräu	4 Beers

Flaucher

Take a walk along the Isar canal, and make a left through the woods and you'll arrive at Zum Flaucher beer garden. One of Munich's oldest, Flaucher is a favorite haunt of bicyclists and hikers who spend the day among the greenery and the afternoon in the shade of a chestnut tree or an umbrella in the beer garden. It is a pocket of activity in an expanse of secluded park and woodland, with plenty of nearby recreational opportunities, including a meandering network of walking and biking trails.

In 1871, Johann Flaucher first opened a restaurant on land that was once a part of the exclusive Wittelsbach hunting preserve. The small restaurant and beer garden business in the woods changed several hands until the 1920s when Ida Bornschlegl took over with a serious mind to keep it. And she did for more than 50 years, finally calling it a gastronomical career in 1979. Another ownership brought renovation to the restaurant and expansion of the beer garden. Finally, in 1989 Hermann Haberl from the Munich hospitality family of the same name bought the property. It's been handed down once again, and in 2000 a Haberl daughter, Antje Haberl Schneider, took over the tap handle at Zum Flaucher.

Flaucher's beer garden covers a wide area, and rows of tables and benches spill over to the other side of the road. The restaurant is primarily a self-service, fast-food affair, but an outdoor full-service dining area is also available. The posted menu lists a hearty assortment of Bavarian beer snacks, and for seafood lovers roasted mackerel on a stick is a special treat. There is a play area for kids.

The beer garden and restaurant complex are in one of the city's more scenic woodland areas. The 12-minute walk from the nearest bus or U-bahn stop is a pleasant trek along the river canal and through the forest. The Haberls are interested in attracting more vacationing visitors, although the local business is thriving. They ought to be taken up on the invitation. Zum Flaucher, a green and shaded summertime sanctuary with good food, beer and relaxing atmosphere, gets 4 beers.

Entrance to Zum Flaucher's beer garden.

Hauptbahnhof
S-Bahn 6 to Perlach
Perlach
Walk out back of station, straight down Stephenson Platz, following map. Option: Take short-cut along walking path, adjacent to station entrance. Don't walk along track! Too dangerous.

Forschungs -brauerei

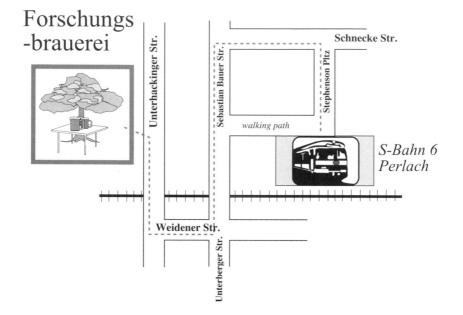

Address ...	Seating ...
Forschungsbrauerei Unterhachinger Straße 76 81737 Munich	450 in Beer Garden 300 in Restaurant
Phone/FAX ...	**Sounds like ...**
(089) 6701169; No FAX	'FORE-Shungs BROW-Er-Rye'
Hours ...	**Web presence ...**
Tues.-Sat.: 11 a.m.-11 p.m., Sun./Hol.: 10 a.m.-10 p.m. Closed Mon.	www.forschungsbrauerei.de
Beer ...	**Rating ...**
St. Jakobus, Pilsissimus	4 Beers

Forschungsbrauerei

In the world of modern research, a small ante room belongs to the process of making beer. Forschungsbrauerei, strictly translated, "experimental brewery," has made a niche for itself, advancing the art along with the science. It's the little brewery that could, matching and surpassing Munich's industrial brewing giants in quality, but choosing to remain small and undiluted by the effects of mass production. So, while the big guys are up to their fill-lines with bottling and exporting demands, Forschungsbrauerei focuses its efforts on a small, select group of customers. Beer drinkers lucky enough to know of this suburban Munich establishment are rewarded with a home-brewed product manufactured and sold solely within the confines of the restaurant and beer garden.

Give credit to Gottfried Jakob whose profit motive was tempered by his credo that he'd never brew a bad glass of beer. In 1924 with diploma in the liberal libation arts in hand, the Weihenstephan-trained Gottfried began experimenting with a small 44-gallon beer making plant. He dispensed the fermented drink sparingly at first, to family and close friends. With each improved formula, Jakob built his own ladder to beer brewing success and demand for his brew grew faster than his laboratory could handle. In 1936 he began a commercial venture, a 500-gallon capacity brewery. At the same time he added a five-table restaurant.

The beer garden as seen from top of the Südhaus (main brewing plant) at Forschungsbrauerei.

That was essentially the end of Jakob's grandiose plans for major expansion. He kept the business based on two personal principles: he would not compromise on the quality of his beer, and he would keep the entire operation within the capability of his family. Jakob never strayed from that path.

Gottfried Jakob passed on in 1958 and the business was handed down first to his son Heinrich, who ran the business along with his brother-in-law Sigmund. Heinrich's wife Karin and sister Lieselotte stayed busy operating the kitchen and office, as they do today. Meanwhile, son Stefan Jakob balanced his time manning the *bierausschank* and pursuing his studies at Weihenstephan, following in his grandfather's footsteps. With a degree in hand, Stefan has now moved from behind the bar to the *Südhaus*, where the brewing process begins. He's now in charge of the family business as well as the tradition.

The family remains proud that they operate no retail outlet, no beer tents and no other guest houses. Their locally and rightfully famous *Pilsissimus* and *St. Jakobus* bock beers are reserved for the fortunate few: those who are there to enjoy it. The restaurant is basic and the menu is filled with Bavarian specialties that are cheap, filling, and tasty. The beer garden has room to seat thousands, but in character the proprietors have kept it to a manageable 400-500 or so. The two-story copper brewing plant at one end of the restaurant seems to gravity feed the entire beer garden, where beer is only served in the traditional and seldom seen clay-fired beer mugs. (Most Munich establishments have gone for the clear, 1-liter glass mugs that are more eye-appealing but less efficient in maintaining the freshness and cold temperature of the beer.) For at least one week out of the year, Forschungsbrauerei not only tries harder but succeeds over the big Munich breweries. The strong beer or "double-

The brewer's art has been pursued for centuries in Munich and the region of Bavaria. Forschungs -brauerei is carrying forward an age-old tradition.

bock" season, a two-week period beginning around "Joseph's Day" on the 19th of March, is well celebrated by Münchners.

Most popular during this time is Forschungsbrauerei's St. Jakobus bock beer. This is truly one of the best-tasting brews in the world. We love this beer but warn its 7.5% alcohol level — by comparison Pilsissimus runs about 5.2% — makes it a healthy but stealthy drink.

While the rest of Munich is restricted to the 14-days of stark bier revelry, Forschungs is allowed an extra week of celebration. For an uncertain reason that is best explained as tradition, the brewery begins its party a week early, thus gaining the spotlight while the big houses downtown are still lining up entertainment and stringing decorations. Score one for the little guys.

Forschungsbrauerei is an unusual and rare find. The freshness of its product and the personal touch of the family-run business see to that. It's a moderate S-bahn ride and a short walk from the station in Perlach. Definitely worth an experimental visit to find out what the Jakob family will brew up next. Forschungsbrauerei gets a 4-beer rating.

Weihenstephan-trained Stefan Jakob (left) and his uncle, Sigmund Steinbeisser, inspect *Südhaus* brewing equipment at the family-run operation.

93

Franziskaner Garten

We welcomed Franziskaner Garten to the previous 5th edition of this book because it literally embodied our entire philosophy here at The Beer Drinker's Guide. Our commitment has always been to include only businesses whose management readily welcomed foreign visitors, regardless of the size or atmosphere of the beer garden itself. Unfortunately, prior to the business changing hands a few years ago, that was a test Franziskaner would not meet. We had visited this beer garden many times. Never was the wirt friendly, cooperative or even close to welcoming when it came to the prospect of outsiders visiting his beer garden. He just didn't seem to care.

Patience. That's what it took. And new management.

Annet and Harald Weber took over Franziskaner Garten in 2000 and gave it new life. They enlisted the support and counsel of Sepp Krätz, well-known wirt of Waldwirtschaft Großhesselohe and several other overachieving Munich beer

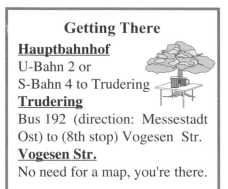

Getting There

Hauptbahnhof
U-Bahn 2 or
S-Bahn 4 to Trudering
Trudering
Bus 192 (direction: Messestadt Ost) to (8th stop) Vogesen Str.
Vogesen Str.
No need for a map, you're there.

gardens. The partnership proved productive and beneficial, fostering a new attitude and a new look to the beer garden.

The new owners trashed the plastic furniture from previous management and replaced it with traditional wood tables, chairs and benches, more befitting a genuine Munich beer garden. That was a good start.

Then the Webers renovated the restaurant — the building itself an historic landmark dating back to 1923 — and

Address ...	Seating ...
Franziskaner Garten Friedenspromenade 45 81827 Munich	2500 in Beer Garden 180 Terrace; 120 in Restaurant
Phone/FAX ...	Sounds like ...
(089) 4300996 FAX (089) 43759211	'FRAN-Ziss-KAN-Er-Gar-Tin'
Hours ...	Web presence ...
10 a.m. to 11 p.m.	www.franziskanergarten.de
Beer ...	Rating ...
Spatenbräu, Franziskaner Weiß	4-1/2 Beers

modernized and centralized the serving area.

To insure a ready supply of brew, a battery of six 100-liter tanks of beer feed the beer garden. Barely enough to meet demand, the tanks require replenishment on a weekly basis. A unique feature of the more efficient serving system includes the use of refrigerated *eisgekühlt* glasses. Every frosted mug is pre-cooled in the basement and brought up to the *ausschank* via an automatic lift before it is filled with Spatenbräu and served to customers. For those who love the local variety of inland seafood, the *Steckerlfisch* stand offers five varieties of roasted fish on a stick.

The Webers regularly book live entertainment in the beer garden as part of local special musical events in July and August. A retractable cover provides some shelter from summer showers and during the winter months, portable heaters beat back the cold for an annual Christmas fest right there in the beer garden. In an interesting sidenote, the Franziskaner wirts actually made the pages of The Guiness Book of World Records when for the fun of it they rolled out the world's largest baked pretzel — weighing in at 397 lbs. (180 kilograms). Typically, Herr Weber has future plans to break his own record with an even larger version of the world's most impressive beer snack. This is a terrific beer garden and restaurant in east Munich, and one you don't even have to stretch your legs for since the bus drops you off directly in front of the entrance. Our compliments to the old chef for selling out — it was about time. And our thanks to the new chefs for bringing back a customer-friendly atmosphere that we have no reservations in recommending to readers of The BDG2M. Franziskaner Garten keeps getting better and was recently named among the top three of Munich's beer gardens in a citywide poll. We agree completely and are happy to give it an upgraded 4-1/2 beers.

Franziskaner Garten proprietors Annet and Harald Weber strike a welcoming pose at the entrance to their restaurant and beer garden.

Hauptbahnhof
U- or S-Bahn to Marienplatz
Marienplatz
U-3 to Thalkirchen
Thalkirchen
Exit U-Bahn station using ramp, not stairs/escalator. Cross the street to Bus 135. Take Bus 135 five stops to Hinterbrühl.
Hinterbrühl
You're there.

Campingplatz (one stop earlier)
MVV added the new 135 bus in Dec. 2004. For those who enjoyed the short, 12-minute walk from Campingplatz through the woods to Hinterbrühl, we're leaving the map. Your choice. Pathway:

Gasthof Hinterbrühl

Bus 135
Hinterbrühl

Golf Course

Benediktbeuer Str.

Two bridges

Isar River

Zentralland Str.

Campground

Bus Stop:
Campingplatz
for alternative
walk

Walking Path

(Note: Mangostin beer garden is just across the street from Thalkirchen U-Bahn stop.)

Address ...	Seating ...
Gasthof Hinterbrühl **Hinterbrühl 2** **81479 Munich**	**1500 in Beer Garden** **300 in Restaurant**
Phone/FAX ...	**Sounds like ...**
(089) 794494 FAX (089) 798724	'GAST-Hoff HIN-Ter-Brool'
Hours ...	**Web presence ...**
10 a.m. to 12 Midnight	www.gasth-hinterbruehl.de
Beer ...	**Rating ...**
Hacker-Pschorr Bräu	4-1/2 Beers

Hinterbrühl

Tired of city life? Wish you could find a little alpine redoubt but no time for a trip to Garmisch, Berchtesgaden or some other Bavarian mountain resort? Hinterbrühl is a low-altitude, high-atmosphere facsimile of the above, and a whole lot easier to get to. It's hard to believe this "mountain lodge" on the banks of the Isar is actually within Munich's city limits (Thalkirchen district). It seems a world and several topographical elevations apart. The 170-year-old, three-story restaurant and beer tavern has more the look of a way-station where knapsackers stop to pitch a lean-to and *lederhosen* and spiked climbing boots are the preferred dress over shirt-sleeves and tennis shoes. A backdrop of a pine-forested hillside adds to the effect as does an expanded 1500-seat beer garden overlooking the river. Those seated nearest the river's edge in summer are treated to a constant parade of party rafters (*Floß*) where the conversation is punctuated every 10 minutes or so by the gradually rising crescendo of an approaching waterborne "oom-pah" band. For a fleeting moment, river-going rafters and landlubber *biergärtler* share a camaraderie in a raised glass of beer and several harmonious bars of a traditional German drinking song before the raft and its revelers disappear in the distance. That is, until the next raft, the next song, and the next beer.

Gasthof Hinterbrühl, with the atmosphere of a Bavarian mountain inn, is within easy reach of the city's public transportation system.

Hinterbrühl's history is a common one: a down-river stopover along the main logging route between the upper forested areas and the lumber mills below. The lumberjack clientele have been replaced by a devoted following of city-slickers, and the process itself is embodied in the still flourishing custom of *Floß*. Yet, the original forest atmosphere remains.

In a little-known historical footnote, Hinterbrühl was once a favorite haunt of Nazi officialdom before and during World War II. The likes of Hitler, Göring and Göbbels were frequent visitors as they considered this a suitable alternative when political business kept them away from their more opulent mountain chalets nestled among Berchtesgaden's pictur-esque snow-capped peaks. When the war ended and scores were settled, 10 Nazis went to the gallows in October 1946. Göring cheated the hangman's rope by committing suicide in his cell. His ashes, along with those of the other Nazi war criminals were strewn into the *Weuzbach*, a stream that runs alongside Hinterbrühl.

Hinterbrühl today is no shrine to anything but outdoor beer drinking enjoyment. The location of this restaurant and beer garden is ideal for long walks along the river, through the woods and general communing with nature. One of the city's largest camping areas, an 18-hole golf course, and the Tierpark Hellabrunn (zoo) are all nearby. The restaurant offers a limited but reasonably priced menu with

The tradition of *Floß*, or party rafting, is as strong today as it was hundreds of years ago when Bavarian lumber-jacks celebrated their harvest by organizing waterborne beer busts on the way to market. This happy group of beer drinkers makes the most of a slow cruise down the Isar.

daily specials. In fact, eating in the outdoor restaurant is one of the more economical moves you can make in Munich. The beer garden serves wood-grilled specialties, including roast pork knuckles, chicken and a variety of sausages. The proprietors are continually striving to improve their establishment. Their expansion of the beer garden from 1200 to 1500 seats was a welcome addition. Even more so was their decision to remain open seven days a week, with no *Ruhetag* (rest day). Previously Hinterbrühl had this strange custom of closing on Fridays, of all days. But no longer. Open now when you are, as they say.

Hinterbrühl is high on tradition and atmosphere in a rare wooded setting that puts the Bavarian alpine region a short U-bahn and bus ride away. It's one of the best in Munich, earning a well-deserved 4 1/2 beers.

A Maß of Hacker-Pschorr Bräu could hardly taste any better than at Hinterbrühl Gasthof on a warm summer afternoon.

99

Hirschgarten

Hauptbahnhof
One of several S-Bahns to Laim

Laim
From platform, walk down stairs and through traffic tunnel. First street after tunnel, turn right. Follow map, walking through park to beer garden.

Park

Fenced Deer Enclosure

Park Entrance

Walking Path

Ginhardt Str.

De La-Paz Str.

Signal light

Winfried Str.

Parking Lot

Tunnel/ Underpass

Stairs

S-Bahn Laim

Tip: Include Hirschgarten in an all-day "Tram 17" tour of outstanding Munich beer gardens. See page 55 for details.

Address ...	Seating ...
Hirschgarten Hirschgartenallee 1 80639 Munich	8000 in Beer Garden 320 in Restaurant
Phone/FAX ...	**Sounds like ...**
(089) 172591; FAX (089) 175706	'HERSH-Gart-In'
Hours ...	**Web presence ...**
9 a.m. to 12 Midnight	www.hirschgarten.de
Beer ...	**Rating ...**
Augustiner, HB Tegernsee, Kaltenberger Bräu	5 Beers

Hirschgarten

Hirschgarten is the biggest beer garden in the world, and doesn't even bother to brag about it. The proprietors have decided the money they save on advertising and glitzy brochures is better spent financing an army of service help to manage the 8,000 guests who invade this place on warm weekend afternoons. This former royal hunting preserve packs them in, beer mug to beer mug, tighter than salt on a pretzel. As big as it is, the beer garden and restaurant occupy a small parkland corner of the palatial grounds surrounding Schloß Nymphenburg. Nearby are lakes, gushing fountains, botanical gardens, parks and of course the palace itself. (We should mention here that the best way to view the Schloß Nymphenburg proper along with Hirschgarten is via the alternate Tram 17 route and Zur Schwaige, see page 55.)

Nymphenburg is one of the more opulent among the Wittelsbach stable of royal estates. It was built in 1664 as a present to the Electress Henriette Adelaide for having given birth to a long-awaited son, Max Emanuel. The palace became the favored summer retreat of several generations of Bavarian ruling families. Within the mirrored halls and gold-leaf and fleur-de-lis embellished ceilings is a unique set of paintings: King Ludwig I's "Gallery of Beauties." The paintings are Ludwig's choice of the most beautiful women in Munich. Those he personally selected to pose for portrait painter Jo-

Families and friends find a meeting place in the Hirschgarten.

seph Stieler included his own daughter-in-law, ladies at court and Lola Montez, the royal mistress (see Menterschwaige). With Ludwig's well-known love for Munich's beer gardens, it's no wonder a section of this massive estate was dedicated to the outdoor beer-drinking art.

The beer garden is so large to be split up in areas of shade, sun and a section of tables with an overhead, retractable ramada standing by in case of any sudden afternoon cloudbursts. Service is available at those covered tables nearest the restaurant. Most, however, are *selbstbedienung* (self-service) and patrons sitting there are welcome to bring their own picnic baskets and wait on themselves. They begin by selecting a glass, liter mug from the rack at the side of the row of fast-food stands. Tradition calls for washing the mug in the steel basins provided (more like rinsing in cold water) and walking around the corner to the *ausschank* for a fill-up of fresh, cold Augustiner beer right from the wooden keg. In fact, there are five beer stations in

all, two dedicated to the dispensing of *Weizen* or wheat beer. In addition to Augustiner, Hirschgarten offers Hofbräuhaus Tegernsee and Kaltenberg beers as well.

The self-serve, cafeteria style row of snack stands offers a wide assortment of Bavarian foods. Lots of sausages, spit-roasted whole chickens, and meat and potato salads are on sale. There's also a mouth-puckering rich cream cheese called *Obatzer* worth trying. It goes great as a spread over torn-off sections of fresh-baked salted pretzel (*Bretz'n*). Fish lovers have only to follow their nose when the mackerel-on-a-stick stand is in operation. The aroma of roasting seafood permeates the entire beer garden. The indoor restaurant at the far end of Hirschgarten has managed a gourmet reputation of its own. Unlike many of Munich's beer gardens, the restaurant here has won the support of a loyal clientele that keeps it open and busy during the winter months when the rest of the beer garden is closed. The Hirschgarten or

The deer that give Hirschgarten its name are well-protected and a special attraction for the kids.

102

"deer garden" actually lives up to its name. At the edge of the beer garden is an enclosure housing dozens of live, well-domesticated Bambis who like to stick their noses through the fence and munch on handouts from passersby. This informal petting zoo is a treat for the kids and a reminder of local history. Centuries ago the Hirschgarten was a staging area for the king's royal hunts. The local four-legged game have nothing to fear these days. They're well protected and cared for and kept off the restaurant's menu. Hirschgarten is the type of beer garden that Munich is famous for: huge, inviting and filled with tradition. Local management isn't hurting for patronage, so they are less keen than most in attracting the notice of the city's hype-conscious tourist industry. One result is that few foreign visitors venture here. They just haven't known about Hirschgarten or how accessible it is with public transportation. (A 10-minute S-bahn ride and a short walk from the busy commuter stop at Laim — pronounced "Lime.")

It's no wonder bragging rights are conferred upon the patrons and not the proprietors of Hirschgarten. With a can't-miss combination of Munich's best-tasting beer, plenty of outstanding eats, and an atmosphere without room for much improvement, word-of-mouth testimonials are all that's needed. Hirschgarten gets the top 5-beer rating.

Visitors to Hirschgarten are treated to the vanishing custom of a trip to the *Krüge* rack to select their own liter glass mug. A quick rinsing, and then around the corner to the beer *ausschank* for a fill-up.

103

Hauptbahnhof
Walk up Bayer Str. (see inset
map) through Marienplatz and
follow main map.

OR

Hauptbahnhof
Take one of several S- or U-
Bahns direct to Marienplatz.

Marienplatz
Walk, following main map.

Hofbräuhaus

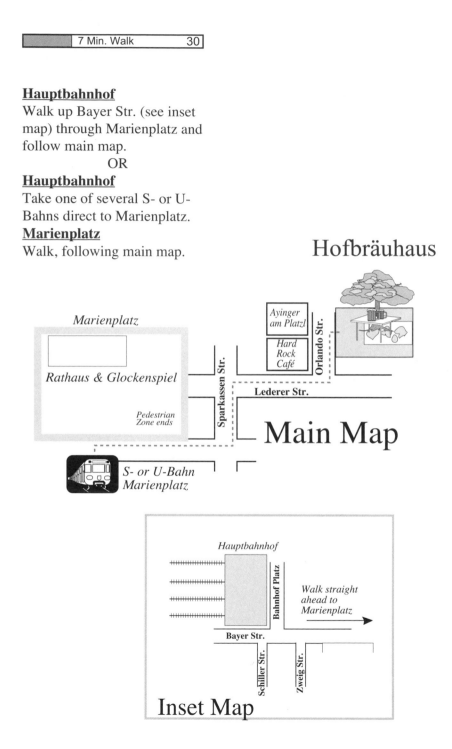

Marienplatz

Rathaus & Glockenspiel

Sparkassen Str.

Ayinger am Platzl

Hard Rock Café

Orlando Str.

Lederer Str.

Pedestrian Zone ends

Main Map

S- or U-Bahn Marienplatz

Hauptbahnhof

Bahnhof Platz

Walk straight ahead to Marienplatz

Bayer Str.

Schiller Str.

Zweig Str.

Inset Map

Hofbräuhaus

No beer establishment in Munich is more renowned, revered — and reviled — than the Hofbräuhaus. To some, the world-famous beer hall is an artificial plastic replica of a real Munich beer hall, wheeled out on an hourly basis for the amusement of a rotating fleet of bused-in tourists. A reasonable fascmile and not much more. To others, it's a veritable shrine to the brewing and beer-drinking arts, worthy of more than a few genuflects from those faithful pilgrims fortunate to pass through its gothic portals. But defenders and detractors take note. The truth, somewhere in the middle, is rendered moot by a Hofbräuhaus that is rafter to rafter of uncompromising and unrelenting fun!

On any given afternoon and evening, a world community, from Americans to Zambians (and more than a few touring Germans), gathers here to hoist a mug, join in a round of "Oans, Zwoa, Gsuffa" and become — if only for the moment — honorary, card-carrying Bavarians. And if the Hofbräuhaus isn't rollicking, pulsating fun the way Munich beer halls really are, then maybe it's the way they ought to be: a place where everybody is welcome and nobody goes away disappointed. The beer and food are plentiful and the high-charged atmosphere is the closest thing to a real party this side of Oktoberfest.

Despite the artificial veneer left from decades of commercialization, the history of this beer-drinking mecca is without question. Bavarian Duke Wilhelm V founded the *Hofbräu* or central brewing house in 1589. Two years later the brewery began producing limited libations for an elite royal clientele, but by 1604 was "exporting" its product beyond the city limits. Soon thereafter the first bock beer was brewed here and, since it was commonly dispensed beginning in May, earned the name *Maibock*. In 1610 the royal brewery expanded its business beyond the Bavarian aristocracy and embraced the thirsty common folk, thus

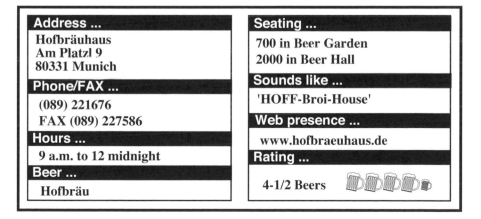

Address ...	Seating ...
Hofbräuhaus Am Platzl 9 80331 Munich	700 in Beer Garden 2000 in Beer Hall
Phone/FAX ...	**Sounds like ...**
(089) 221676 FAX (089) 227586	'HOFF-Broi-House'
Hours ...	**Web presence ...**
9 a.m. to 12 midnight	www.hofbraeuhaus.de
Beer ...	**Rating ...**
Hofbräu	4-1/2 Beers

founding its reputation as the "people's brew." When rampant mid-19th century inflation threatened to place beer among a growing list of unattainable luxuries, a royal decree was issued freezing the brewhouse's prices and preserving for "the military and working classes a healthy and wholesome drink." A good thing, too, because lesser provocations were stirring revolution all over Europe. The Bavarians, with a Hofbräuhaus continuing to dispense their venerable brew at dependable prices, remained contented and left the militant unpleasantries to their Prussian cousins up north.

The Hofbräuhaus was moved to its present location in 1828 and rebuilt in much its current style in 1897. In the years just after World War I, this was the site for much plotting and intrigue. Hitler and his fledgling Nazi party moved their political rallies to the Hofbräuhaus' spacious inner sanctum when his fiery oratory began drawing large crowds. The blood-red, white and black banners with the Nazi *Hackenkreuz* (Swastika) were an oft-seen adornment to the eaves of the Hofbräuhaus during the years between the wars. As if paying the price for the conflagration that followed, the Hofbräuhaus was 60 percent destroyed in World War II and not completely rebuilt until the late-1950s.

Today it is a meeting place for the world. Visitors to its cavernous beer hall, restaurant, beer garden, and second-story massive festival hall will sense the history behind this place — despite the touristy surface outer layer. But along with a perception of the past is a wonderful enjoyment of the present. Like no other place on earth, fun is infectious at the Hofbräuhaus. At some time during the evening, you will fall prey and become one of the crowd of singing, shouting, swaying beer drinkers. Since chances of being left a table to one's self are slim, the opportunity for striking up conversations

Panoramic mid-1800s drawing of HB's courtyard (today's beer garden).

with fellow travelers in a multitude of languages is practically assured. (Here you would even be forgiven for sitting, unknowingly of course, at a *Stammtisch* for *der Altbayern*, a table reserved for genuine Bavarian aboriginals.) If you don't think you'll get caught up in it all, you just haven't been there yet. One young visitor from Sweden did. He made beer-drinking history at the Hofbräuhaus when he set the world record for fastest chug-a-lug of a one-liter stein of beer. The 22-year-old med student accomplished the feat in 4.4 seconds. (Kids, don't try this one at home!)

The immediate neighborhood keeps changing around the Hofbräuhaus. The one-time Platzl am Platzl turned Planet Hollywood is now a Hard Rock Cafe. Not much change there. Just outside the Hofbräuhaus to the right is Ayinger am Platzl, which is worth a visit to try some good beer. Also, outside to the left on Münz Str. is a new Augustiner am Platzl, offering again great beer and a welcome addition to the local diversity.

The Hofbräuhaus lives up to its billing as a "must-see" on every travel itinerary computer print-out. Yes it's commercialized and yes its service has suffered with the loss of real competition, such as occurred with the closure of Mathäser Bierstadt a few years ago. But passing this off as a thinly layered tourist trap would be missing the point: Hofbräuhaus is a cauldron of bubbling fun and enjoyment, spiced with good beer, food and just about all that one could ever ask of a Munich beer hall. You'll seldom have a bad time here. We give it 4-1/2 beers because, while not perfect, it's still one of the best beer-drinking experiences in Munich or the world for that matter.

Meanwhile, on the inside the atmosphere was calmer but still busy in HB's Great Hall or *Schwemme*.

107

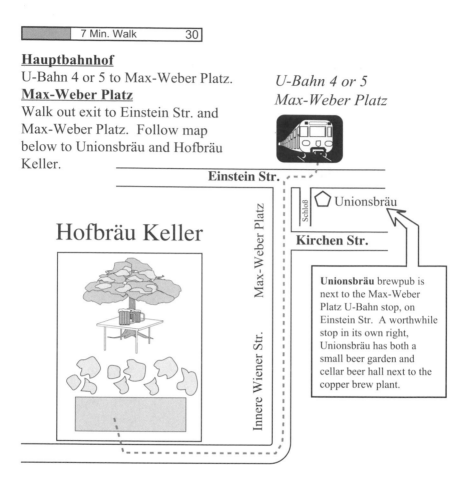

Hauptbahnhof
U-Bahn 4 or 5 to Max-Weber Platz.

Max-Weber Platz
Walk out exit to Einstein Str. and Max-Weber Platz. Follow map below to Unionsbräu and Hofbräu Keller.

U-Bahn 4 or 5
Max-Weber Platz

Einstein Str.

Hofbräu Keller

Max-Weber Platz

Innere Wiener Str.

Schloß

Unionsbräu

Kirchen Str.

Unionsbräu brewpub is next to the Max-Weber Platz U-Bahn stop, on Einstein Str. A worthwhile stop in its own right, Unionsbräu has both a small beer garden and cellar beer hall next to the copper brew plant.

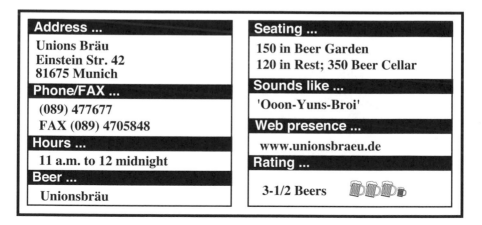

Address ...

Unions Bräu
Einstein Str. 42
81675 Munich

Phone/FAX ...

(089) 477677
FAX (089) 4705848

Hours ...

11 a.m. to 12 midnight

Beer ...

Unionsbräu

Seating ...

150 in Beer Garden
120 in Rest; 350 Beer Cellar

Sounds like ...

'Ooon-Yuns-Broi'

Web presence ...

www.unionsbraeu.de

Rating ...

3-1/2 Beers

Hofbräu Keller
and Unionsbräu

Two worthy watering holes in the city's Haidhausen artists' quarter are Hofbräu Keller and Unionsbräu brewpub. Just around the corner from each other, the two establishments offer both the atmosphere of a large traditional Bavarian beer garden as well as the intimacy of a cellar beer hall with its own craft-brewed beer.

Unionsbräu

First up is Unionsbräu, just across the street from the Max-Weber-Platz U-Bahn stop. A small but growing brewpub, the Unionsbräu comes complete with a cellar beer hall, restaurant, courtyard beer garden and historical pedigree of its own. Established in 1885 as one of Munich's larger beer emporia, by 1922 it was associated with the fast-growing Löwenbräu brewery. It continued operation until World War II but was almost completely destroyed in a bombing raid. In the late 1980s the building that houses the brewpub today was rebuilt and designated a protected historical monument. Entering the picture at that time was Ludwig Hagn, the man who is best known around Munich for running the Löwenbräu Festival Tent during Oktoberfest. As one might expect, Herr Hagn was especially enamored of the building's previous role in housing a brewery. After a few years of brick-by-brick restoration and plenty of painstaking detail, a brewpub emerged and Unionsbräu opened its

Unionsbräu wirt Ludwig Hagn in his micro-brewing plant.

109

doors in July 1991. The cellar brew plant at one end of the 350-seat Braukeller beer hall produces an unfiltered *Helles* (light) and *Dunkles* (dark) lager, as well as a seasonal strong bock beer dubbed, naturally, "Unimator". The courtyard beer garden has room for 150 with several wooden modules arranged for circular group-sit. The brewpub is fast gaining reputation for live music offerings, especially dixieland jazz and swing bands that play regular weekend events in the beer hall. The wirt, whose family has been active in the annual Oktoberfest since the 1950s, has the beer hospitality business in his blood and it shows at Unionsbräu. This is a great place to begin a Haidhausen pub crawl that leads around the corner to Hofbräu Keller, one of Munich's most traditional beer establishments.

Hofbräu Keller

The Hofbräu Keller, easily mistaken for its better known cousin, the Hofbräuhaus, is a sprawling restaurant and beer garden on Wiener Platz frequented by a large number of urban dwellers who want a taste of traditional *Gemütlichkeit* without having to travel long distances to enjoy it. Predictably, the "keller" versus the "haus" leans heavily on the outdoor beer garden atmosphere to attract its clientele. Not without its roots in local history, HB keller is also near the site of the infamous Burgerbräu Keller, where in 1923 Hitler hatched his ill-fated "Beer Hall Putsch." While the Burgerbräu has been leveled and a modern cultural center erected in its place, the Hofbräu Keller has survived. But just barely. Built in 1893, the beer emporium flourished for many years and became a well-frequented haven for Munich's cultural elite. As the center of activity shifted to other sections of the city, the Hofbräu Keller fell on hard times. The imposing multistory building that houses the restaurant and banquet hall was totally bombed out during the War in the same raid that decimated Unionsbräu. Just when it looked safe to go back into the beer garden, another stroke of bad luck occurred in the late 1980s when a fire gutted a portion of the main structure to the bare stone of its foundation.

Still, it came back, with a completely refurbished interior and expanded and improved beer garden. The outside paint is fresh again, and the self-service food stands are back in operation. The food served up in the restaurant and in the

Address ...	Seating ...
Hofbräu Keller **Innere Wiener Str. 19** **81667 Munich**	**1900 in Beer Garden** **600 in Restaurant**
Phone/FAX ...	**Sounds like ...**
(089) 4599250 FAX (089) 4483587	'HOFF-Broi Kell-Er'
Hours ...	**Web presence ...**
9 a.m. to 12 midnight	www.hofbraeukeller.de
Beer ...	**Rating ...**
Hofbräu	3-1/2 Beers

110

garden is excellent, and the beer, after all, is HB. In fact, Hofbräu Keller has improved substantially since it was mentioned in the first edition of this guide in 1991. And it has added some unusual variety to go along with the beer and high-carb pupus. The cellar of the building that houses the restaurant is also home to Maratonga Tanzcafe, a dance hall and cocktail lounge with a South Pacific flavor and enough aging lounge lizards to populate an entire Lawrence Welk concert. Another recent addition at one end of the beer garden is the chrome-plated and highly polished "Sausalitos," a Mexican cantina with plenty of salt-rimmed cocktails and errant shots of tequila. New and unusual tenants aside, Hofbräu Keller retains much of its old charm, and the interior rooms appear unscathed from the time when the intelligentsia and political movers and shakers from all over Munich were counted among its devoted followers. Tenacity breeds admiration and this is an enduring facility, to be sure. Teamed with Unionsbräu around the corner the two serve up a bit of Munich old tradition along with a new wave of craft brewing that greatly enhances the beer drinking experience. All things considered we give Hofbräu Keller and Unionsbräu together 3-1/2 beers.

A Family day outing in the Hofbräu Keller beer garden.

Hauptbahnhof

U-Bahn 4 to Richard-Strauss Str.

Richard-Strauss Str.

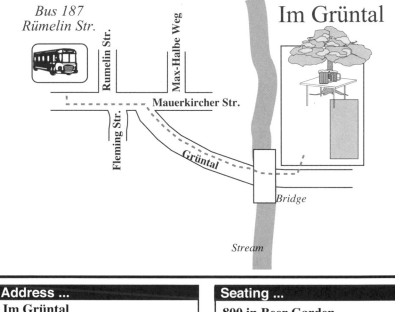

U-Bahn □

Bus 187/188

Denninger Str.

Exit to Bus 187 (Rümelin Str.) (Bus stop location shown above.)
Bus 187 eight stops to end of line at Rümelin Str.*

*Weekends: Slight hitch in the Sat. & Sun. schedule. Bus 187 does not run to Richard-Strauss U-Bahn stop. So, from Richard Strauss U-Bahn stop on weekends take Bus 188 one stop to Herkomerplatz and then resume journey with Bus 187 to Rümelin Str.

Rümelin Str.

Note: Bus makes turn around at end of the line, so direction to beer garden is behind you as you exit. Walk 3 minutes, following map.

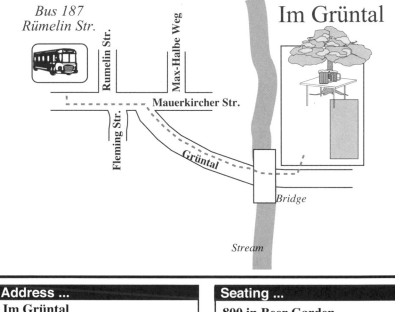

Bus 187
Rümelin Str.

Rumelin Str.

Max-Halbe Weg

Im Grüntal

Mauerkircher Str.

Fleming Str.

Grüntal

Bridge

Stream

Address ...	Seating ...
Im Grüntal **Im Grüntal 15** **81925 Munich**	**800 in Beer Garden** **240 in Restaurant**
Phone/FAX ...	**Sounds like ...**
(089) 9984110 FAX (089) 981867	'Em-GROON-Tall'
Hours ...	**Web presence ...**
11 a.m. to 11 p.m.	www.kuffler.de
Beer ...	**Rating ...**
Paulanerbräu	**3-1/2 Beers**

Im Grüntal

Previous editions of this guide have referred to Im Grüntal as "the most expensive beer garden in Munich." That wasn't our conclusion, it was the prevailing sentiment of just about anybody you ask. Munich beer garden people are pretty firm and outspoken in their opinions — the best beer, the most friendly, the most beautiful, the one with the most celebrities . . . you name it, beer drinkers in Munich have something to say about it. So, we were somewhat surprised by the rebuttals that were forthcoming from Im Grüntal management. They were quick to point out that, regardless of the price of a Maß, they had resisted raising the cost of a beer for nearly 10 years. Maybe so, but at € 7.10 a liter, it's a pretty hefty price tag to begin with. Now, forget all that. Im Grüntal is expensive — but it's worth it! And that's the deal.

This is an outstanding place. The setting is right out of a Thoreau novel, complete with babbling brook running through the premises. In addition to some of the best Bavarian fare available anywhere, the restaurant sports a menu filled with international favorites, such as French and Italian dishes, as well as wild game, including venison and wild boar.

The atmosphere is quiet, relaxing and seldom overcrowded. There is no self-service and picnic baskets are prohibited. However, the house makes up for this by providing excellent service and superior food that even *Oma* would have had trouble coming up with. Im Grüntal's accommodating beer garden (800 seats) is smartly landscaped and well-buffered from the residential area nearby. Major renovations were completed in 1998. All new furniture in the beer garden and major wall resurfacing of the building interior was done carefully and did not detract from the traditional look and feel of the place.

Here is a beer garden where the focus is on relaxation and casual conversations. It's a great place to take a date you want to impress and a chance to hob-nob with Munich's upper-crust. All those beautiful people and members of the *Biergarten-Schickeria* (beer garden chic) crowd who hang out at Im Grüntal add to the high-brow atmosphere of the place, not necessarily to the company's profit margin. Chances are the most prominent of the *prominente* will also appear the most casual. Although Im Grüntal stands several rungs up the luxury ladder, the atmosphere is laid-back and short-sleeve shirts with open collars are more than acceptable. The restaurant and beer garden go back about 100 years which makes Im Grüntal a relative newcomer on the epicurean block. This is a place where gourmet tastes are satisfied and the beer (Paulaner) is one of the best in Munich. Expensive, sure, but a terrific value. Im Grüntal earns a value-added 3-1/2 beers.

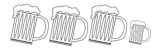

Hauptbahnhof
S-2 to Allach.
Allach
Exit station on Oertelplatz (look for picture of bus). Take Bus 160 (direction "Steinkirchen") or 165 (direction "Westfriedhof") to Friedhof Untermenzing, 4th stop.
Friedhof Untermenzing
Walk about 3 minutes down Eversbusch Str. to beer garden.

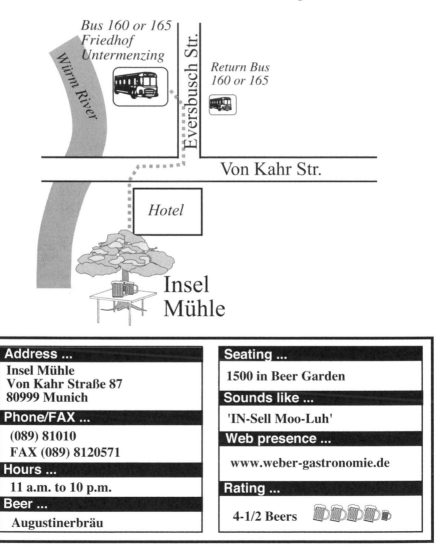

Address ...	Seating ...
Insel Mühle Von Kahr Straße 87 80999 Munich	1500 in Beer Garden
Phone/FAX ...	**Sounds like ...**
(089) 81010 FAX (089) 8120571	'IN-Sell Moo-Luh'
Hours ...	**Web presence ...**
11 a.m. to 10 p.m.	www.weber-gastronomie.de
Beer ...	**Rating ...**
Augustinerbräu	4-1/2 Beers 🍺🍺🍺🍺🍺

Insel Mühle

An Insel is an island. A Mühle is a mill. The two words aptly describe this old farm house and mill turned beer garden on the banks of the Würm River. Well, not exactly at the water's edge. This large expanse of a beer garden is actually an island encased in the fast-flowing river, where the loud, constant roar of rushing water drenches the area along with the mist thrown up by the cascading torrent. Towering trees — some of the most majestic of any Munich beer garden — fill the area and provide a blanket of shade that takes the bite out of the warmest summer days. The wooded areas nearby are favorite haunts of joggers, walkers and cyclists. The verdant surrounding is little changed over the past five centuries since the mill first began operation. The old water wheel is still there, posted as a welcoming sentry at the entrance to the beer garden. Although last used to turn a modern turbine, the wheel was around centuries ago, grinding grains and help-ing to feed local Untermenzingers in good times and bad. Records show the first miller, around 1500, was named Peter Wildenrother; the last, Herr Unsöld, shut down operation in 1910 and turned it into a guest house.

The hotel next door, in the old farm house, is a family-run business today. The gourmet cuisine is left to the hotel restaurant while the beer garden caters to the paper-plate-and-fast-*obatzer* crowd. And there are plenty of filling eats to go around. Insel Mühle features a fully stocked *schmankerl* stand with hearty fare at reasonable prices. Of course, the beer flows about as smoothly as the river and drives this beer garden the way the Würm drove its grinding wheel centuries ago. That beer is now Augustiner in place of the former Löwenbräu brand, which has to be listed as an improvement.

Insel Mühle qualifies as a *geheim tip* — best-kept secret — since few Münchners even know about it. But that's changing, and you can help. Now that you know about this outstanding beer garden in Munich's western region, tell the locals about it. It's an island of enjoyment and easily worth the S-bahn, bus, and short walk to get here. Insel Mühle gets 4-1/2 beers.

The beer garden at Insel Mühle is literally within the confluence of the Würm River.

115

Hauptbahnhof
S-Bahn 6 to Planegg
Planegg
Heide Volm is across the street from the station.

To Kraillinger Brauerei: Exit S-Bahn station down the stairs and to the left catch Bus 967. Take Bus 967 four stops to Mitterweg. Kraillinger Brauerei and beer garden is across the street from the bus stop. The bus runs every 40 minutes.

Note: Second stop is at Alter Wirt beer garden. Also, Bus 967 doesn't run on Sundays, but it's not much of a walk from the S-Bahn station. Head straight down the street to Margareten Straße and then turn right. Keep going — past Alter Wirt — until you get to Kraillinger Brauerei, about a 20 minute walk.

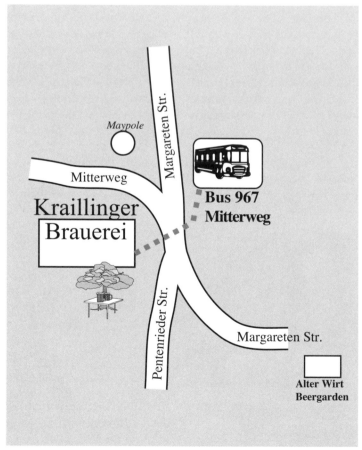

Kraillinger Brauerei
Heide Volm and Alter Wirt

In the past we've recommended a trip to Kraillinger Brauerei, with Heide Volm and Alter Wirt thrown in as a bonus. That may be changing. Kraillinger is still a worthy venue, to be sure, but Heide Volm and especially Alter Wirt are looking more like stand-alone attractions themselves. Of course, that's all good news. The three together provide ample reason to take the S-Bahn ride to the outskirts of the city and maybe walk a few blocks to enjoy them all.

Heide Volm is about as convenient as any beer garden could be. It's right across the street from the Planegg S-Bahn stop. It does plenty of business, and has a spacious restaurant in what might be the ugliest, square-brick, nondescript building imaginable. It has this "newness" that

A Bavarian combo plays a special event in Kraillinger's beer garden.

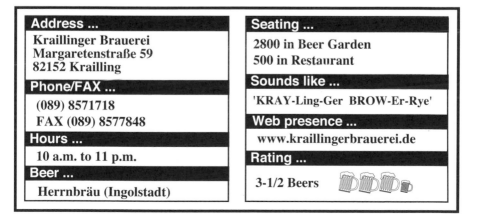

Address ...	Seating ...
Kraillinger Brauerei Margaretenstraße 59 82152 Krailling	2800 in Beer Garden 500 in Restaurant
Phone/FAX ...	**Sounds like ...**
(089) 8571718 FAX (089) 8577848	'KRAY-Ling-Ger BROW-Er-Rye'
Hours ...	**Web presence ...**
10 a.m. to 11 p.m.	www.kraillingerbrauerei.de
Beer ...	**Rating ...**
Herrnbräu (Ingolstadt)	3-1/2 Beers

Willi Kuttenburger literally grew up in the shadow of Kraillinger Brauerei's wooden kegs.

He still participates in special events hosted by the beer garden and is the first to lend a hand in tapping a new keg.

seems to never wear off. No matter how many times we check on it, Heide Volm looks like it just came out of the box and will never be properly broken in. It's like borrowing a brand new car and enjoying the ride but never getting over the fear you might put a scratch in it.

That said, the beer garden is another story — tons of room (1400 seats) and live entertainment on most weekends. Stay out of the factory-looking restaurant and enjoy the beer garden instead and you just might be inclined to linger here at Heide Volm. We recommend you move on, though, to enjoy both Alter Wirt and

Kraillinger Brauerei.

You can take a bus to Kraillinger or walk, because it isn't that far from the Planegg S-Bahn station. If you happen to arrive on a Sunday, you will have to walk because the bus doesn't run that day. If you do walk, just before arriving at Kraillinger you'll pass by the Alter Wirt, which is pretty good all by itself. A change of ownership a few years ago made all the difference. They've created a pleasant beer garden right next to the Würm river. The place serves Augustiner beer, a good thing, and has an indoor theater that features live entertainment

---

Heide Volm
Bahnhof Str. 51
82152 Planegg

Seating: 1400
Beer: Hacker-Pschorr
Phone: (089) 8572029
Hours: 10 a.m to 12 Midnight daily.
Web: www.heidevolm.de

and cabaret shows. Also, Alter Wirt has adopted a "sports bar" theme, as evidenced by the monitors strategically placed among the patrons. They claim it's the best place to catch your favorite soccer — er, fußball — team in action. As you might expect, this fast-improving beer garden attracts a younger crowd and a lot of energy in its small but lively beer garden where they still serve a Maß of Munich's best beer for € 5.80.

Finally we come to Kraillinger Brauerei. Truth in advertising compels an outright admission that the brauerei is not a brewery. It used to be, but the brewhouse closed down about 25 years ago, leaving only the beer garden and restaurant in its place. Now it gets its beer from Herrnbräu in Ingolstadt.

The personification of the tradition that is today Kraillinger Brauerei (named after the Kraillinger section of the city where it is located) is Willi Kuttenburger. There are photos on the wall of Willi throughout his life — Willi as a child, Willi as an adult, Willi in his later years — but always Willi with the beer he loves so well. Willi still appears at special events to help tap that first wooden keg of beer, just as he has for most of this past century. He maintains a hand in the business and is owner of the land and buildings that house Kraillinger Brauerei today. Kraillinger *Wirt*, Peter Schweizer, is quick to refer to Willi Kuttenburger with admiration and respect befitting a local brewing legend. He does Willi proud in the business he runs, adhering closely to the best Bavarian traditions for beer gardens. The expanded beer garden now approaches 2800 seats, most them taken up with permanent wood tables. Four large *Schmankerl* stands provide a steady supply of snacks, grilled sausages, *Obatzer* (creamed cheese) and beer. Prices here are very economical as you might expect.

Teamed together, this is an excellent beer garden experience. Heide Volm and Alter Wirt have both improved since the previous edition, and frankly Kraillinger Brauerei has slipped a bit. Still we rate the three-way combo with a 3-1/2 beer-rating complete with expectations for a wonderful day in the beer garden(s).

Alter Wirt
Margareten Str. 31
82152 Krailling

Seating: 700
Beer: Augustiner
Phone: (089) 89198444
Hours: 10 a.m to 11 p.m.
Web:
www.alterwirtkrailling.de

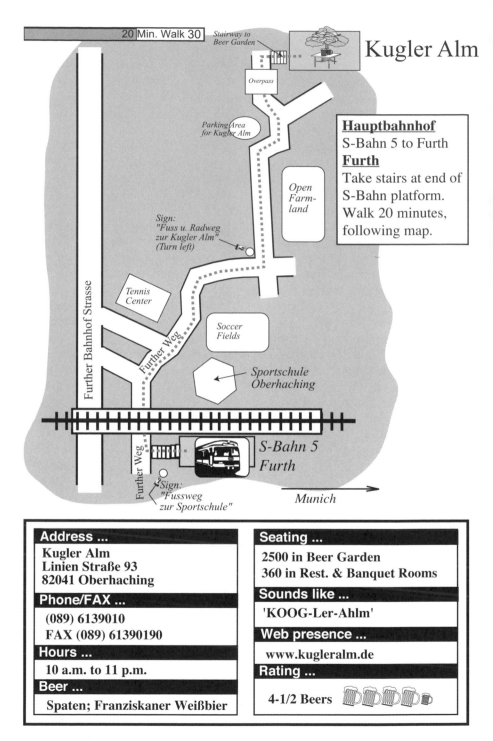

Kugler Alm

20 | Min. Walk | 30

Stairway to Beer Garden

Overpass

Parking Area for Kugler Alm

Open Farm-land

Sign: "Fuss u. Radweg zur Kugler Alm" (Turn left)

Hauptbahnhof
S-Bahn 5 to Furth
Furth
Take stairs at end of S-Bahn platform. Walk 20 minutes, following map.

Further Bahnhof Strasse

Tennis Center

Further Weg

Soccer Fields

Sportschule Oberhaching

Further Weg

S-Bahn 5
Furth

Sign: "Fussweg zur Sportschule"

Munich

Address ...	Seating ...
Kugler Alm Linien Straße 93 82041 Oberhaching	2500 in Beer Garden 360 in Rest. & Banquet Rooms
Phone/FAX ...	**Sounds like ...**
(089) 6139010 FAX (089) 61390190	'KOOG-Ler-Ahlm'
Hours ...	**Web presence ...**
10 a.m. to 11 p.m.	www.kugleralm.de
Beer ...	**Rating ...**
Spaten; Franziskaner Weißbier	4-1/2 Beers

120

Kugler Alm

For years we overlooked this beautiful beer garden for one specific reason: it was a 45-minute walk to get there! Unfortunately, no bus service is available from the Deisenhofen S-Bahn station and unless you happen to have a bicycle with you, that's a pretty long trek to get a beer. Even longer coming back. Well, we're happy to report we've found a back door to Kugler Alm. Instead of the Deisenhofen station, we now recommend a route from the Furth station, one stop earlier, then a walk through a sports training school and open farmland. At just over 20 minutes, the walk to Kugler Alm now fits our model of a reasonable effort to enjoy one of Munich's best beer gardens.

Nobody could ever question the credentials and legacy of Kugler Alm. After all, this is the place where the Radler was invented and first served. By now, you probably know that a Radler is a simple mixture of beer and lemon-lime soda (you know, 7-Up). The "discovery" of this particular libation was the work of Franz Xaver Kugler, a one-time railroad worker whose powers of observation included the realization that working on the rails was hot and thirsty work. Thus, the entrepreneurial Franz saw the opportunity in 1895 to begin dispensing fresh beer to his railway brethren and Kugler

Kugler Alm used to be just too far to walk, but not any more.

Franz Xaver Kugler, the "discoverer" of the *Radlermaß*

Alm, the beer garden soon followed.

The business flourished and expanded, but the real coup occurred on a hot Saturday in July 1922. As it is today, this beer garden has always been somewhat remote, requiring additional means to get there. The most common mode of transit was by bicycle, still a popular method to this day. After a couple of Maß, a shaky ride back home on two wheels is risky at best. Looking for a way to maintain his clientele and keep them alive and coming back for more, Franz tried mixing half beer and half *lemonade*. Call it the first "light beer" if you want, but the drink caught on and Franz named it after those most ready to benefit from a lower-alcohol drink — bicyclists or "Radlers" as they're called in German. Oh, sure, we're not talking about a cure for cancer here — maybe more a cure for what ails you — but Franz Kugler will always hold a place in Munich beer lore for inventing a simple means to allow devoted beer drinkers the opportunity to hang longer and enjoy another round.

Lower-octane drinks are a great innovation, but don't think for an instant that they dominate the preference list of those who visit Kugler Alm. Lots of regular beer is flowing and thousands will show up on any given day to enjoy it.

Sundays are usually reserved for an Oompah band, and if the weather is good, the place will get full. Luckily, there is plenty of room here, and more than one beer garden. Through the entrance archway an Obstgarten or "orchard garden" lies straight ahead. The shady area is buffered from the main beer garden, and provides a refuge for several hundred beer drinkers who want a little more con-

Bicycle or "Radler" traffic is heavy at Kugler Alm.

122

versation and less celebration. The large beer garden, with plenty of traditional wood tables and benches, fronts on a large *Schmankerl* stand serving some of the best barbecue ribs served anywhere.

There is space for more than 2,300 in the large beer garden, with tables snaking their way back and behind a second serving building, ensuring convenient access to an excellent selection of Bavarian dishes and beverages.

Most of the available seating is self-service, and patrons are encouraged to bring food and stage their own picnic so long as they purchase their drinks from the *Bier Ausschank*. A huge children's play area at a far end of the beer garden will keep the kids occupied.

There was never a doubt that this was a very appealing beer garden and worthy of a prominent place in The BDG2M. But now that the practicality of getting there has been solved, it's a pleasure to include this beer garden once again.

A 20-minute walk is not asking too much to enjoy one of Munich's best beer gardens and visit the place where the Radler was born. Kugler Alm gets a high recommendation and an inventive 4-1/2 beer rating.

An afternoon in the sun at Kugler Alm. (The man with the beer paid too much for those sunglasses.)

123

Hauptbahnhof
U-Bahn 5 to Neuperlach Zentrum.

Neuperlach Zentrum
Look for bus icon, take "people mover" moving ramp and look for bus stop on left as you exit. Take Bus 55 (direction "Waldperlach") to Waldperlach end of the line.

Waldperlach
Follow map to beer garden, just a few minutes walk.

Address ...	Seating ...
Wirtshaus Leiberheim Nixenweg 9 81739 Munich	2500 in Beer Garden 300 Rest. and Banquet
Phone/FAX ...	**Sounds like ...**
(089) 4300000 FAX (089) 43739598	'VERTS-House LIE-Ber-Hime'
Hours ...	**Web presence ...**
10 a.m. to 11 p.m.	www.leiberheim.de
Beer ...	**Rating ...**
Brauerei Erharting	4-1/2 Beers 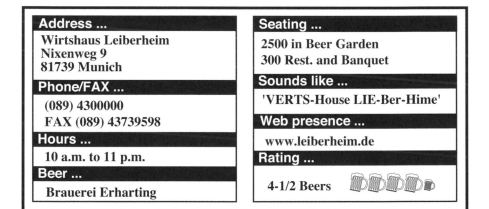

Leiberheim

When Eduard Ordnung returned from World War I, without the use of his right leg and with an Iron Cross around his neck, a world-wide depression was looming. Even war heroes had to struggle to eke out a living in 1918 and Ordnung opened a beer garden in one of Munich's outlying suburbs. Leiberheim, named in honor of his wartime infantry unit, the Royal Bavarian Leibregiment, weathered the hard times and prospered. It is today one of Munich's largest beer gardens, and many would argue one of its most beautiful. Among mixed stands of pine and chestnut trees, Leiberheim accommodates 2,500-plus visitors on summer afternoons. The husband-and-wife team of Thomas and Katrin König, who also run the beer garden at Aumeister, took charge of Leiberheim a few years ago and have made major improvements. A 180-seat terrace garden was added with table service. The restaurant was totally renovated and the beer garden equipped with new tables and benches and given an even more inviting atmosphere than before. The menu was expanded to include Italian specialties to go along with the mainstay Bavarian-style dishes you would expect. Outdoor food stands are now cen-

Leiberheim today is home to both the neighborhood *Kameraden* along with a steady troop of new customers attracted to the major improvements to the restaurant and beer garden.

tralized and more accessible, making self-service in the beer garden a welcome alternative. The beer served is Erharting, from one of the area's smaller breweries.

A recent innovation we hope will last, and maybe catch on elsewhere is Happy Hour (yup, that's what they call it). During the summer, Monday through Thursday, it's 10 percent off everything in the beer garden from 2:30 to 6 p.m., 10 a.m. to 4 p.m. Friday and Saturday. (Sorry no Happy Hour on holidays.) Happier still

for the youngsters is the children's play area, one of the nicest we've ever seen. A huge sandbox play structure at the far end of the beer garden is reminiscent of that fort we all wanted when we were kids but our parents invested in accordian lessons instead.

The interior of the lokal is consumed mostly by a stage and auditorium used to host special Bavarian folk theaters. *Bayrischer Abends*, as they are known, are a speciality of Leiberheim during the

Formerly on display in the restaurant, the founder's pre-World War I uniform suffered water damage and was sent out for preservation. It is now housed in a museum in Chiemgau.

fall and winter months. The programs, usually lasting until late in the evening, feature semi-professional Bavarian entertainers in renditions of music, folk dancing and humorous skits (unless you're familiar with the language, most of the humor flies several feet above your head). The traditional folk theater was introduced at Leiberheim in 1920, with 215 "premiers" since 1946. Information and reservations can be had by calling (089) 609-8830. Inside the lokal, Leiberheim's atmosphere is much more upbeat than before. Most of the faded photographs and discolored paintings of military men that formerly graced the walls are gone. What's also noticeably missing is the glass-and-wood paneled display case that formerly housed two full-dress military Leibregiment uniforms, dating back to before World War I. Major storms hit the area in January 2004 and flooded the restaurant. The uniforms were water-damaged and had to be sent out to be restored.

Today, these uniforms have been rescued and are in a museum in Chiemgau where they are still on public display. One, a captain's parade uniform with sword, dated back to 1912 and the last days of the Kaiser's Imperial Guard. Ordnung's Knight's Cross is also in the museum with other collected military artifacts.

Ironically and tragically, Leiberheim's founder, who was wounded severely in 1916 during combat that earned him his high military honor, died in his sleep during a 1945 bombing raid at the close of World War II. It is in his spirit that a diminishing few of the old *Kameraden* still find their way to Leiberheim. These are men who grew up together, fought together, and now grow old together. They can be seen today in the middle of a raucous card game, suddenly pausing to raise their glass and their voices to an old marching song in the memory of others who served and are now gone.

Ordnung's legacy lives on at Leiberheim, but not to the beat of a militant drum. The emphasis here is peaceful co-existence amid a patter of suburban socialization. Interestingly, the spacious beer enclave is able to thrive and prosper on a word of-mouth existence. Available local tour guides seem bent on protecting its anonymity by ignoring one of the city's largest beer gardens. On the other hand, on those summer afternoons when 2,500 seats are barely enough, greater notoriety hardly seems a problem. When the roll call is sounded, Leiberheim stands at attention with a stalwart 4-1/2 beers.

Hauptbahnhof

U-Bahn 1 to Stiglmaier Platz. Exit U-Bahn
station following signs toward Seidl and
Dachauer Str. Basically, you're there.

Löwenbräu
Keller

Sand Str.

Dachauer Str.

Nymphenburger Str. ⟍ Stiglmaier Platz

*U-Bahn
Stiglmaier Platz*

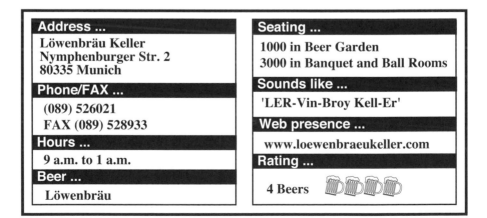

Address ...	Seating ...
Löwenbräu Keller
Nymphenburger Str. 2
80335 Munich	1000 in Beer Garden
3000 in Banquet and Ball Rooms
Phone/FAX ...	**Sounds like ...**
(089) 526021
FAX (089) 528933	'LER-Vin-Broy Kell-Er'
Hours ...	**Web presence ...**
9 a.m. to 1 a.m.	www.loewenbraeukeller.com
Beer ...	**Rating ...**
Löwenbräu	4 Beers

Löwenbräu Keller

Name recognition. That's what Löwenbräu the beer has. Few English-speaking visitors to Munich will fail to recognize the famous "Lion's Brew" logo. And if they ask for it, few German-speaking natives will likely understand them. What is commonly pronounced in English as "Low-in-brow" flows easily off the German tongue as "Ler-vin-broy." Despite the dueling diphthongs, Löwenbräu ranks as one of Germany's most international brands. In 1997, Löwenbräu and Spaten merged into a single company and in 2003 Belgian InBev (formerly Interbrew) bought them both. Ownership transfers notwithstanding, production has continued unabated and Löwenbräu continues to produce an abundance of liquid product, sold in more Munich beer gardens than any other. As is often the case, Löwenbräu's reputation travels better than its beer. In Munich this is just another good-tasting beer, and by no means the popular favorite. (Augustiner Edelstoff holds that honor.)

Löwenbräu the beer hall and beer garden does much better. An annex to the massive brewery on Nymphenburger Straße, Löwenbräu Keller has been a locally preferred beer oasis since it opened

The Löwenbräu Keller from an artist's rendering in 1885. The original facility accommodated 8,000 guest until it was heavily damaged in World War II.

its doors for business on June 14, 1883 with four regimental bands to mark the occasion. The original structure was massive, with interior and beer-garden seating for some 8,000 guests, or about twice what is available today. On Dec. 17, 1944 a heavy bombing raid reduced the huge *Festsaal* (ballroom) to rock and rubble. Rebuilt after the war to smaller dimensions (encroachment from the thriving brewery helped here), Löwenbräu Keller was reinstated with much of its original flavor and atmosphere. In 1986, a fire again destroyed part of the building, requiring yet more rebuilding and renovation. By 1987, the establishment was back together again, featuring a massive ballroom (2,000 seats) and a beer garden to accommodate 1,000 guests.

Löwenbräu Keller ranks as one of Munich's largest and most sumptuous.

Its abundance of interior rooms (*Stüben*), cavernous restaurant and voluminous menu make this one of the city's most popular dining spots. The Pils-Pub, with its large circular bar, is a favorite with guests who want to quaff suds into the late evening. Returning home after one Maß too many is no problem since the nearest U-bahn stop is right across the street. Löwenbräu Keller is filled with rooms and don't be shocked by the name of one of them. The Dachauer Stübe reflects a common German innkeeper's custom of adopting the names of surrounding villages. It is in no way intended to hallow the dark and historically brief period when the medieval town played unwilling host to the Third Reich's first and most-infamous concentration camp. (See Schlossberg, in Day Trips, a beer garden in Dachau itself.)

Löwenbräu Keller attracts a heavy after work crowd to the beer garden.

The beer garden is large though somewhat gerrymandered to fit within the confines of the available space and the large traffic artery that borders the entire brewery complex. On summer afternoons it is filled to capacity with brewery and other blue-collar workers pausing for a refreshing break before heading home.

Two seasonal occasions are especially well celebrated at Löwenbräu Keller. When the Fasching or Carnival season (marking the beginning of Lent) reaches its peak in mid-February or early March, Löwenbräu Keller throws some of the rowdiest parties and masquerade balls in all of Munich. Several weeks later, in mid-March, the strong beer season (*Starkbierzeit*) begins and Löwenbräu Keller is again the scene of a little festive craziness, hawking its own "-ator" strong beer, Triumphator.

Strong beer calls for strong men, and Steyrer Hans was by far mightiest of them all. Legend or history, probably a little of both, holds that one day in Löwenbräu Keller the Munich master butcher and lionized folk hero caused more than a few patrons to spill their beer by a feat of strength not equaled since. Hans, it is claimed — here comes the legend — was able to lift a 508-pound boulder with his middle finger! That late-19th century herculean feat has inspired the annual *Steinheberwettbewerb* at Löwenbräu Keller. The boulder lifting contest is a main attraction when the strong beer starts to flow. Contestants are given a break Hans never needed, because they are allowed to use both hands. Any lift of a foot or more is considered world-class and calls for the hoisting of several more liters of suds in celebration. Löwenbräu Keller is a year-round attraction and the home of excellent traditional Bavarian cuisine along with the city's most widely dispensed beer. The lion on the label stands for a roaring good time. Löwenbräu Keller checks in with a 4-beer rating.

The lion, a popular emblematic figure throughout southern Germany, is seen on the royal Bavarian coat of arms, along with the characteristic blue-and-white checkered pattern (eagles are favored up north). The king of beasts quaffing a mug of beer is an iconic symbol seen often at the Oktoberfest. (No, there never were lions roaming wild in prehistoric Germany.) The lion is a worldwide symbol of strength and potency, and a natural selection for ambitious princes and brewers alike.

Hauptbahnhof
S- or U-Bahn to Marienplatz.
Marienplatz
U-Bahn 3 to Thalkirchen.
Thalkirchen
Exit U-Bahn station using the ramp (not the stairs/escalator). Walk a block to the beer garden.

(Note: Across the street is bus stop for travel to Gasthof Hinterbrühl.)

Address ...	Seating ...
Mangostin Maria-Einsiedel Str. 2 81379 Munich	550 in Beer Garden 250 in Restaurants
Phone/FAX ...	**Sounds like ...**
(089) 7232031; FAX 7239847	'Man-GHOST-Inn'
Hours ...	**Web presence ...**
4 p.m. to 12 Midnight weekdays, 12 Noon to Midnight weekends	www.mangostin.de
	Rating ...
Beer ...	
Löwenbräu	4-1/2 Beers

Mangostin

Mangostin has been around nearly two decades and is showing real staying power. Few thought this strange mix of Bavaria and the Far East could survive (a beer garden with ice carvings and sushi?), but it has. It has thrived. It began simple enough. Just a casual conversation over a couple of beers between two home-grown Bavarians — one an accomplished chef, the other a savvy entrepreneur—in a Bangkok bar years ago. That discussion led to the building of a business and the first and only Asian beer garden in Munich. Dr. Erich Kaub and Joseph Peter took an early first step in 1989 with "Thai Week" at Seehaus in Englischer Garten. The experimental oriental food fair was such a hit that the two budding businessmen pooled resources and began looking for other opportunities. The plan was to somehow take the traditional German beer garden and season it with the spice and flair of the Far East.

The two entrepreneurs found a failing beer garden, bought it, and began renovating it. They developed rock gardens and other oriental landscaping. They planted tropical ferns alongside domestic bushes, bamboo next to chestnut trees. The old restaurant was completely gutted and a new one molded in its place. Each renovated room was given a new Asian decor, highlighted with amber and black-

Mangostin's terrace dining area has recently undergone renovation and expansion of the menu has continued the Far East gastronomical theme.

varnished furnishings. When Mangostin opened its doors in early spring 1990, Munich had never seen anything quite like it. The shaded traditional Bavarian beer garden had been absorbed completely into an oriental theme park where culinary tastes from east meet west.

The outdoor self-service food and drink stands of the Mangostin Garden offer an unusual choice of Mai-Tais from the tropical fruit bar or a fresh Maß of Löwenbräu beer. Inside are three more restaurants featuring original cuisine from Thailand, Japan and Malaysia. One, the Lemon Grass, offers Thai specialties, seafood, and "open wok" oriental cooking. Keiko Japanese restaurant dishes up sushi (raw fish), Tempura, and Sukiyaki.

Papa Joe's Colonial Bar and Restaurant features snacks and hors d'oeuvres and plenty of comfortable rattan chairs for sitting around and enjoying exotic fruit-based cocktails (careful you don't poke your eye with an umbrella). The ice carvings, billed as the only such epicurean embellishments in all of Europe, begin as 5-ft.-high blocks of ice. The figures are chosen by customer request, carved and given a rotating place of honor in one of the restaurants. Mangostin today sells more cocktails and wine than beer, alluding to the shift in customer base and the increasing number of Asian businessmen among its patrons. It has expanded its sushi bar and now boasts the ability to accommodate all customer orders to get exactly what they want, as fresh as it can possibly be delivered. Although Joseph Peter is still a partner, Roland Kuffler, the Munich gasthaus impresario, is also part owner. His hand and experience will likely continue to add improvements to both the menu and the ambience. Certainly there is no real comparison to this unique establishment any-

Ever wonder what happened to that artifact unearthed in the first reel of the movie *The Exorcist*? It may have been given new life as a courtyard sentry at Mangostin-Asia.

where in Munich. Its popularity continues to grow and during the summer months both the restaurant and beer garden fill up with the speed of a fast hand with an abacus board.

Seats in the beer garden can be had on a first-come basis, but a table in one of the restaurants usually requires a reservation, or a long wait at the Colonial Bar. Inside prices are generally high, outside much more reasonable. No surprise for an establishment of this quality.

Mangostin is the best of not just both, but several worlds. It works on many different levels, one being that which appeals to lovers of Munich's beer gardens and lokals.

The planners, owners and builders of Mangostin were smart enough to augment but not replace the Bavarian beer garden experience. They have created that rare and truly distinctive atmosphere that has to be enjoyed to be appreciated. Mangostin gets an inscrutable 4-1/2 beer rating.

Eat, drink, or just raise a Maß in Prosit! A crowded Munich beer garden on a warm afternoon is a welcome venue for all of the above.

Hauptbahnhof
Take one of several U- or S-Bahns to Marienplatz.
Marienplatz
U-Bahns 3 or 6 to Universität.
Universität
As you exit the U-Bahn station, walk toward the Victory Gate on Ludwig Str. The last street just before the gate (Adalbert Str.), turn left and walk to the beer garden. It's about a 9-minute walk.

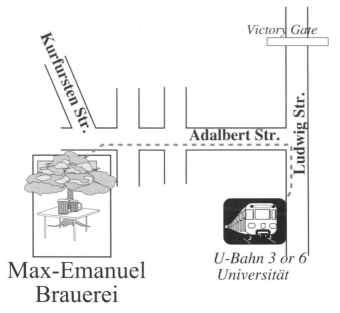

Max-Emanuel
Brauerei

(**Note on Opening Hours:** In summer, the beer garden is open 11 a.m. - 11 p.m.; Inside bar and lokal, 11 a.m. - 1 a.m., to 3 a.m. on Fridays. From November to April hours are 5 p.m.- 1 a.m.)

Address ...	Seating ...
Max-Emanuel Brauerei **Adalbert Straße 33** **80799 Munich**	**700 in Beer Garden, 110 Rest.**
Phone/FAX ...	**Sounds like ...**
(089) 2715158; FAX 2714038	**'MAX-Ee-Man-Yoo-Ell** **Brow-Er-Rye'**
Hours ...	**Web presence ...**
11 a.m. to 1 a.m.	**www.max-emanuel-brauerei.de**
Beer ...	**Rating ...**
Löwenbräu **Franziskaner Weisse**	**3-1/2 Beers**

Max-Emanuel Brauerei

Max-Emanuel Brauerei is a multi-faceted beer garden and student lokal in the heart of Schwabing, just down the street from Ludwig Straße and the Victory Arch. It's a student hang-out first class, but with a lot of extra appeal to a cross-section of Munich's beer garden crowd. For one thing, there's the spacious beer garden, totally unexpected in this purely residential block of apartments. The well-shaded courtyard beer enclave serves up a choice of half or full liters of Löwenbräu beer and a rotating number of "blueplate" specials, including fish and vegetarian dishes. The outdoor restaurant adds a little zing to the standard Bavarian menu with Greek gyros dishes (mutton grilled on a revolving spit) with lots of tzatziki (a sauce made of yogurt and diced cucumber). On weekends a pub-grub menu is invoked with four different schnitzel dishes, spare ribs and 10 pasta plates to choose from, all in an economical range of € 5.50 to € 6.50.

Indoors is a wood-paneled typical student lokal. There are sturdy oak tables and benches with plenty of room to carry on conversations about politics, culture,

Max-Emanuel Brauerei, in the middle of Munich's student quarter.

the arts and partying. A big-screen TV in one corner alludes to a renewed interest in finding things to do while eating nachos and hot buffalo wings. Of special note is the daily 4-6 p.m. Happy Hour, when a liter of beer can be had for € 3.90 instead of the usual € 6.50. During the afternoon and early evenings the lokal is dominated by the university crowd and affords an excellent opportunity for younger visitors to meet and get to know their Munich peer group. The conversations are friendly and many a university co-ed or local bohemian will welcome the chance to ply an English major or satisfy a lively curiosity regarding foreign guests. In the evenings, the mood swings to dancing. Rock and roll and a "50s Record Hop" on Sundays, chic dance style of the month on Wednesdays and Fridays and whatever else might be in vogue. In fact, Max-Emanuel wirt Stephan Gloxhuber proudly proclaims his establishment to be the "oldest Salsa club in Munich".

Max-Emanuel Brauerei is a beer garden and lokal that caters to a primarily young crowd. But like so many establishments in Munich, it attracts all age-groups and discriminates against none. All visitors are welcome here, and a trip to this beer garden in the center of the city's student quarter is a class worth making. Its report card shows 3 1/2 beers.

Max-Emanuel's commodious courtyard beer garden is a popular oasis that attracts a young crowd yet welcomes all age groups.

138

Vaulted arches and gothic interiors give Munich's beer halls a monastic
appearance, alluding to their religious roots.

Hauptbahnhof
U-Bahn 2 to Silberhorn Str.
Silberhorn Str.
Tram 15 or 25 to Menterschwaige (15 min.)
Menterschwaige
Walk, following map.

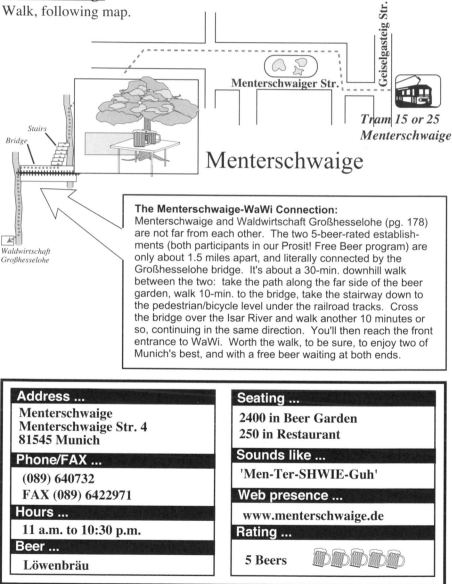

The Menterschwaige-WaWi Connection:
Menterschwaige and Waldwirtschaft Großhesselohe (pg. 178) are not far from each other. The two 5-beer-rated establishments (both participants in our Prosit! Free Beer program) are only about 1.5 miles apart, and literally connected by the Großhesselohe bridge. It's about a 30-min. downhill walk between the two: take the path along the far side of the beer garden, walk 10-min. to the bridge, take the stairway down to the pedestrian/bicycle level under the railroad tracks. Cross the bridge over the Isar River and walk another 10 minutes or so, continuing in the same direction. You'll then reach the front entrance to WaWi. Worth the walk, to be sure, to enjoy two of Munich's best, and with a free beer waiting at both ends.

Address ...	Seating ...
Menterschwaige Menterschwaige Str. 4 81545 Munich	2400 in Beer Garden 250 in Restaurant
Phone/FAX ...	**Sounds like ...**
(089) 640732 FAX (089) 6422971	'Men-Ter-SHWIE-Guh'
Hours ...	**Web presence ...**
11 a.m. to 10:30 p.m.	www.menterschwaige.de
Beer ...	**Rating ...**
Löwenbräu	5 Beers

Menterschwaige

O nly in Munich would a beer garden play a role in that oldest of life's dramas: the eternal love triangle. And on a royal stage no less. Menterschwaige, today a favorite among Munich's beer garden frequenters, was once a part of the royal estate of King Ludwig I. Ludwig, you may remember, married Princess Therese von Sachsen-Hildburghausen in 1810 and gave the city the excuse it needed to launch the world's rowdiest keg party, Oktoberfest.

The marriage of the soon-to-be king and queen of Bavaria progressed swimmingly for awhile. But, the king's wandering eye eventually fell on the lovely image of the self-styled Spanish dancer Lola Montez (she was born Irish) and

troubles began. The illicit love affair blossomed and when the queen got word of it, the lithe Lola was forced to leave town. Well, almost anyway. Ludwig, still in the throes of his mid-life crisis, hid her away in a cathedral of his youth, the Menterschwaige.

Here in a hut the young Prince Ludwig had once reserved as a commune of sorts for befriended artisans and architects, dubbed the "Alt England,"the king continued his nightly trysts with Lola. For a month the steamy romance played on. When the emotional fires dwindled, the Spanish lady and the Bavarian monarch parted company. Lola went on to a successful cabaret career in Gold Rush-era San Francisco. For Ludwig, however, the

Towering chestnut trees cover the beer garden at the Menterschwaige.

141

relationship — which some still insist was only platonic — contributed to his downfall. Despite his many architectural gifts to Munich and his kingdom, the monarch was besieged by public reprobation for his scandalous affair with Lola. The final straw occurred when he tried to raise the price of beer. His subjects might have forgiven a little royal infidelity, but never the attempt to pad the royal purse at the expense of their public brew. Ludwig abdicated in 1848 and retired to his country estate to follow his true love as Munich's celebrated patron of the arts. As for Lola, she became a religious recluse in her later life and died in 1861 at the young age of 43. She is buried in Brooklyn, NY.

The romantic interlude of some 150 years ago is today a curious footnote to the history of Menterschwaige. The sprawling beer garden and restaurant ex-

King Ludwig I, in coronation robes, fell for Lola and from grace in the Menterschwaige.

Lola Montez entertained the King of Bavaria before she went on to dance for California miners during the Gold Rush.

hibit little of their royal past, although the hut where Lola and Ludwig met is still there and available for specially catered events. The remainder of the complex has more the look of a traditional Munich establishment, with abundant shade from stands of mature chestnut trees. After major renovation of the restaurant and expansion of the beer garden in 1999, Menterschwaige now accommodates some 2,400 guests. Most of the tables are uncovered, thus self-service is the rule. The fast-food and grill stands offer an unusually wide variety of cooked meats, sausages and salads. The portable crepe stand which occasionally graces the beer garden is a hint of the French influence seen on the menu inside the restaurant (the high prices are another clue). A small courtyard serving area with linen-covered tables on the far side of the restaurant commonly hosts wedding receptions, private festivities and other more-formal affairs. A well-designed and strategically located children's play area at a far end of the beer garden will keep the kiddies occupied. Menterschwaige is what Münchners often refer to as a *Geheimtip*, a close-hold secret known only to the more enlightened and knowledgeable of the city's beer-drinking crowd. And there are evidently plenty who are in on the secret. On a warm weekend summer day the beer garden is full to overflowing with the locally rich and famous, as well as the well-represented everyday middle class. Menterschwaige is a little more upscale than most, and the prices inside the res-

taurant reflect that fact. However, the real draw is the large beer garden where the cost of an afternoon is more reasonable. It has plenty of class and is often compared with Waldwirtschaft Großhesselohe as an excellent choice for a traditional Munich beer garden (see the "Wa-Wi connection," pg. 140). It's easy to see what attracted the King of Bavaria to this area — in addition to Lola Montez, of course. It gets a top 5-beer rating. We're pleased to report that along with their top rating, Menterschwaige has joined our Prosit! Free Beer offer (coupon at back of the book).

The hut Ludwig called the "Alt England" survives to this day on the other side of the restaurant. The interior has been refurbished in the same manner and style that Lola left it. Menterschwaige makes it available for special occasions.

143

Hauptbahnhof
U-Bahn 5 to Michaelibad
Michaelibad U-Bahn Stop
Exit using escalator (not ramp) and follow bus sign - St Michael Str.
(Ostseite). Take bus 195 one stop to Heinrich-Wieland Str.
Heinrich-Wieland Str.
Walk across street, following map, to
beer garden.

(Note: From Heinrich-Wieland Str., if you continue with
Bus 195 for 12 more min. and 12 more stops to Vogesen Str.
you'll be at Franziskaner Garten front door, pg. 94)

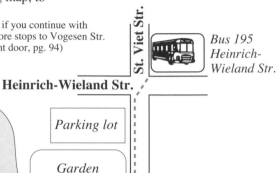

St. Viet Str.

Bus 195
Heinrich-
Wieland Str.

Heinrich-Wieland Str.

Parking lot

Garden

Lake

Ost Park

Michaeligarten

Address ...	Seating ...
Michaeligarten Feichstraße 10 81735 Munich	3000 in Beer Garden 250 on Terrace
Phone/FAX ...	**Sounds like ...**
(089) 43552424 FAX (089) 43552413	'MICK-Ah-Ale-Lee Gar-Ten'
Hours ...	**Web presence ...**
10 a.m. to 12 Midnight	www.michaeligarten.de
Beer ...	**Rating ...**
Löwenbräu	5 Beers

Michaeligarten

Most of Munich's beer gardens have a history reaching back several centuries. Their loyal patrons include several generations of families who have frequented the same establishment since *Opa* was just a teenager. Customers of Michaeligarten, on the other hand, might not be old enough to vote. This beer garden in Munich's Ost (East) Park shatters the mold by having secured its niche among the city's most popular establishments in barely the time needed for the varnish to wear off the wood. It is testament that a beer garden need not be old to be good. Real good.

Built along with Munich's Ost Park in 1973, Michaeligarten is a prize of a beer garden with lots of neo-tradition. The foreground is a large (albeit manmade) lake, with a fountain of water that sprays a continuous cascade. The adjacent area is rolling green hills criss-crossed by walking paths that roam throughout the park. It's a place where Münchners bring the entire family on warm weekend afternoons to let the kids play in the water or along the shores of the lake.

Michaeligarten's owners were smart enough to allow for plenty of room to expand and have taken advantage of it. The beer garden was expanded by half — from 2000 to 3000 seats — and is now one of the finest in the city. Obviously patterned after Seehaus, in the Englischer

Michaeligarten's lakeside location adds to the beer garden's relaxing atmosphere.

Garten, the experience is similar, but with more reasonable prices and a better chance at finding an empty seat.

Michaeligarten is made for relaxation. The lake and park setting is enough to take 20 points off anyone's blood pressure. Since the blueprint is primarily self-service (the lakeside terrace has table service), the economics are much more in favor of the customers. The large *Schmankerl* stand, with lots of flavorful Bavarian-style snacks, is a cut above most fast-food-and-beer outlets. After an afternoon here and enough to eat and drink, the impulse is to spread a blanket down by the lake and check one's eyelids for holes.

Michaeligarten attracts large crowds but few tourists. It's a great find and among the very best Munich has to offer, even if it is of a relatively recent vintage. The attention by its proprietors to the enjoyment of their guests is obvious in this always improving beer garden. You could search Munich for a better beer garden today and not find one. Michaeligarten gets a maximum 5 beers and a top recommendation.

The beer garden offers plenty of seating right up to the water's edge.

The end of a day at the end of a beer, lakeside at Michaeligarten.

Hauptbahnhof
S-Bahn 7 to Mittersendling.
Mittersendling
Take **exit at far end of platform** and walk down stairs under tracks and up the next stairs to the asphalt foot path. Follow path along tracks, turn right through tunnel and straight to beer garden.

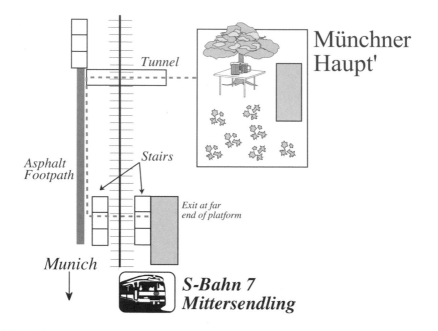

Münchner Haupt'

Tunnel

Asphalt Footpath

Stairs

Exit at far end of platform

Munich

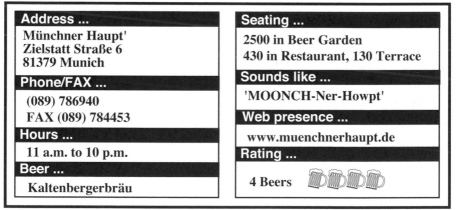

S-Bahn 7 Mittersendling

Address ...	Seating ...
Münchner Haupt'	**2500 in Beer Garden**
Zielstatt Straße 6	**430 in Restaurant, 130 Terrace**
81379 Munich	
Phone/FAX ...	Sounds like ...
(089) 786940	**'MOONCH-Ner-Howpt'**
FAX (089) 784453	Web presence ...
Hours ...	**www.muenchnerhaupt.de**
11 a.m. to 10 p.m.	Rating ...
Beer ...	**4 Beers**
Kaltenbergerbräu	

Münchner Haupt'
(formerly Schießstätte)

We're having real trouble keeping up with the name of this beer garden. (Identity theft is a crime, isn't it?) Well, the former Schießstätte, and before that the former Königlich Bayerische Biergarten, and before that . . . well, never mind. Fact is, this is now known as Münchner Haupt', a shortcut for "Königlich privilegierte Hauptschützengesellschaft München 1406". That's the name of the centuries-old shooting club that owns and runs the beer garden and restaurant housed in a Victorian-style mansion. Founded before Columbus sailed for the New World, the club is still a bastion of German chauvinism where women are allowed sparingly and members gather to destroy a few targets along with a large number of brews.

Whatever you call it, Münchner Haupt' is both beautiful and spacious. The 2,500-seat beer garden has been designed with about half the anchored wooden tables in the shade of 100-year-old chestnut trees and the rest in the open for those who want to take in some late-season rays before fall turns to winter. New management — thus the name change — are justly proud of the Kaltenberg Beer they serve and its history. Prince Leopold, a Wittelsbach ruler, established the Kaltenberg palace brewery several hundred years ago and the suds served the royal family in some unusual ways. Next to the salt tax, income generated by the royal brewing business kept the House of Wittelsbach in deep sauerkraut for many years. On the "medicinal" side, Duke

Emanuel drank a full liter of beer every noon and evening for his entire healthy life. The strangest use of the suds occurred in 1823 when the Bavarian national theater caught fire. Cold winter temperatures froze the local water supply and the fire was eventually doused, you guessed it, with beer. Maximilian I, a bit of an ingrate, later rebuilt the national theater with money raised by hiking the beer tax.

The Kaltenberg beer at Münchner Haupt' is as tasty as the better-known brands and cheaper than most. In fact, everything about this establishment is easy on the pocketbook with no compromise in the quality or service. The business promotes seasonal fare, including special programs during the March strong beer season and a Christmas and New Years celebration. The crowd on weekends is large and families are especially at home here. We've mapped a backdoor shortcut to this worthy establishment. From the end of the S-Bahn platform it's a short walk along an asphalt footpath and then a hard right through a railroad underpass to the shooting club and beer garden.

What's new here along with the name is a 130-seat terrace restaurant, with a cover when raining and portable heaters when winter. Call it what you will, Münchner Haupt' is well worth your visit. We haven't changed our opinion nor high recommendation. It gets 4 beers.

Hauptbahnhof
Walk, following map.

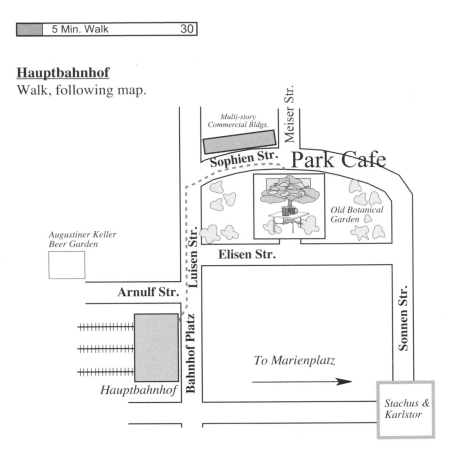

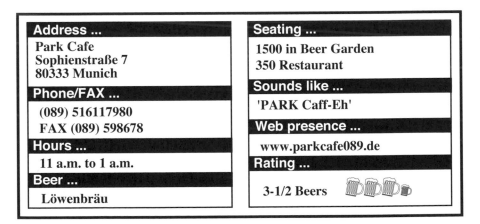

Address ...	Seating ...
Park Cafe Sophienstraße 7 80333 Munich	1500 in Beer Garden 350 Restaurant
Phone/FAX ...	**Sounds like ...**
(089) 516117980 FAX (089) 598678	'PARK Caff-Eh'
Hours ...	**Web presence ...**
11 a.m. to 1 a.m.	www.parkcafe089.de
Beer ...	**Rating ...**
Löwenbräu	3-1/2 Beers

150

Park Cafe

The century was just beginning and there was no finer nightclub in all of Munich than the Park Cafe. Gentlemen in tophats and tails and their ladies in chic evening gowns danced the night away on polished black marble floors below crystal chandeliers. Couples relaxed on stuffed velvet settees or gathered around the long mahogany bar to talk politics or the latest trends from Paris. Others strolled through the botanical gardens, just outside.

The velvet, marble, mahogany, and crystal are mostly gone now. The botanical gardens are now referred to as "old" and the new replacement gardens are several miles across town. But the luster of the Park Cafe's golden age is slowly returning, thanks to Chris Lehner, a local entrepreneur who took over the Park Cafe several years ago. At the time, the place still consisted of a restaurant, a nightclub and a beer garden, cobbled together in strained peaceful coexistence. Lehner closed the business, called in the architect and builders and started over. Nine months and undisclosed thousands of Euros later (he won't talk about how much) the "new" Park Cafe was reborn, and reopened in February 2007. The three original pieces are still there: a restaurant, a *Tanzlokal* (dance club) and a beer garden. What's new is an integrated experience with something designed to appeal to each and every visitor. Inside the former nightclub is a totally refurbished modern restaurant and cafe bar, designed for adults this time. A central stage plays host on a near daily basis to live bands that cover the gamut from pop to rock to jazz. The restaurant is filled with polished wood tables and refurbished fixtures along with an expanded menu that features traditional Bavarian specialties. For the first time in local memory, one can arrive at the Park Cafe during the day and actually walk through the front door.

The beer garden is now an extension of the remodeled building and the botanical gardens. Currently at 1500 seats, plans are underway for expansion. Huge flower-filled urns and decorative statuary punctuate long rows of wood tables in the beer garden. Periodic jazz, Big Band and dixieland groups also entertain here. The beer garden has both service and self-serve sections (again, look for the tables that are uncovered). The *Tagesschmankerl* menu insert offers daily specials and better deals for light inexpensive snacks when dining outside. Park Café still holds the distinction as the closest beer emporium to the main train station, an important note for those in a hurry. A flurry of construction has taken place in the neighborhood and now you have to look closely to make sure you don't miss Sophien Str. in the shadow of one of the multi-story office and residential buildings that now dominate the area.

The Park Cafe, with its new look, remains a unique blend of boisterous bistro and Bavarian beer garden. It gets a commendable 3 1/2 beers.

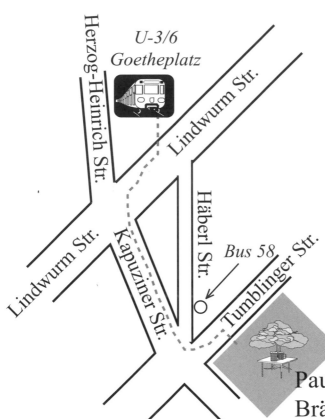

Hauptbahnhof
U-1 or U-2 to Sendlinger Tor.

Sendlinger Tor
U-3 or U-6 to Goetheplatz

Goetheplatz
Walk down Kapuziner Strasse, following map. (Take short cut down Häberl Str. if you prefer. Bus 58 on Häberl Str. will take you directly back to Hauptbahnhof.)

U-3/6
Goetheplatz

Herzog-Heinrich Str.

Lindwurm Str.

Lindwurm Str.

Kapuziner Str.

Häberl Str.

Bus 58

Tumblinger Str.

Paulaner
Bräuhaus

Address ...	Seating ...
Paulaner Bräuhaus **Kapuzinerplatz 5** **80337 Munich**	**850 in Beer Garden** **400 in Beer Hall/Restaurant**
Phone/FAX ...	**Sounds like ...**
(089) 5446110 **FAX (089) 54461118**	**'Pa-LAH-Near-BROW-House'**
Hours ...	**Web presence ...**
10 a.m. to 1 a.m.	**www.paulanerbraeuhaus.de**
Beer ...	**Rating ...**
Paulaner House-brewed	**4 Beers**

152

Paulaner Bräuhaus

It's puzzling why Munich isn't filled with brewpubs where beers are crafted right on the premises. Despite a ready and willing customer base, opportunities to drink straight from the tap are relatively rare. That makes Paulaner Bräuhaus an especially inviting venue. The brew house and beer garden on Kapuzinerplatz are busy brewing and serving up gravity-fed suds that rival those found anywhere — or nowhere else, for that matter.

The history behind this place is rich with local brewing lore. Early roots of an important branch of the Paulaner brand reach back to 1889 when two brothers, Eugen and Ludwig Thomas after being schooled in the brewing capital of Pilsen, began hand-crafting beers on this site.

The Bräuhaus, centrally located in a residential area of Munich.

They opened their doors of what was then called Zum Thomasbräu and began offering a pale lager that was way ahead of its time. The popularity of this first-ever Münchener *Helles* bottom-brewed beer was enormous and would eventually become the foundation of the Munich beer trade. The Thomas Brothers expanded their own business and the brewery, at one point bridging the space from Kapuzinerstrasse to Maistrasse.

The beer the brothers introduced in Munich revolutionized the industry and literally altered the tastes of the beer-drinking public. In the next several decades the Munich brewing business exploded, and the Thomas Brothers found themselves adrift in a sea of competition. Eventually the Paulaner brand absorbed Thomasbräu the brewery and its variety of beers.

A century after the Thomas Brothers made their mark, a portion of the old brewery was renovated and restored in the old style. In October 1989, the Paulaner Bräuhaus re-opened for business with a brand new brew plant and a lot of built in tradition. The interior was rebuilt around the huge copper kettle that dominates the inner *Schwemme* or beer hall. Surrounding open space is taken up with lots of benches and stand-up drinking perches. They're reminiscent of a century ago when locals graced the smoke-filled inner-sanctum and discussed the virtues of a new Pilsener-style beer that had never before been seen or tasted. It's easy to see that the very essence of the *Bier Kultur* that sprang up in Munich began right here in the Bräuhaus. The building retains many smaller areas that were sectioned off to create the restaurant and beer hall to go along with the brewery. In an usual twist, those seeking a little quietude are invited to retreat to the alcove library (no, really, with books!) and sample a few brews among the leaves.

The library exit leads to the outside beer garden with terrace-style, umbrella-covered tables with service. In the back are more open wooden tables with benches where self-service is allowed. A recent innovation is a "beer garden lounge" complete with oversized and heavily padded and upholstered arm chairs and coffee tables where folks can gather in panel discussions regarding the benefits of imbibing beer.

Most Paulaner beers are available here, including Pils, Dunkles and even a light wheat beer to go along with a non-alcoholic lager. The restaurant is adequate, with a solid offering of Bavarian dishes, Daily *Tageskarte* full-course specials are available at cheap prices. Plus, a sample of any three beers is yours for around 3 Euros. Happy hour discounts on the beers are good until 5 p.m. during weekdays.

The real treat are the home-brewed beers. Braumeister Ulrich Schindler is justifiably proud of his list of brews, particularly his unfiltered "Thomas Zwickl" lager. The cloudy pale, lager with the yeast still suspended follows the old recipe first developed by the Thomases themselves. The "Zwickl" in the name comes from the German term for the small tasting tap used to test the beer while it is still fermenting. One taste of this lager and it's easy to understand the urge to pull the Zwickl often. The other Paulaner Bräuhaus mainstay is the "Hefe-

Brewers in Germany have been held in high esteem for centuries and awarded their own coat of arms (above). Brewing in Bavaria was first undertaken by ecclesiastical beer makers. The six-pointed star shown in the 1730 copper engraving (left) is yet another historical symbol of the beer-making art.

Weissbier Naturtrüb," a top-brewed un-filtered wheat beer. Additionally, the brewhouse offers a seasonal third beer — a bock, Märzen, even a kölsch — that is available upon request.

The Wirt and brewery folks are proud of their establishment and quite willing to entertain an impromptu tour of the brew plant, when time permits. (They ask that you call first (089) 5446110 to reserve a brewery tour for small groups.) During a walk-through of the brew plant, visitors are shown an operation that adheres to centuries-old beer-making tradition, yet still manages to produce a product that remains pure and unique. Several Munich walking tours actually schedule a tour of Paulaner Bräuhaus as part of their normal itinerary.

This is an outstanding lokal, one part beer hall, another beer garden, and still a third part micro-brewery. Add to that the great home-brewed products, the convenient location and the relatively short walk to get there, and Paulaner Bräuhaus holds and brews its own with a strong 4-beer rating.

The beer garden has table service as well as the more traditional wooden tables with bank seating where self-service is allowed.

Hauptbahnhof
U-Bahn 2 to Silberhorn.
Silberhorn
Tram 15 or 25 one stop to Ostfriedhof (direction: Max-Weber-Platz).
Ostfriedhof
Follow map a short walk across railroad bridge, up Hoch Str. to entrance to beer hall and garden.

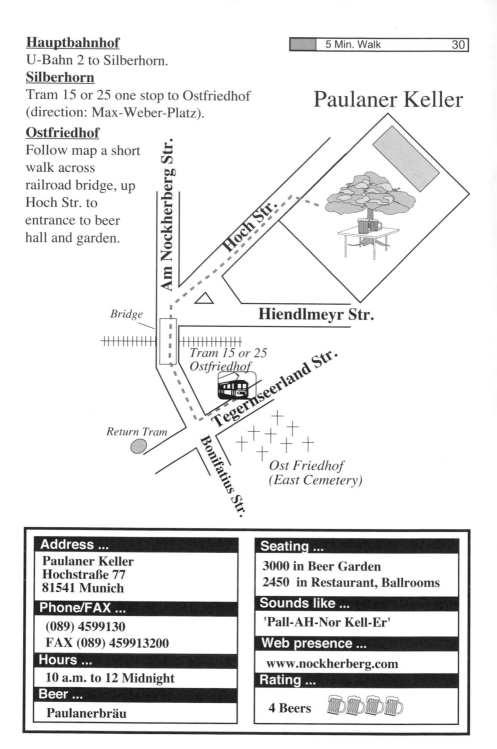

Paulaner Keller

Am Nockherberg Str.

Hoch Str.

Bridge

Hiendlmeyr Str.

Tram 15 or 25
Ostfriedhof

Tegernseerland Str.

Return Tram

Bonifatius Str.

Ost Friedhof
(East Cemetery)

Address ...	Seating ...
Paulaner Keller **Hochstraße 77** **81541 Munich**	**3000 in Beer Garden** **2450 in Restaurant, Ballrooms**
Phone/FAX ...	**Sounds like ...**
(089) 4599130 **FAX (089) 459913200**	**'Pall-AH-Nor Kell-Er'**
Hours ...	**Web presence ...**
10 a.m. to 12 Midnight	**www.nockherberg.com**
Beer ...	**Rating ...**
Paulanerbräu	**4 Beers**

156

Paulaner Keller

The major fire that destroyed Paulaner Keller in 1999 is now only a memory. The main complex is rebuilt and the beer garden reopened in 2003 to huge returning crowds of nostalgic Munich beer garden dwellers. Missing was at least some of the atmosphere that only a centuries-old *wirtshaus* could lend. The new outside *schmankerl* stands are square-pillared and sterile, more suited to a post office than a central food service area for one of Munich's most treasured beer emporia. Inside, the restaurant and banquet rooms are newly furnished and covered in fresh wood. Behind the long bar, highly polished copper brewing vessels embellish the *bierschank* and reflect the newness of the place. It all reminds you that a true Munich beer establishment is a lot more than simple furniture, walls and buildings. Putting it back together again can't totally restore its soul. That will probably

The rebuilt *Wirtshaus* and beer garden at Paulaner Keller have a new look but an old tradition that keeps customers coming back for more.

157

take another century or two.

Still, it's a new condition, but an old tradition. What hasn't been lost is Paulaner Keller's focus on beer, "stark" beer. One trip to the Nockherberg — the hill overlooking the Isar and home to the "new" Paulaner Keller — and one quickly learns what keeps them coming back. Formerly "Salvator" Keller, Paulaner Keller has taken the name of its better-known and well-regarded Paulaner brew, the liquid mainstay of the Salvator-Paulaner-Thomasbräu brewery next door. In addition to Paulaner — a typical Munich-style golden lager — the world-famous Salvator doppelbock strong beer (7.9 % alcohol) is served here year-round.

That may not seem like such a drawing card until one realizes that most other breweries in Munich — and throughout Germany for that matter — feature the seasonal strong beer only during a relatively short two-week period beginning around "Joseph's Day" on the 19th of March. This is the so-called *Starkbierzeit*, or strong beer time, when heavily-malted brews approaching 8 percent (vol.) alcohol are dispensed with impunity.

The history of Paulaner Keller is well integrated with its beer. Early in the 17th century, the Paulaner monks immigrated from Italy and established a monastery in Munich. Soon thereafter, in 1629, they brewed a special-occasions beer, dubbed Sankt Vaters Bier, or sacred father's brew, owing to its purported miraculous healing powers. Certainly, aches and pains were temporarily postponed under its influence, but the truth was, potency aside, the beer tasted lousy.

That changed when Barnabas Still entered the Paulaner order a century or so

The rebuilt Paulaner Keller has one of Munich's most impressive *bierschanks*.

later. Brother Barnabas, the son of a well-reputed local brewer, transformed the suds into something divine. By 1770, the beer — known simply around Munich by the slang-shortened "Salvator" name — was being widely dispensed. At a time when religious orders were heavily regulated by the secular authorities, Münchners found it easy to look the other way so long as the powerful brew kept flowing. Barnabas, certainly no fool, would take the trouble to keep the local duke, Karl Theodor, well supplied with his product. Finally, the by now well-oiled duke granted Paulaner Brothers, Inc. exclusive rights to freely market their beer on the 26th of February, 1780.

With secularization of the cloisters two decades later, the Paulaner brewery fell into private hands. In 1836, a brewer named Zacherl was able to petition King Ludwig I to break with tradition and allow the sale of strong beer to be moved up from April to the days just after the beginning of Lent (mid-February to first week in March). Thus, the stage was set for the Starkbier season, with Salvator leading the way. The tradition survives, and Salvator is today widely imitated, but seldom duplicated. A search of local trademarks lists more than 120 registered strong beers, many of which borrow the -ator suffix to advertise their added vigor.

They range from the better known copycat brews (for some reason "Imitator" is not one of the 120) such as Triumphator, Optimator, Delicator, Maximator and Animator, to the lesser known but nevertheless graphic, Vitamator, Sufficator, Multiplicator and Raritator.

Originally renovated and expanded in 1899, the most recent post-fire rebuilding includes six *Stüben* (small bars) with seating for 600; three large banquet halls or ballrooms to hold up to 2,000; a beer garden with seating for 3,000. Next to the Hofbräuhaus, this is the best known among Munich's beer palaces.

The Paulaner Keller is like a magnet during Starkbier time, attracting thousands of locals to answer the "call of the Berg" and join in festivities that resemble a corner Oktoberfest. On normal days, the place is filled with armies of brewery workers imbibing their own hard day's work. Most branded beer styles are poured here, including light, dark, bock and wheat beers, as well as an unfiltered *kellerbier* variety only available on site.

When the sun is shining, an early afternoon arrival is recommended to insure seat availability in the beer garden. Waiter or waitress service is available at the tables with table cloths; the rest are self-service (*selbstbedienung*).

A Munich mainstay that gets inexplicably snubbed by outsiders, the newly rebuilt Paulaner Keller should be high on the list as a beer hall and beer garden with still plenty of the old tradition in a spanking new package. An outstanding selection any time of year, its commodious interior makes it especially amenable to an off-season visit (such as during the strong beer festival) when foul-weather plans are in order. Paulaner Keller earns 4 industrial strength beers.

Sankt Emmerams Mühle

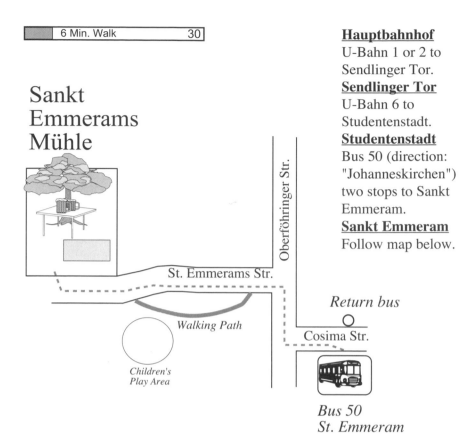

St. Emmerams Str.

Walking Path

Children's Play Area

Hauptbahnhof
U-Bahn 1 or 2 to Sendlinger Tor.
Sendlinger Tor
U-Bahn 6 to Studentenstadt.
Studentenstadt
Bus 50 (direction: "Johanneskirchen") two stops to Sankt Emmeram.
Sankt Emmeram
Follow map below.

Return bus

Cosima Str.

*Bus 50
St. Emmeram*

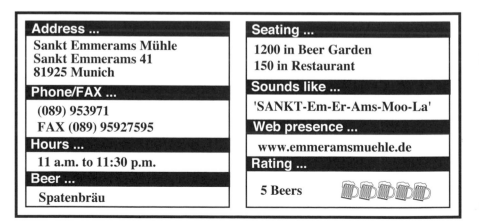

Address ...	**Seating ...**
Sankt Emmerams Mühle Sankt Emmerams 41 81925 Munich	1200 in Beer Garden 150 in Restaurant
Phone/FAX ...	**Sounds like ...**
(089) 953971 FAX (089) 95927595	'SANKT-Em-Er-Ams-Moo-La'
Hours ...	**Web presence ...**
11 a.m. to 11:30 p.m.	www.emmeramsmuehle.de
Beer ...	**Rating ...**
Spatenbräu	5 Beers

Sankt Emmerams Mühle

Not the river but the stream . . . down by the old Sankt Emmerams Mühle. Anybody who is somebody, and everybody who is anybody at one time or another can count themselves among the patrons of this diamond among Munich's rural beer garden treasures. Lifestyles of the rich and famous converge daily with the workaday existence of the city's middle-class multitudes at the one-time paper mill-turned-restaurant and beer garden near the Isar River.

Historically, the Sankt Emmerams locale is connected with the city's founding. In 1158, King Henry the Lion destroyed a nearby toll bridge over the Isar at Oberföhring that had been a lucrative venture of his rich royal uncle. He built his own money-making crossing a few miles upstream at a village called Munichen. The city was thus chartered as a consequence of Henry's medieval entrepreneurship.

"The Mill of Saint Emmerams" was in existence in the 14th century. The mill stayed busy — first with the conversion of grains and later production of paper — for several hundred years. As a sideline, the mill management began serving food and beverages to customers in 1825 by

A production crew films a scene for German television at Sankt Emmerams.

Customers arriving to Sankt Emmerams Mühle pedal or stroll their way along the pathway that borders the beer garden.

converting adjacent offices and waiting rooms into a restaurant and outdoor beer garden. The mill and restaurant were reconstructed in 1866 in the style they appear today. When the milling business ground to a halt after World War I, the

The old paper mill, still standing, behind the beer garden.

gastronomical side of the house took over. Over the years, the proprietors or *wirts* have taken painstaking care to preserve the restaurant's centuries-old atmosphere. With a devotion to detail, they have even gone so far to use 19th-century timbers and other antique building materials for interior renovations.

The result is an unspoiled, living museum piece that has become almost as famous as the entourage of big name entertainers and film stars who visit here. Sankt Emmerams' guest book reads like a Who's Who of international celebrities. ABBA, Led Zepplin, Tina Turner, Rod Stewart, and Donna Summer have all paused for a brew in the shady beer garden. Famous international and local film personalities have stopped here. Former tennis great Boris Becker would pause for a beer between sets. The Bavarian political king himself, Franz Joseph Strauss after whom the Munich airport is named, once held court here. But most patrons of Sankt Emmerams Mühle don't come to see or be seen. Most are everyday Münchners who arrive on foot or by bicycle, after a walk or ride along one of the many scenic pathways that meander through the countryside and terminate at the far side of the beer garden. They bring their own food and spread their own table-cloths and are not intimidated by any luminary sitting nearby. Thus it is with Munich's beer gardens, where several hundred years of custom and tradition have created the ultimate classless society. When every seat is the same, the best seat in the house is the one that is available. And the celebrity is the one who gets there first. The rush for seating is a little calmer since management expanded the seating capacity by 50 percent from what it was a few years ago. Today the beer garden holds 1200 seats with the addition of a new section behind the restaurant and adjacent to the old mill itself. The pinnacle quality of food, beverage, and service at Sankt Emmerams Mühle is enough to make every customer feel like a VIP, and at a price a commoner can afford. Making it even more affordable is Sankt Emmerams' participation in the BDG2M's Prosit! beer offering (check coupon page). The country inn atmosphere in a setting of rolling hills, and grassy meadows is a rare experience that shouldn't be missed. Sankt Emmerams Mühle justly deserves the reputation it has earned of being among Munich's very best. It gets an unqualified 5 full beers!

The beer garden at Sankt Emmerams Mühle.

163

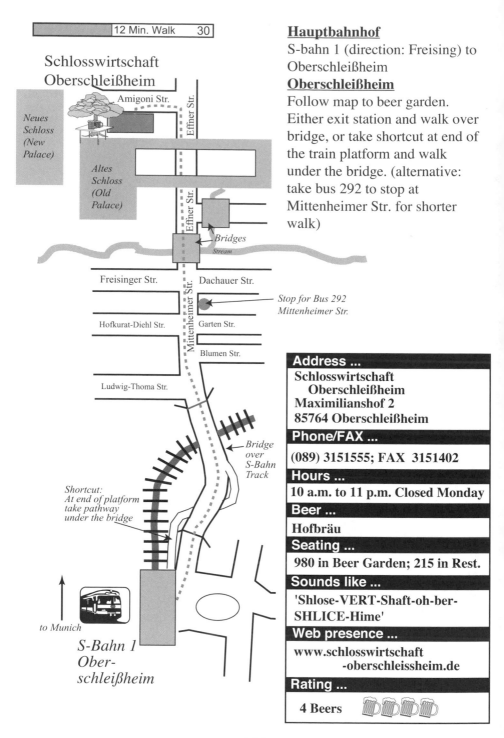

Schlosswirtschaft Oberschleißheim

Amigoni Str.

Effner Str.

Neues Schloss (New Palace)

Altes Schloss (Old Palace)

Effner Str.

Bridges

Stream

Freisinger Str.

Mittenheimer Str.

Dachauer Str.

Stop for Bus 292 Mittenheimer Str.

Hofkurat-Diehl Str.

Garten Str.

Blumen Str.

Ludwig-Thoma Str.

Bridge over S-Bahn Track

Shortcut: At end of platform take pathway under the bridge

to Munich

S-Bahn 1 Ober- schleißheim

Hauptbahnhof
S-bahn 1 (direction: Freising) to Oberschleißheim

Oberschleißheim
Follow map to beer garden. Either exit station and walk over bridge, or take shortcut at end of the train platform and walk under the bridge. (alternative: take bus 292 to stop at Mittenheimer Str. for shorter walk)

Address ...

**Schlosswirtschaft
    Oberschleißheim
Maximilianshof 2
85764 Oberschleißheim**

Phone/FAX ...

(089) 3151555; FAX 3151402

Hours ...

10 a.m. to 11 p.m. Closed Monday

Beer ...

Hofbräu

Seating ...

980 in Beer Garden; 215 in Rest.

Sounds like ...

**'Shlose-VERT-Shaft-oh-ber-
SHLICE-Hime'**

Web presence ...

**www.schlosswirtschaft
        -oberschleissheim.de**

Rating ...

4 Beers

164

Schlosswirtschaft Oberschleißheim

B eer gardens annexed to royal Bavarian palaces are few in number. Zur Schwaige and Hirschgarten come to mind. Also gracing that elite list is the Schlosswirtschaft Oberschleißheim, with a history stretching back more than 400 years. It really began in the year 1597 when Herzog Wilhelm V (the same Duke who founded the Hofbräuhaus) bought a sprawling estate in his home town of Schleißheim. He retired a year later and headed home for a little peace and tranquility, living out the rest of his life in relative seclusion. In the period 1617-1623 his son Maximilian took the family

charge and built on this site what's known today as the "Alte Schloss" or old palace. This royal structure was renowned as one of the best examples of Baroque architecture in all of Bavaria until much of the palace was destroyed during World War II. The main building was reconstructed in 1970-72 and today is open to the public. The imposing "Neue Schloss" or new palace was commissioned by Elector Max Emanuel with the assumption he would someday ascend to become the next Emperor (he was wrong) and would need suitable housing. The New Palace was begun in 1701 under design of Enrico

The "Neue Schloss" at Oberschleißheim was completed in 1726.

Zuccalli and finished in 1726 under architectural direction of Joseph Effner. When completed, the palatial complex and gardens rivaled those of palaces in Vienna and Versailles, although Max Emanuel's status was never so vaulted. After his unsuccessful run for Emperor, he returned from exile in France with little fanfare. Yet, judging by his digs, one could at least surmise that if he could not be a king, he could certainly live like one.

Of course where there is a Schloss, there is usually a Schlossbrauerei and this is where the Schlosswirtschaft got its start. After all, it was literally an exclusionary right of the royal Wittelsbach family to brew ales and wheat beers in Bavaria at the time. With this royal monopoly in place the palace administration was obliged to offer some liquid solace to the traveling public. Sometime in the early 1800s a country inn was established and a brewery operated on the palace grounds. The completion of a rail line to Landshut further expanded the Wirtschaft business. The place became a haven for artists and artisans in the region, especially painters and writers who streamed to the beer garden to raise a brew in honor of their most recent masterpiece.

In 1912, Bavaria's first Flughafen (airport) was built nearby. Early aviators quickly turned the Schlosswirschaft into a neighborhood bar or *Kneipe*. Many can still be found having left their signature in the guestbook, including Germany's most

The spacious beer garden at Schlosswirtschaft Oberschleißheim is just around the corner from one of Bavaria's most prominent palaces.

famous World War I flying ace, Manfred von Richthofen.

The restaurant and beer garden today are a thriving operation in a bucolic setting. The beer garden is spacious and well-shaded with mature chestnut trees. A large *schmankerl* stand lines one side of the beer garden, with plenty of opportunity to serve yourself to moderately priced beer and high-carb (thus great tasting) snacks. The restaurant is a major part of the business and stays busy even during the winter season when the beer garden is closed. Occasional group tours visiting the palaces will stop by the beer garden for a lunch or beer.

Latest in a long line of locally famous innkeepers, the Blaß Family runs the operation and maintains a high level of quality and traditional service. On a clear and sunny day, this is an outstanding destination to enjoy an invigorating beer garden folded into no less than a historic, palatial estate. We give the royally rooted Schlosswirtschaft Oberschleißheim a high recommendation and four crowning beers.

Museum Hours: The Alte Schloss is open to the public from 10 a.m. to 5 p.m., closed Mondays. The Neue Schloss is open April-September, 9 a.m. to 6 p.m.; October-March, 10 a.m. to 4 p.m. Closed Mondays.

A four century head start has provided a mature stand of shade trees for the beer garden.

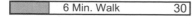

Hauptbahnhof
S-Bahn to Marienplatz.
Marienplatz
Follow bus (not tram) sign and
exit for Bus 52 for Tierpark.
Take bus to final stop at
Tierpark (Zoo).
Tierpark
Walk, following map.

Siebenbrunn

Schon Str.

*Bus 52
Turnaround*

Tierpark Str.

Siebenbrunnen Str.

*Entrance
to Zoo*

Address ...	**Seating ...**
Siebenbrunn Siebenbrunner Straße 5 81543 Munich	1400 in Beer Garden 140 in Restaurant
Phone/FAX ...	**Sounds like ...**
(089) 650848 FAX (089) 62230636	'SEE-Bun-Broon'
Hours ...	**Web presence ...**
11 a.m. to 12 midnight	www.siebenbrunn-muenchen.de
Beer ...	**Rating ...**
Spatenbräu	4 Beers

Siebenbrunn

Grab the kids and head for the zoo. And after the kiddies have dragged you through several miles of four-legged exhibits from six continents, wouldn't a tall cool one go good right now? As luck would have it, a short detour from Munich's zoo entrance is Siebenbrunn, one of the city's more attractive beer gardens. It's now better than ever with a steady ration of live entertainment and a near doubling of the beer garden, from 800 to 1400 seats.

Siebenbrunn ("Seven Springs") was there long before any nearby zoological undertaking. In the 18th century the area was a part of the royal hunting preserves of Bavarian Duke Karl Albrecht. In 1732, another avid royal huntsman, Baron von Preysing, sent his emissary in search of a suitable location for overnight resting of the royal hunting nags. Siebenbrunn, with plenty of running water and nearby game — albeit belonging to someone else — seemed an ideal stopover point. So, the baron's people got with the duke's people and struck up a 60-day temporary lease agreement, one assumes with some option for renewal. The prototypical time-share plan was followed by an early example of squatters rights. Suddenly, Siebenbrunn was under new management and stables were erected on the site.

The normal evolution prevailed, and the spirit of the hunt was replaced by other spirits, most notably those sold across the bar of the local country tavern. The horse barn was turned into a restaurant of sorts, and one can imagine the natural incentive to develop an area with lots of outdoor seating. Historical records reveal the ownership dispute was settled by 1763 when the property was officially sold to a count with the prophetic name of Maximilian von Baumgarten (literally "tree garden"). Later this was a cottage factory turning out sandals and boots. The sole of the business wore thin, and by the early 19th century Siebenbrunn was back to being a lokal and beer garden again.

Siebenbrunn has survived floods (1899) and bombs (1944) and thousands of tourists on safari. It's an excellent example of a traditional Munich beer garden. With plenty of summer shade and an outdoor *bühne* or stage, the wirt wants you to think of this place as the "Live Music" beer garden, with a group ready to boogie every afternoon around 4 p.m. You can catch traditional Bavarian, as well as folk, country and western, and even an occasional Elvis impersonator daily in the beer garden.

The restaurant and lounge, with one of the longest bars seen anywhere, has an unusual menu. Customers are invited to select raw and rare meats like kangaroo and South African antelope and have them cooked to order. (Someone had better go over to the zoo and do another head count.)

Siebenbrunn is a perfect day-trip for the kids, but you don't have to answer the call of the wild to make the trip worthwhile. Siebenbrunn gets 4 well-earned beers.

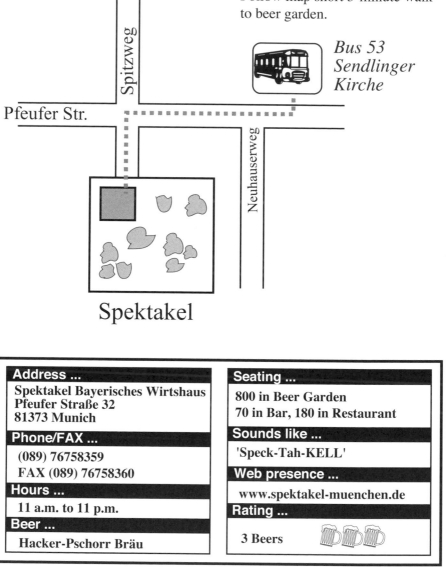

3 Min. Walk 30

Hauptbahnhof
S-Bahn 7 to Harras.
Harras
Cross the street to Bus 53. Take Bus 53 three stops to Sendlinger Kirche.
Sendlinger Kirche
Follow map short 3-minute walk to beer garden.

Bus 53
Sendlinger
Kirche

Spitzweg

Pfeufer Str.

Neuhauserweg

Spektakel

Address ...	Seating ...
Spektakel Bayerisches Wirtshaus Pfeufer Straße 32 81373 Munich	800 in Beer Garden 70 in Bar, 180 in Restaurant
Phone/FAX ...	**Sounds like ...**
(089) 76758359 FAX (089) 76758360	'Speck-Tah-KELL'
Hours ...	**Web presence ...**
11 a.m. to 11 p.m.	www.spektakel-muenchen.de
Beer ...	**Rating ...**
Hacker-Pschorr Bräu	3 Beers

Spektakel
(formerly Tannengarten)

What used to be the Tannengarten — with or without *Tannenbäume* (pine trees) — is now Spektakel Bayerisches Wirtshaus. Along with a new name, Spektakel inherits a history that reaches back to 1889 when the beer garden was first opened. It was a neighborhood beer garden then and it remains today, a durable institution in the Sendlinger section of Munich. Local chroniclers note that the historically significant "farmers revolt" of 1705 took place around the corner. A December parade winding through the neighborhood is held in honor of the revolutionary event and a painting depicting the battle still hangs in Spektakel's banquet room.

With the new name comes an improved beer garden and a totally renovated restaurant. What was formerly plain "tables, chairs and not much more" decor is now a completely rebuilt interior with lots of unfinished lumber, crossbeams, platforms, corner nooks, and small balconies for dinner customers to enjoy. Twice each evening (7:30 and 9:30 p.m.) is a "gewitter" show. The 10-minute computer-controlled show, complete with thunder (heavy bass), lightning (flashing lights) and flowing water (in-line irrigation), treats patrons to a bit of an electronic, well, "spektakel" to go along with their *wienerschnitzel*. Not exactly something from DreamWorks, but modestly entertaining.

Outside, the beer garden still offers plenty of shade from a stand of mature, fully foliated chestnut trees. This is still a great place to experience a traditional Bavarian beer garden, with both a self-service and a terraced service area offering a full menu of tasty food specialties. Adding some spice are a few unusual concoctions, like a Tex-Mex chili dish, lasagne and even a vegetable strudel (say what?). A new centralized serving area now caters to brown-baggers looking for a little lift from their own culinary limitations, one of many capital improvements and upgrades to go along with the new Yellow Pages listing.

Sure, there are those who will not appreciate the change. No amount of new glitter with the *gewitter* will impress them. But, for those who are looking for a beer garden with a little something extra, Spektakel (not crazy about the name) delivers. And while Spektakel isn't spectacular, it's certainly making progress. To us, that's worth a commendable 3 beers.

Hauptbahnhof
U-Bahn 1 to Gern.
Gern
Exit on Tizian Str. and follow map 100 yards to beer garden.

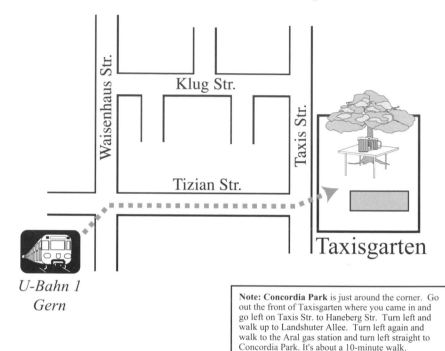

Klug Str.

Waisenhaus Str.

Taxis Str.

Tizian Str.

Taxisgarten

*U-Bahn 1
Gern*

Note: Concordia Park is just around the corner. Go out the front of Taxisgarten where you came in and go left on Taxis Str. to Haneberg Str. Turn left and walk up to Landshuter Allee. Turn left again and walk to the Aral gas station and turn left straight to Concordia Park. It's about a 10-minute walk.

Address ...
Taxisgarten
Taxis Straße 12
80637 Munich

Phone/FAX ...
(089) 156827
FAX (089) 1595019

Hours ...
10 a.m. to 11 p.m.

Beer ...
Spatenbräu

Seating ...
1500 in Beer Garden
250 in Restaurant and Banquet

Sounds like ...
'TAX-Ees-Gar-Tin'

Web presence ...
www.taxisgarten.de

Rating ...
3-1/2 Beers

Taxisgarten

Germany's martial past is legion. There are few countries in the world whose citizens are more sensitive to a record of two world wars in the space of a century, and many thousands of casualties that were taken on all sides during the conflicts. The fabric of collective guilt has been woven through this republic. Today's Germany, economically strong and a leader in the European Union, has outlived its warrior past and is foremost among western democracies in both its abhorrence to war and highest regard for peace. Yet the reminders remain, even in its beer gardens.

Taxisgarten, established in 1920, was dedicated to the rehabilitation of wounded veterans of World War I. The enterprise was originally the property of the *Vereins Kriegs- und Korperbeschädigte* (Association of War-wounded) and served as a social gathering point for those whose service would forever bear the scars of war.

The bonds of national sacrifice were strong and Taxisgarten's patronage remained exclusively former military. A building to house the association was constructed. And, in a tragic irony, the entire complex — structures and beer garden — was consumed during the century's second conflagration, World War II. Post-war rebuilding was accompanied by a rejection of all things bellicose and belligerent. The organization of war veterans opened its doors to the neighborhood and Taxisgarten became a quiet haven for conversations dominated less by war stories than the mundane issues of the day. The restaurant and beer garden were completely renovated in 1988. The last remaining memorial to its martial origins is seen over the restaurant entryway. The overhead portal relief displays a helmeted German soldier accompanied by an inscription. The word *opfer* is used, which in German can mean either "sacrifice" or "victim." The semantic contradiction is left to speak for itself. Taxisgarten fits much better the peaceful mold.

The shady, 1,500-seat beer garden is a neighborhood mainstay and a green oasis in a residential surrounding of stairwell apartments and onion-domed churches. The *speisekarte* or menu features the standard selection of roasted chicken, pork shank, and (not so standard) meaty spareribs. The same folks serving up great barbecued entrees at Am Hopfengarten, Chinesischer Turm and Kugler Alm (Haberl) are in charge here as well. Fresh-baked pretzels are also a local favorite, along with plenty of Bavarian-style snacks. The beer garden draws from a local crowd of young professionals, families and an entourage of students. It's easily accessible, with the Gern U-Bahn stop only a football field away.

This is a prime example of a Munich beer garden that relies on a loyal patronage encouraged by a conscious management effort to provide both quality and service. Taxisgarten gets 3 1/2 beers.

173

Hauptbahnhof
Take one of several S- or U-Bahns direct to Marienplatz.
Exit train station mall toward "Rindermarkt".
Marienplatz
Walk, following map. (Note: Hofbräuhaus is nearby.)

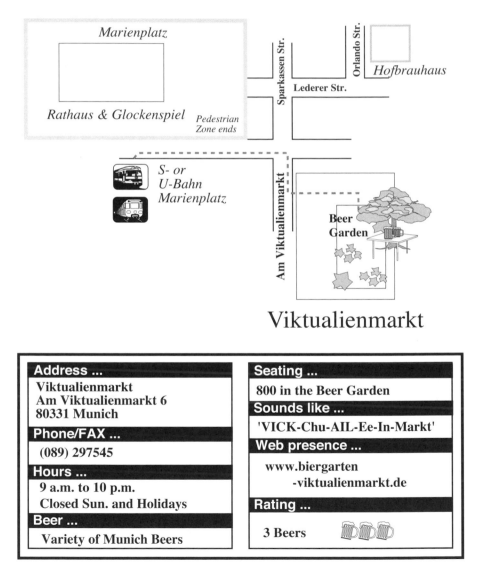

Viktualienmarkt

Address ...	Seating ...
Viktualienmarkt Am Viktualienmarkt 6 80331 Munich	**800 in the Beer Garden**
	Sounds like ...
Phone/FAX ...	'VICK-Chu-AIL-Ee-In-Markt'
(089) 297545	**Web presence ...**
Hours ...	www.biergarten -viktualienmarkt.de
9 a.m. to 10 p.m. Closed Sun. and Holidays	
	Rating ...
Beer ...	
Variety of Munich Beers	3 Beers

Biergarten
Viktualienmarkt

This is a place best visited on a Saturday morning or early afternoon. That's when the weekly Viktualienmarkt, the city's central food market, is in full swing. Everything from *Suppe* to *Nuß* and a million other daily necessities (as in victuals) are hawked here. It's where Münchners come to shop 'til they drop — or, rather, stop to enjoy a Maß of refreshing beer. Viktualienmarkt, a Munich tradition since 1807, is no touristy museum piece. It's a living, thriving activity. The Saturday morning ritual of bartering, haggling, and buying has changed little in the past two hundred years. A colorful display of wares from all over Germany and Europe attests to Munich having served as a southern and northern European trade center for centuries.

The beer garden is wedged in the market's middle, in the center of a ring of flower, fresh fruit, vegetable, meat and other produce stands. Marked at one end by a towering May Pole, the beer garden is anything but hard to find. The greatest concentration of people is there, and seats are at a premium. Numerous food stands and outdoor restaurants are a part of the market complex. Helping yourself to nearby food selections and smuggling them back to your seat in the beer garden is no crime. Interspersed among the beer garden patrons is a series of statues commemorating Munich's six most popular folk singers and comedians. The fountain figures represent Karl Valentin (1882-1948) and his partner Liesl Karlstadt (1892-1960). Also enshrined in permanent bronze are the comedians Weiss Ferdl (1883-1949) and Ida Schumacher (1895-1956), the singer Roider Jackl (1906-1975), and actress Elise Aulinger (1881-1965).

It's hard to separate the beer garden and the market. And they probably shouldn't be. That also means that when the Saturday-morning-to-afternoon market is ended, the beer garden is just another pretty place. When the market is on, Biergarten Viktualienmarkt gets 3 beers. When it's off . . .

Viktualienmarkt is just around the corner from the Marienplatz, in the heart of Old Town.

Hauptbahnhof
U-Bahn 6 or S-Bahn 7 to Harras
Harras
Exit station on Meindl Str. (look for picture of bus).
Take Bus 54 to last stop, Lorettoplatz (15 minute ride).
Lorettoplatz
Follow map. Beer garden is about 1/4 mile walk in the woods.

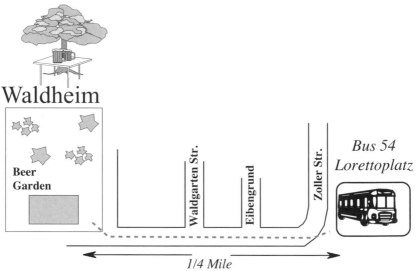

Waldheim

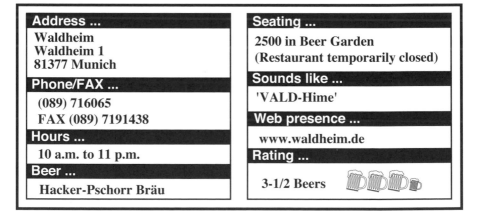

Address ...	Seating ...
Waldheim Waldheim 1 81377 Munich	2500 in Beer Garden (Restaurant temporarily closed)
Phone/FAX ...	**Sounds like ...**
(089) 716065 FAX (089) 7191438	'VALD-Hime'
Hours ...	**Web presence ...**
10 a.m. to 11 p.m.	www.waldheim.de
Beer ...	**Rating ...**
Hacker-Pschorr Bräu	3-1/2 Beers

Waldheim

Those who enjoy the outdoors and don't mind following bread crumbs back to the hotel should make the trip to Waldheim. Although only about a quarter-mile from the nearest bus stop, this impressive beer garden is at the edge of Munich's wooded outback. The Waldheim, or "forest home" is true to its name. It must be the place where Hansel and Gretel, in search of the sinister Gingerbread House, stopped off for a quick beer. Waldheim management has all but abandoned the adjacent inside restaurant, reserving it during the summer months only for special-event bookings and concentrating instead on improving the beer garden. Somehow, that still works for us. The crowd here tends toward the outdoors type, with lots of backpacks and hiking boots mixed in with a briefcase or two and the usual shirtsleeves in abundance on a warm summer day. It's a meeting place for older singles and nomadic bands of nature-lovers who spend their weekends in the woods. The beer garden now has plenty of self-service areas and has been expanded to accommodate 2,500 thirsty pathfinders. Waldheim is at a major crossroads for a series of hiking and bicycle trails that wind through the woods. It's a great place to experience a little nature and you don't have to be a Boy Scout to enjoy it (is there a merit badge for beer drinking?). Few beer gardens in Munich are so secluded and yet have this much to offer. A little bit off the beaten path, but a great choice for those who like to walk. Waldheim gets 3 1/2 beers.

Towering trees at Waldheim.

Waldheim is a wooded oasis with plenty of natural wonders to go along with the food, beer and the company.

Hauptbahnhof
S-Bahn 7 to Großhesselohe/Isartal bahnhof

Großhesselohe/Isartal bahnhof
Visit station brewpub. Walk, following map straight up Kastanienallee to one-way street, Georg-Kalb Str. Walk right (against traffic) as street turns to left and straight to beer garden.

Also, check out the Wa-Wi/Menterschwaige connection. Details on pg. 140.

Waldwirtschaft
Großhesselohe

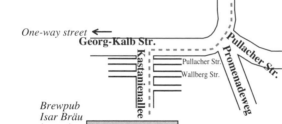

One-way street ←
Georg-Kalb Str.

Pullacher Str.
Wallberg Str.

*Brewpub
Isar Bräu
in station*

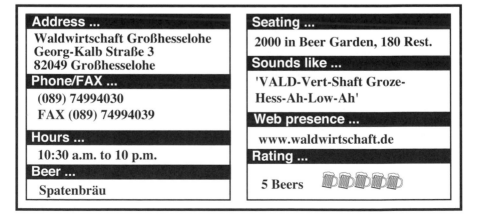

*S-Bahn 7
Großhesselohe
Isartal Bahnhof*

Address ...	Seating ...
Waldwirtschaft Großhesselohe **Georg-Kalb Straße 3** **82049 Großhesselohe**	**2000 in Beer Garden, 180 Rest.**
Phone/FAX ...	Sounds like ...
(089) 74994030 FAX (089) 74994039	'VALD-Vert-Shaft Groze- Hess-Ah-Low-Ah'
Hours ...	Web presence ...
10:30 a.m. to 10 p.m.	www.waldwirtschaft.de
Beer ...	Rating ...
Spatenbräu	5 Beers

178

Waldwirtschaft Großhesselohe

If Sepp Krätz had wanted to run for Mayor of Munich in 1995 he might have won. At least he would have commanded the *Biergärtler* vote. Sepp and his beloved "Wa-Wi" (pronounced Vah-Vee and short for Waldwirtschaft Großhesselohe) were busy manning the frontlines of Munich social protest that year. It began when the Waldwirtschaft was sued in court after a group of unyielding Großhesselohe neighbors complained about late-night "noise" emanating from the beer garden. It seems their quietude was being thrashed by the clinking of thousands of liter mugs of beer coming together in late-night *Prosits*. The neighborhood naysayers prevailed for a while (Germans do love their peace and quiet) when magistrates ruled that Wa-Wi and its ilk would have to cease serving beer after — ready for this? — 9 p.m. Sepp was mad as hell and not about to take it

any more. He went back to the courts and eventually to the streets where he was joined by many thousands of beer-loving garden dwellers in one of the largest public protest rallies Munich had ever seen. It became known as the Great Beer Garden Revolution of 1995 and it ended up legalizing the right of Münchners everywhere to enjoy their beer long after the sun had set, just as they had for centuries before. The lesson: Don't mess with Sepp and don't mess with Munich's beer gar-

The 1995 "Beer Garden Revolution" (above) sent thousands into the streets.

Regular live jazz and Big Band programs are a special attraction at 'Wa-Wi'.

179

dens! More than a decade after Sepp's public stand, his beer garden has only grown and prospered. Waldwirtschaft Großhesselohe remains today a mix of the best of old German tradition and modern day musical enjoyment. Nestled high atop a hillside overlooking the Isar Valley, Wa-Wi is center stage for some of the liveliest jazz and Big Band sounds in all of Bavaria. Everyday during summer months visitors to the garden and restaurant are treated to musical programs by bands from all over Europe, even Polish and Czech ensembles whose contemporary sounds belie their eastern origins.

But don't let the modernity of the music fool you. This beer dispensary has roots reaching back hundreds of years.

The "Schweiger Hesselohe" was mentioned in official proclamations as early as 776, when it was listed as a region under control of the Bavarian Duke Tassilos. The first beer tavern was established in the 15th century and business has been fermenting steadily ever since. In 1779 a new wrinkle was added in the form of a farmer's market, which attracted more visitors and more customers for the foamy brew. Around 1800, a dance pavilion was established, and along with

An evening Maß of Beer and the time to enjoy it is on the menu now that the opening hours of Wa-Wi and other Munich beer gardens have been secured. It took a near revolution and major public protest in1995, but Münchners today enjoy their beer gardens late into the evening as a matter of local law.

it the Waldwirtschaft name. The place became an instant hit with Munich's young crowd who at last had a place to meet where, one would imagine, the beer was cold but the romance was not. In 1852 the railroad reached Großhesselohe. With customers now arriving by the carload, history records that on a good day 10,000 visitors staggered down the slopes of the Waldwirtschaft. A high-water mark was reached on Easter Sunday 1900 when some 11 thousand liters of beer were dispensed — still a local record.

The Spaten Brewery, which itself had been around since 1397, bought the Waldwirtschaft Großhesselohe in 1930, thus fulfilling a long-awaited dream of the brewery's patriarchal Sedlmayr family. It was Gabriel Sedlmayr's dying wish of a century earlier to someday have the Wa-Wi as one of his own. The beer must have been flowing freely in that Big Beer Garden in the Sky the day they brought this one into the fold. The restaurant and beer garden today are patterned around the celebrated jazz musical blueprint that gives the Wa-Wi its individuality. Tables, benches and chairs radiate from the center bandstand likes spokes on a wheel. Benches line the beer garden's outer edge, affording visitors a breathtaking view of the lush, green Isartal river valley below.

Well-foliated chestnut trees provide abundant shade throughout, and a children's play area in one corner keeps the small-fry engrossed while the adults enjoy a cool beer and food selections from the several *Schmankerl* stands nearby.

The Waldwirtschaft Großhesselohe boasts an excellent indoor/outdoor restaurant for more formal dining, featuring a wide selection of traditional Bavarian dishes.

All this and jazz music, too, is almost more than one could ask. A bonus, though, is that many of the summer help come from Ireland or Britain or the former Eastern Bloc countries where English is a popular second language taught in school. Thus the mother tongue is all that's needed in getting exactly what you want, when you want it.

We're pleased to have them as a participant in our Five-Beer Club Prosit! offering as well.

Thanks to Sepp Krätz and his activism for preserving one of the very best beer gardens in Munich and the time — into the late evening — for all to enjoy it. Wa-Wi weighs in with a revolutionary 5-beer rating!

Note: The nearby train station arrival point offers an unusual and refreshing diversion, since it has been refurbished into one of Munich's growing number of microbreweries. The brew, manufactured on the premises, is a type of *weizen*, or wheat beer. **Isar Bräu's** combination restaurant and small outdoor platform cafe also offers Hofbräuhaus Traunstein brand libations for those who prefer the more familiar *helles* style of beer. Prelude to a visit to Wa-Wi should include a brief tour of this facility's glass-enclosed polished copper brewing plant. The cleanliness throughout is an encouraging introduction to the patently Bavarian art of brewing. The Isar Bräu brewpub and restaurant has a beer garden of its own (left) and a small Pils Bar, adding to its appeal as a warm-up to Wa-Wi.

Hauptbahnhof
Take one of several S-Bahns direct to Marienplatz.
Marienplatz
Walk short distance, referring to map. Note that
Hofbräuhaus is just around the corner from Weisses
Brauhaus. Donisl and Andechser am Dom are also
nearby at other end of Marienplatz.

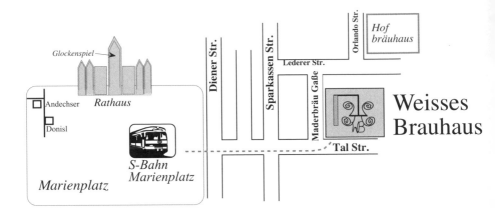

Address ...	Seating ...
Weisses Brauhaus Tal Straße 7 80331 Munich	840 in Restaurant 80 on Outside Terrace
Phone/FAX ...	**Sounds like ...**
(089)2901380; FAX 29013815	'VICE-Iss Brow-House'
Hours ...	**Web presence ...**
7 a.m. to 1 a.m.	www.weisses-brauhaus.de
Beer ...	**Rating ...**
Schneider Weiße Karmeliten Kloster Urtyp	3 Beers

Weisses Brauhaus

Straight through the Marienplatz, just past the end of the pedestrian zone on the historic Tal Straße, is the Weisses Brauhaus. The name signals both the long history of this establishment as a former brewery and also the featured brew, Schneider Weissbier. The Tal Strasse was along a major trade route during the middle ages, leading from Salzburg to Augsburg. The adjacent street, Maderbräugasse, is named after an old Munich brewing family who practiced their trade in the area for centuries. The building that houses Weisses Brauhaus was a brewery as early as 1540 and probably for decades before that. In 1872, Georg Schneider bought out the Maderbräu brewery and turned from the traditional lagers to producing a wheat or

weizen beer, often called weiss or "white" beer. Thus, the Weisses in this case refers to the brew and not the exterior chalk-colored facade.

Schneider had earned his brewing spurs running the Weisses Hofbräuhaus around the corner, where the present-day Hofbräuhaus is located. He was able to turn both Maderbräu and the associated guest house into a thriving business. Eventually, the brewery had to move, but the beer restaurant and lokal stayed on.

Today there is even more of the Weisses Brauhaus to like. A major renovation a few years ago added a second story and 160 more seats to help accommodate the continuous retinue of thirsty and hungry visitors who course through the restaurant and beer hall.

The Weisses Brauhaus today is especially popular among students and others who pause for a beer or a sumptuous meal before or after a trip to the Hofbräuhaus. The atmosphere here is busy, but not hectic. The food is outstanding and plentiful, including house specialities of roasted pork and beefshank, and various grilled sausages. It's not a bad idea to do as the locals do and catch your breath and a good meal at the Weisses Brauhaus before wading into the Hofbräuhaus around the corner. Weisses Brauhaus, with one of the best menus in Munich, earns 3 beers.

Zur
Schwaige

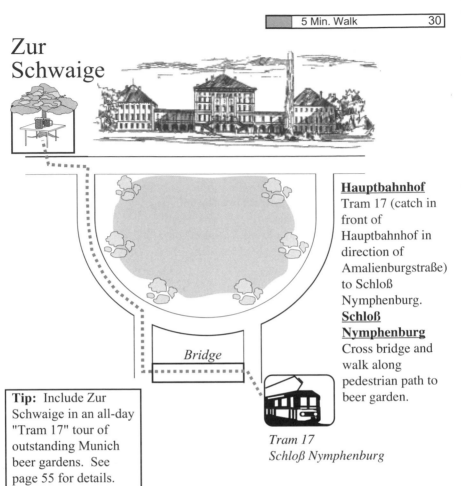

Hauptbahnhof
Tram 17 (catch in front of Hauptbahnhof in direction of Amalienburgstraße) to Schloß Nymphenburg.

Schloß Nymphenburg
Cross bridge and walk along pedestrian path to beer garden.

Bridge

Tram 17
Schloß Nymphenburg

Tip: Include Zur Schwaige in an all-day "Tram 17" tour of outstanding Munich beer gardens. See page 55 for details.

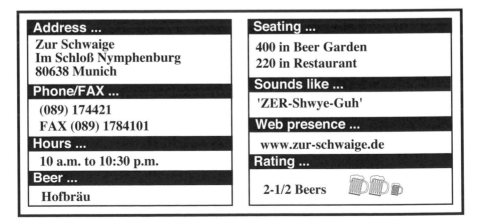

Address ...
Zur Schwaige
Im Schloß Nymphenburg
80638 Munich

Phone/FAX ...
(089) 174421
FAX (089) 1784101

Hours ...
10 a.m. to 10:30 p.m.

Beer ...
Hofbräu

Seating ...
400 in Beer Garden
220 in Restaurant

Sounds like ...
'ZER-Shwye-Guh'

Web presence ...
www.zur-schwaige.de

Rating ...
2-1/2 Beers

Zur Schwaige

Location, location, location. If real estate agents were tour guides, this would be the sales pitch for Zur Schwaige beer garden. It happens to be on the grounds of Schloß Nymphenburg (Nymphenburg Palace), an opulent and historic Munich landmark. Zur Schwaige is probably more restaurant than beer garden, with stuffy upper-crusty tablecloths, cloth napkins, fine silverware and high prices. Fortunately, though, the moderate price of a brew in the beer garden is more to the liking of beer drinkers on a budget. Stay away from the menu and and don't make a move toward the pricey indoor restaurant and you won't get hurt. Although today it shares acreage with Munich's most famous royal residence, Zur Schwaige was actually here first. The building that houses the restaurant and encloses the stand of trees that shades the beer garden was in place in the early 1600s. By 1714 it was incorporated into the palace complex (see section on Hirschgarten for additional information about Nymphenburg Palace). Primary attraction, of course, is still the opportunity to rest the feet while downing a cool one in this shady beer garden. A visit to the palace can consume a morning and a lot of energy roaming from one corridor to the other. For serious beer drinking — and eating for that matter — save the heavy stuff for nearby Hirschgarten. Meanwhile Zur Schwaige can suffice for a break from all the touristy responsibilities of cramming several hundred years of history in a 30-minute walking tour of the palace. Zur Schwaige's location and window of opportunity give it 2 1/2 beers.

Schloß Nymphenburg Museum Hours:
Tues.-Sun. 9 a.m.-12:30 p.m., 1:30 -5 p.m.

The welcoming committee greets visitors to the palace beer garden.

An afternoon in a traditional Bavarian beer garden is worth the trip.

Day Trips

How far would you go for the definitive beer-drinking experience? If you said to Munich, Germany and back, then you probably won't mind an hour or two more on a fast and comfortable train to enjoy a couple brews at a world-class beer hall or beer garden. Fact is, there are some spots that are just too good to miss, and too near to overlook. Albeit, one is technically in another country (Salzburg, Austria) but that shouldn't stop anyone from taking a short ride across the border to enjoy one of the best beer hall/garden combos in the entire world. Others are nearer to Munich but will still eat up most of a day in transit to and from.

In the case of Dachau, the Schloßberg beer garden comes as a totally unexpected beer-drinking experience in the middle of historical ambiguities that are just too obvious to be explained. Bräustüberl Tegernsee is the social centerpiece of a popular lakeside resort. It's the little brewery that could with both the audacity and tenacity of a new leadership team to challenge the most famous beer hall of them all, Hofbräuhaus — and then pull it off.

Also worthy of a little extra time on the road are Weihenstephan and Kloster Andechs. Both are beer pilgrimages with strong religious roots that have given way to even stronger cloister-brewed beers. In this edition, we've found nearby beer gardens for both of these excellent venues that definitely add to the trip.

New in this edition as well is a beer garden-brewery experience in Liebhards in the Munich suburb of Aying that will appeal to every beer drinker.

So pack the lunch, the camera and get ready to make a day of it and venture beyond Munich's city limits to some of the finest beer oases found anywhere.

View of Salzburg, Austria, and the Salzach River, in the vicinity of Augustiner Bräu brewery, beer garden and beer hall in the Mülln section of the city.

187

Hauptbahnhof

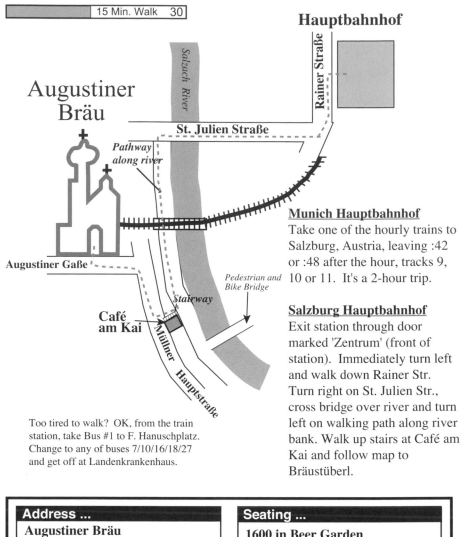

Augustiner Bräu

Salzach River

Rainer Straße

St. Julien Straße

Pathway along river

Augustiner Gaße

Pedestrian and Bike Bridge

Stairway

Café am Kai

Müllner Hauptstraße

Munich Hauptbahnhof
Take one of the hourly trains to Salzburg, Austria, leaving :42 or :48 after the hour, tracks 9, 10 or 11. It's a 2-hour trip.

Salzburg Hauptbahnhof
Exit station through door marked 'Zentrum' (front of station). Immediately turn left and walk down Rainer Str. Turn right on St. Julien Str., cross bridge over river and turn left on walking path along river bank. Walk up stairs at Café am Kai and follow map to Bräustüberl.

Too tired to walk? OK, from the train station, take Bus #1 to F. Hanuschplatz. Change to any of buses 7/10/16/18/27 and get off at Landenkrankenhaus.

Address ...	Seating ...
Augustiner Bräu **Augustinergaße 4** **A-5020 Salzburg, Austria**	**1600 in Beer Garden** **1400 in Rest. & Beer Hall**
Phone/FAX ...	**Sounds like ...**
(0043) 662-431246; FAX 662-43124620	**'Ah-Gus-TEEN-Er Broi'**
Hours ...	**Web presence ...**
Weekdays: 3-11 p.m. **Sat., Sun., Hol.: 2:30-11 p.m.**	**www.augustinerbier.at**
Beer ...	**Rating ...**
Augustinerbräu (Salzburg)	**5 Beers** 🍺🍺🍺🍺

Augustiner Bräu Salzburg

Europe is small, remember that. With the emergence of the European Union and a common currency, it got even smaller. Cultures may vary, but distances between countries are bridged easily with a short ride on a fast train. That makes a world-class beer garden like Augustiner Bräu in Salzburg, Austria, within practical reach of a day trip from Munich.

By now you may be thinking beer gardens named Augustiner are becoming as commonplace as good-tasting beers with the same name. Credit the industrious Augustin brethren. While the rest of

Europe was inventing the Renaissance, they were busy opening beer outlets all over southern Bavaria and the Austrian Tyrol. So it was that the Arch Bishop Wolf-Dietrich founded the monastery in the Mülln section of Salzburg in 1605. By 1621, the brothers were actively brewing and consuming beer. The brothers may have quaffed a few too many brews and neglected their prayers because Kaiser Ferdinand handed the whole cloister over to the Benedictine order in 1835. The entire operation then went public and has been a prime watering hole ever since.

A two-hour train ride from the Munich

Augustiner Bräu beer garden is full of thirsty Austrians and visitors on a warm summer afternoon.

main train station is all it takes to land in Salzburg hauptbahnhof. That makes the timing just about perfect, since Augustiner doesn't open up until the early afternoon. A 15-minute walk across the river to the bräustüberl is immediately met by the smell of fermenting malt and hops, indicating that this beer brewed on the premises is as fresh as it gets. From Augustiner Gaße side entrance, the visitor walks through towering Gothic arches and long fresco-painted hallways, past a well-supplied *schmankerl* (fast-food) stand, a souvenir stand, a delicatessen, butcher shop and bakery, and finally out the back to the hill-top beer garden.

A large beer hall with plenty of wood tables and benches to seat 1400 is at one end. During winter months the spacious interior allows plenty of room to keep the party in full bloom. There is even a hot water basin at one end to take the chill off the beer when the temperatures head south to the freezing point. But during the warm summer-to-fall months most of the activity is centered on the well-shaded, 1600-seat beer garden.

Although table service is available, most of the customers choose the age-old tradition of selecting a porcelain *krug* from the nearby racks and lining up at one of several *ausschanks* for a gravity-fed fill-up. The style of beer is dark, rich, and strong, a version often served by monastic breweries. The Austrian tradition of fast, friendly service at a modest price is

Interior beer hall at Augustiner is ready for business with tables, chairs and benches to seat 1400.

in evidence here. And now that you can use euros, you don't even have to take a beating on the currency exchange. That makes a half liter of beer here cheaper than most beer gardens in Munich. Head Brew Master Christian Spatzenegger adds a personal touch by roaming from table to table, hoisting a brew with the customers as he makes certain they enjoy themselves and have plenty to eat and drink. Well prepared for the task, the food stands offer a wide variety of hot and cold wurst, roasted meats, sandwiches, salads, cheeses *(obatzer!)* , breads, pastries, and desserts. The brewery, of course, will never run out of beer. It keeps 40 large wooden kegs aging at all times, insuring a steady supply of some of the best-

tasting brew found anywhere.

Salzburg, the birthplace of Mozart, is a must stopover on many European itineraries. The churches, monuments, magnificent nearby alpine scenery (The Sound of Music was filmed here) are well worth the visit and trains to Salzburg leave Munich Hauptbahnhof hourly, so why not?

The Augustiner Bräu, long on tradition, short on price, and filled with warm atmosphere and friendly service is an important addition to any visit to the Austrian capital. You don't think we'd send you all that way for a beer garden that wasn't one of the best. Augustiner Bräu Salzburg earns five full hearty beers.

Selecting a beer mug and giving it a quick rinse before a fill-up is an old tradition.

Tegernsee Bahnhof

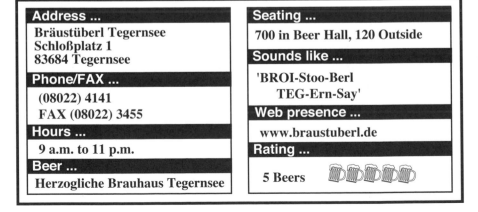

Hauptbahnhof
Take BOB train to Tegernsee
(about 1-hour ride).

(On most days a train leaves München Hauptbahnhof each hour at 42 minutes after the hour on track 34. Check to make certain your car goes to Tegernsee.)

Tegernsee Bahnhof
Walk, following map.

(Return trains leave Tegernsee at 27 minutes after the hour; first train in the morning is 6:27 a.m., last train returning to München is 10:27 p.m.)

What about BOB?
Bayerische Oberland Bahn ("BOB") operates trains directly from Munich Hauptbahnhof to Tegernsee. If you already have an MVV Tageskarte or equivalent, the cost of the ride from Munich as far as Holzkirchen is covered. You pay the difference from Holzkirchen to Tegernsee, around € 5 each way. Don't want to hassle with catching a train on the DB side of the Hauptbahnhof? Instead, take the S-Bahn 2 line using your MVV ticket directly to Holzkirchen and get off. Then buy a roundtrip ticket from there to Tegernsee via BOB. (Caution: When riding BOB, make sure that "Tegernsee" is the clearly marked destination on the car you are on, so you don't end up in Lenggries or Bayrischzell instead.)

Bräustüberl Tegernsee

Tegernsee (Lake Tegernsee)

Address ...	Seating ...
Bräustüberl Tegernsee **Schloßplatz 1** **83684 Tegernsee**	**700 in Beer Hall, 120 Outside**
Phone/FAX ...	**Sounds like ...**
(08022) 4141 **FAX (08022) 3455**	**'BROI-Stoo-Berl** **TEG-Ern-Say'**
Hours ...	**Web presence ...**
9 a.m. to 11 p.m.	**www.braustuberl.de**
Beer ...	**Rating ...**
Herzogliche Brauhaus Tegernsee	**5 Beers** 🍺🍺🍺🍺🍺

Bräustüberl Tegernsee

Tegernsee, about 30 miles south of Munich, plays weekend host to thousands of resort-minded Münchners looking for a convenient getaway to the nearby alpine countryside. With a beautiful lake surrounded by a half-dozen picture-postcard villages and relatively fast accessibility by car or train, the Tegernsee region has much to offer — including one of the best beer hall breweries in all of Germany. This Bavarian mountain valley got its start more than 1200 years ago, when in 746 Benedictine brothers founded an abbey. And we all know what the monks liked to do best. So, the cloister was a brewery before Munich was even an upstart village. At the peak of its influence the religious community of Tegernsee held ownership of more than 12,000 farms including vineyards near Vienna and in northern Italy. In the 15th century its monastic library contained 80,000 volumes and was more extensive than those of the Medicis and the Pope. In fact, had things been slightly different, it might have been Tegernsee that got all the attention and folks today might be heading in the opposite downhill direction on Satur-

Just as it has for centuries, the setting afternoon sun peers through a window of Tegernsee's famous Bräustüberl.

day mornings. We should be happy with the way things turned out. That cloister brewery and meditation room of a millennium ago has become the bustling Bräustüberl Tegernsee today. The affiliation with the clergy is mostly ended — secularization severed the ecclesiastical ties in 1803. The monastery was taken over by the Bavarian royal family and with the help of the famous German architect Leo von Klenze, the abbey was transformed into the summer residence of Bavarian kings. There remains a connection to this day with the Wittelsbach monarchy, stemming from Duke Karl Theodor and later Duke Ludwig Wilhelm. The royal family tree still has a small branch with a financial interest in the brew house. Thus, the brewery that supplies the Bräustüberl is still known as the Herzoglich Bayerische Brauhaus Tegernsee and sports the distinctive logo of a crowned "T" flanked by an "H" and a "B" on either side.

The similarity to the Hofbräuhaus emblem so ubiquitous in Munich is not coincidental. Bräustüberl Tegernsee is just bold enough to feel it is in real competition with the world-famous Hofbräuhaus. Those who operate the Bräustüberl are quick to mention the royal bloodline that at least puts it in the same league with the Hofbräuhaus. Moreover, according to local accounting, the beer business at Hofbräuhaus has a way to go to match a daily output at the Bräustüberl. The all-time pouring record at Bräustüberl Tegernsee is 4,200 liters of beer in a single day! The average weekend daily consumption still runs around 2,500 liters.

One of the best things to happen at the Bräustüberl is the arrival of a new wirt,

Peter Hubert. Young and energetic, Herr Hubert has improved the operation with innovative promotions and a renewed emphasis on satisfying his patrons. He and his staff are developing programs that put the customer first. For example, the Bräustüberl has teamed up with "BOB," Bayerische Oberland Bahn — the independent rail line and primary transportation to and from Munich — to offer a free beer to those who leave the car at home and the driving to BOB. Just present your BOB ticket at the Bräustüberl upon arrival. There are plenty of other daily specials and promotions, and you can read about them in the Bräustüberl's own locally produced and published house organ, the aptly named "Bräustüberl-Zeitung."

One thing the new wirt has not changed is the tech-driven system that keeps the beer hall running smoothly and the suds flowing freely. He's not about to risk running out of beer, not with a brewery next door. The proof is seen in a tour of his cellarworks, with barrel after barrel of fully loaded brew. A computer-controlled distribution system feeds this massive beer emporium and maintains at the ready 18,000 liters of chilled beer, just in case unexpected friends should drop by for the world's largest Stammtisch. The brewery produces some 5 million liters of beer annually, about 600,000 of those sold across the tables at Bräustüberl Tegernsee. Despite its relatively small but thirsty constituency, the Herzoglich Bayerische Brauhaus is one of the leading beer producers in Bavaria, holding its own with more than 800 other breweries. The house features three primary styles of beer: Dunkeles Bock (dark and strong), Tegernsee Spezial (the normal Helles gold-colored lager), and a low-alcohol

Leicht beer that tastes much better than its low-yield might indicate.

Bräustüberl Tegernsee does seem a lot like the Hofbräuhaus, but with a few exceptions. Crowded with people, hardly a seat to be found, heavy vaulted arched corridors filled with smoke — Bräustüberl sports the look of the prototypical Bavarian beer hall. A full house, inside and out, will push a thousand people, but you'll find few foreigners among its lively patrons. Few outsiders even know it exists. Plenty of Germans do, and they don't mind sharing it with friends from out of town who happen by. There is much of the country hospitality at the Bräustüberl that is unfortunately lacking in some of the beer houses in the city. Here you won't be a tourist so much as a guest. The locals are among the friendliest anywhere. The service is fast, the beer is cold, and the food is modestly priced and filling. Menu specialities include Weißwurst and Leberkäse, with plenty of grilled meat and Bavarian-style dishes to choose from.

There is no regular live entertainment, but the loud and raucous crowd noise would probably drown it out anyway. There is excitement in the air at the Bräustüberl and an outstanding beer-drinking experience to be had. We're happy to again rate it to the max — 5 beers and a strong recommendation to take a daytrip to one of the best beer halls in all of Germany.

Oh, one other thing, Peter Hubert has added us to his list of customer-friendly innovations by joining the Prosit! free beer offer. So, a great beer hall experience just got better. Don't miss a visit to Bräustüberl Tegernsee.

You may want to find a place to stay overnight if you visit the Bräustüberl Tegernsee. There are many hotel rooms and *Fremdenzimmers* (bed & breakfasts) available in this resort area. The Travel Offices for the various villages around the lake can help. Here are their telephone numbers, by village: Tegernsee (08022) 180140, Bad Wiessee (08022) 86030, Gmund (08022) 750527, and Rottach-Egern (08022) 671341. A bus line circulates among all the villages, with a stop just around the corner from the Bräustüberl.

The author, left, joins Bräustüberl Wirt Peter Hubert in a *Prosit* to one of the best beer halls anywhere.

Getting to Kloster Andechs

From Munich Hauptbahnhof, take S-Bahn 5 to Herrsching (40 minutes). Herrsching train station has taxi and bus service to Kloster Andechs. Metered taxi ride costs about € 13 each way. MVV buses 951 and 956 run several times a day. Most frequent service is via the private Rauner bus line ("Ammersee Reisen", www.ammersee-reisen.de). Look for the "H" bus stop. A one-way Rauner ticket costs € 2.20 and it's a 10-minute ride. Here's a combined Rauner and *MVV (boldface italic)* schedule:

Monday through Friday

Rauner bus or *MVV bus* departs from Herrsching train station:

Rauner bus or *MVV bus* departs Kloster Andechs to return to station:

8:04 a.m. (Bus 956)	*7:39 a.m. (Bus 951)*
10:05 a.m. (Bus 951)	*11:11 (Bus 956)*
11:00	11:15
11:24 (Bus 956)	*12:41 p.m. (Bus 956)*
12:00 p.m.	1:50
1:40	*1:59 (Bus 951)*
3:00	4:10
4:00	5:20
4:43 (Bus 951)	5:50
5:40	*5:59 (Bus 951)*
6:40	6:50

Saturday, Sunday, and Holidays

Rauner bus or *MVV bus* departs from Herrsching train station:

Rauner bus or *MVV bus* departs Kloster Andechs to return to station:

7:53 a.m. (Bus 951, Sun. and Hol.)	*7:38 a.m. (Bus 951, Sat.)*
9:45	*9:58 (Bus 951, Sun. and Hol.)*
10:05 (Bus 951, Sat.)	10:00
11:00	11:10
11:35	11:45
12:00 p.m.	12:10 p.m.
1:20	*1:38 (Bus 951, Sat.)*
2:25	1:50
4:00	2:40
4:35	4:15
4:33 (Bus 951, Sat.)	4:50
5:13 (Bus 951, Sun. and Hol.)	*5:38 (Bus 951, Sat.)*
5:40	5:50
6:40	*6:38 (Bus 951, Sun. and Hol.)*
	7:00

Kloster Andechs
and Seehof

Kloster Andechs is a beer pilgrimage not to be missed, after a short bus ride up the hill from the Herrshing S-Bahn station. And making this day trip even more worthwhile is nearby Seehof, a short 5-minute walk around the corner from the station.

First, Kloster Andechs. This was one of those best-kept secrets guarded — religiously no doubt — by the Benedictine brethren for centuries. On a hill overlooking the banks of the Ammersee, who could blame these monks 900 years ago for brewing the finest beer around, and then keeping it all to themselves. Then, in one of those historical acts of universal justice, Count Bertold IV decreed in 1128 that the monastic monopoly should end. His fiat required the most pious among his various fifedoms to make an annual pilgrimage, with cross and candle, to Andechs, a journey they welcomed with hardly a complaint.

When a local legend began circulating that a blind woman from Widdersberg made the trek to Andechs and miraculously recovered her sight in 1274, business really took off. The brothers were suddenly swamped. In addition to holy relics, the religious visitors also began venerating the spirited brew.

Today, the "Sacred Mountain" plays host to thousands of modern day pilgrims, some there just to pray and meditate. The vast majority with more secular tastes comes to sample the local libation. Not that man lives by beer alone. The Kloster Andechs' 15th century Gothic church would make the pages of even the most discriminating tour book. The Benedictine abbey, endowed in 1455 as one of the last such monasteries of the Middle Ages, should not be overlooked. But, readers of this book are reminded to also consider the 3500-seat terraced beer garden that literally rings the church and monastic grounds.

The brewing tradition begun by monks

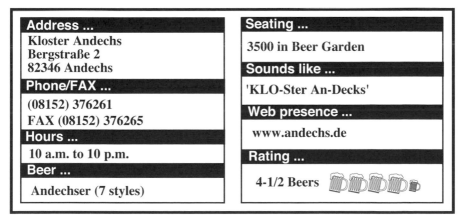

Address ...	Seating ...
Kloster Andechs Bergstraße 2 82346 Andechs	3500 in Beer Garden
Phone/FAX ...	**Sounds like ...**
(08152) 376261 FAX (08152) 376265	'KLO-Ster An-Decks'
Hours ...	**Web presence ...**
10 a.m. to 10 p.m.	www.andechs.de
Beer ...	**Rating ...**
Andechser (7 styles)	4-1/2 Beers

The beer hall at Kloster Andechs.

in the 15th century was a natural offshoot of local farming activities. Beer was brewed on the premises until 1972 when increasing demand caused the brothers to move the plant to a more spacious site—a meadow at the foot of the mountain—where they continue production today. Each year the brewery turns out 1.9 million gallons of beer, in seven different varieties. Most of it is served in the monastery's centuries old *Bräustüberl* (beer hall) or in the brick-floored terrace beer garden. As one might expect, all is self-service here, including the food stands that offer a sturdy variety of Bavarian snacks. The beer is a little more potent than average and half-liter steins are available at all times. The price is right, at around € 5 per liter. The real pleasure is to be able to sit back, relax and enjoy a tall cool one in a medieval setting with a commanding view of the entire valley.

On a good day, the 270-degree panorama takes in the entire countryside, from Wendelstein to the Allgauer Alps. The cloister has a gift and souvenir shop that sells mementos and books covering local history of the monastery and beer garden. Kloster Andechs is a full-day journey, including a 40-minute train ride (S-Bahn 5) from the Hauptbahnhof to Herrsching. There is difficulty in finding a frequent bus that runs from Herrsching the 5-mile up-hill trip to the Kloster. Taxis from the train station are an alternative, but they run around € 13 each way. The city-run buses (951 and 956) are sporadic, and run only two or three times a day. A more frequent and dependable choice is the private-run Rauner bus line (Tel: 08152-3457) that has a regular schedule directly to the Kloster Andechs. A single ticket costs € 2.20 each way. The bus schedule supplied on the first page of this section consolidates the Rauner and the MVV bus schedules. The two lines together provide suitable alternatives to reach

Kloster Andechs in reasonable time. This is truly a beer drinker's pilgrimage where the home-made beer is hearty, strong and malty and always cellar-chilled. Religious beer-drinking experiences are rare. Kloster Andechs, along with Seehof (see below) get an ecumenical 4-1/2 beers.

'The Sacred Mountain' from a mid-17th century engraving.

Seehof Herrsching

Before heading up the hill, walk around the corner to Seehof. This is an outstanding beer garden experience, literally on the banks of the Ammersee, adjacent to the boat landing. At one end of a walking promenade, constant foot traffic pauses here to enjoy a cold half-liter of Hofbräu beer or a quick bite from the outside *schmankerl* stand. The Gasthof Seehof hotel, restaurant and beer garden was established in 1898, offering rooms and sustenance to visitors traveling the Ammersee via one of the several steam-

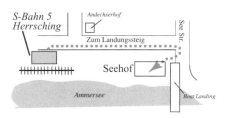

ships traversing the lake. For many years the business was owned and operated by the Löwenbräu brewery, but changed hands after a refurbishment in 1996 and now belongs to the Munich Hofbräuhaus.

Seehof
See Str. 58
82211 Herrsching
Seating: 500
Beer: Hofbräu
Phone: (08152) 9350
Hours: 10 a.m to 11 p.m.
Web: www.seehof-ammersee.de

Hauptbahnhof
S-Bahn 6 to Aying (about a 35-minute ride).
Aying
Following map, walk from S-bahn station to Liebhards and Ayingerbräu
Brewery.

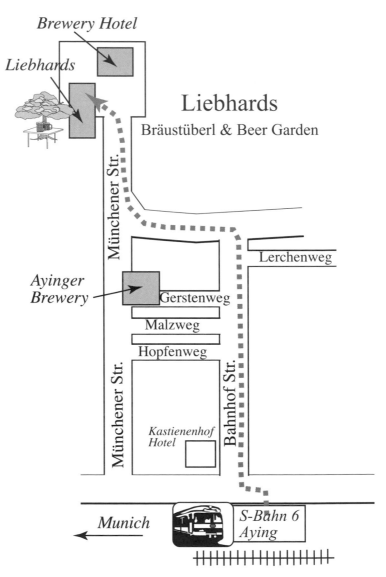

200

Liebhards Bräustüberl
(Ayingerbräu)

Sometimes in one's quest to learn about beer, total immersion is required. In Munich, that philosophy is best expressed in the country village of Aying, about a 35-minute S-Bahn ride from the city center. If you've been paying attention, you've already put together the name of the town with the beer produced here, Ayingerbräu. But there's more. The Ayinger brewery has literally opened its doors to those wanting to learn all they can about the brewing art. And nearby

The Liebhard brewing crew in 1906.

Address ...	Seating ...
Liebhards Bräustüberl Münchener Str. 2 85653 Aying	500 in Beer Garden, 150 Rest.
Phone/FAX ...	**Sounds like ...** 'Leeb-HARDS-Broy-Stoo-Berl
(08095) 1345 FAX (08095) 8956	**Web presence ...** www.liebhards-aying.de (bräustüberl) www.ayinger.de (brewery & hotel)
Hours ... 10 a.m. to 1 a.m.	
Beer ... Ayingerbräu	**Rating ...** 3-1/2 Beers

The beer garden at Liebhards in the country suburb of Aying.

Liebhards restaurant and beer garden — run by the same folks who bring you the beer — is the most appealing tasting room imaginable. Top it off with the opportunity to stay overnight at the adjacent brewery-owned-and-operated hotel and you've got yourself the complete beer experience — *Bier Erlebnis* — and a good reason to spend a day in Munich's countryside.

The roots of this rural brewing business reach back more than a century, to February 2, 1878, when Johann Liebhard wrote in his day book: "Today, we served our first beer", thus joining Liebhard Brauerei with nearly 6,000 brewing businesses throughout Germany at the time. More than a century later, with 90 percent of that number diminished, the lineal descendant Ayinger Brauerei continues as a regional, mid-size brewing presence. Once literally a cottage industry, the family-run business was without a male heir for its first two generations of brewers. Johann Liebhard's eldest daughter Maria married August Zehentmair in 1904. The son-in-law continued the brewery under the Zehentmair name until World War I intervened and August went off to fight.

Brewery Tours

The Ayinger Brewery offers one-hour tours: Tuesdays, 11 a.m.
Thursdays, 6 p.m.
Saturdays, 10 a.m.
Cost is € 7 for adults, € 5 for children. Covered during the tour is a complete overview of the brewing process, from the raw materials to a sampling of the end product. Tour participants are invited to test the *Zwicklbier*, directly from the brewing vessel. Tours include a film and a light and sound show. Tours are in German, with some facility for other languages, including English. English-only tours can be arranged for group tours in advance. To make reservations:
Tel: (08095) 8890
email: brau.erlebnis@ayinger.de

Brauereigasthof Hotel

The hotel offers inn-style rooms, including breakfast for around € 150-€ 190 for a double; € 100-€ 160 for a single. All rooms have bath and WC, radio, phone and TV.
Tel: (08095) 90650
FAX: (08095) 906566
email: hotel@ayinger.de

Returning to Aying in 1918, with the German economy in shambles, August found his small village brewery and its modest affiliated restaurant hanging on by a slender financial thread. The entire Zehentmair family pooled resources and nursed their struggling brewery through the bad times to build the prosperous business that exists today.

The third leg of the enterprise, the Brauereigasthof hotel, was given its start in 1923. The brewery expanded its reach and a delivery truck purchased in 1929 allowed for the first "shipments" of the Ayinger brand to guest houses all over Munich. That customer base has since expanded to the United States, Austria, Italy and eastern Europe. The Zehentmair eldest daughter, another Maria, married Franz Inselkammer in 1932. Four years later, Franz, following the lead of his son-in-law predecessors, took over the family business.

The Inselkammer couple expanded, renovated and modernized every aspect of the business. They renovated the restaurant and beer garden and totally rebuilt the hotel to a 34-room inn catering to out of towners and those visiting the brewery. The comprehensive makeover of the hotel wasn't finished until 2002.

Franz died in 1986, Maria in 2001. Together they had three sons: Franz, Jr., the eldest was schooled in the brewing arts at Weihenstephan and runs the brewery today; son Peter operates the Ayinger Platzl outlet, just outside the Hofbräuhaus; and August heads a local construction firm. Franz's wife, Angela, is in charge of the hotel and spearheaded its most recent renovation. The original brewery is now the bottling and distribution plant. The new brewery –

one of the most modern in all of Germany – was completed and reopened in 1999. It's now able to be run by a small staff, usually outnumbered by the visitors touring the plant. The Ayinger Brewery produces nine different styles of beer, and visitors are treated to a taste of most of them, along with a sampling of bread made from the spent grain. (See boxed information regarding tours.)

Of course a tasting of these excellent beers is only a start. After a tour of the brew plant, Liebhards Bräustüberl and beer garden beckon as a place to finish what was begun at the end of a *Zwickl* spigot used to sample the final-stage beer as it emerges from the *Südhaus* of the brewery (included in the tour). With the ambience of an ancient country inn, the beer garden at Liebhards has been in business in one form or another for the past 300 years. In its most recent incarnation, in 1994, it was officially renamed to memorialize Ayingerbräu's founder. Johann Liebhard would be proud of the level of service and the quality of product served here. A daily *Tageskarte* menu offers three-course meals at around € 7.50.

This is a relaxing beer garden, directly across the parking lot from the Brauereigasthof hotel and the obligatory *Maipole*. There is interior seating as well, with a coterie of *Stammtisch* attesting to the local appeal of this historic establishment. We recommend making the trip to Aying for the beer and everything you ever needed to know about it. The entertaining and complete beer experience gets 3-1/2 beers.

Hauptbahnhof
S-Bahn 1 to Freising (about a 30-minute ride).

Freising
Exit the train station to the right (local buses) and take bus 638 five stops to Weihenstephan. (Stop is "Weihenstephan," not to be confused with earlier bus stop at "Weihenstephaner Str.") Walk about 5 minutes up the hill, following the map.

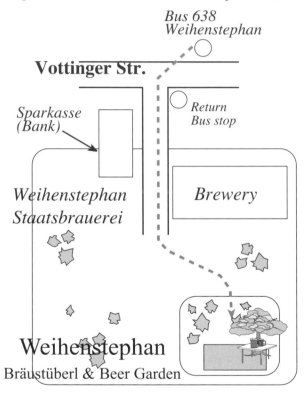

Bus 638
Weihenstephan

Vottinger Str.

Sparkasse
(Bank)

Return
Bus stop

Weihenstephan
Staatsbrauerei

Brewery

Weihenstephan
Bräustüberl & Beer Garden

How to visit *both* Weihenstephan and Plantage — Bus 638 (to Weihenstephan) and Buses 620/621 (to Plantage) have a common stop at "Kriegerdenkmal," one stop before (or after) the S-Bahn station. For example, returning from Weihenstephan, exit bus 638 at Kriegerdenkmal, cross the street and take Bus 620/621 in opposite direction to Wallberg Str. to visit Plantage.

 (Important S-Bahn Note: When on S-1, make certain the car you are on is not headed to the airport. It should say "Freising." Train splits at Neufahrn.)

Weihenstephan
and Plantage

Weihenstephan, the ancient brewery and one-time monastery in Munich's outlying suburb of Freising, still requires the better part of a day's travel in order to lift a *Maß* of its heavenly brew. The trip is just a little more appealing now that Plantage, a nearby forested beer garden, has been added to the itinerary.

Weihenstephan Bräustüberl

What gives Weihenstephan a reputation of near legendary proportions is its status as one of the oldest still-operating breweries in the world. Whether it's the oldest is a matter for historical purists to decide. Local literature holds that the monastery brewery was operational in 1040 as the very first outlet under the auspices of those world-famous Benedictine Brothers. And if that is true, then Weihenstephan certainly qualifies as the most senior among suds producers. But there is no written record that the brewery was able to actually sell its beer publicly, an im-portant distinction.

The earliest documented account holds that Bishop Otto von Freising granted the Weihenstephan monks that right in 1146. Nevertheless, sometime between 725 when the Weihenstephan Cloister was founded and the mid 12th century when it was granted or renewed distribution rights, the monastery became well-versed in the manufacture of Munich's most durable product. Secularization of the ecclesiastical breweries in 1803 was only the beginning for Weihenstephan. When the Bavarian government took control of this and some 200 other cloister breweries they also saw to the temporal side of business by establishing schools to advance the brewing arts. In 1852 a brewing curriculum was begun and by 1930 a full-fledged "college" was established under the Technical University of Munich, continuing to today.

Hardly a class teaching project, the state-run and university-affiliated opera-

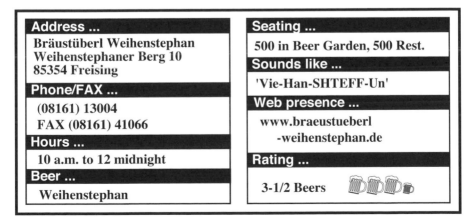

Address ...	Seating ...
Bräustüberl Weihenstephan Weihenstephaner Berg 10 85354 Freising	500 in Beer Garden, 500 Rest.
Phone/FAX ...	**Sounds like ...**
(08161) 13004 FAX (08161) 41066	'Vie-Han-SHTEFF-Un'
	Web presence ...
Hours ...	www.braeustueberl -weihenstephan.de
10 a.m. to 12 midnight	**Rating ...**
Beer ...	
Weihenstephan	3-1/2 Beers

tion is today a modern brewing plant in every way. During a one-hour tour of the facilities, the public is shown a modern, state-of-the art brewery where 40,000 gallons of beer are produced daily. A dozen different types are brewed, with most available for sampling in the shaded Bräustüberl (beer garden and restaurant) at the top of the hill.

The beer garden is small but comfortable and offers a view of the rolling grassy hills that make up the brewery and university grounds. The restaurant serves typical Bavarian dishes at a more than reasonable price. In fact, this beer garden is one of the most affordable anywhere, attesting to the generous state subsidies that keep prices within range of the limited budgets of the students who are enrolled here. With an eye toward promotional marketing, the brewery's well-stocked souvenir shop sells mugs, coasters, T-shirts and other Weihenstephan memorabilia at give-away prices.

Among Weihenstephan's liquid offerings available on tap in the beer garden are the usual *helles*, *dunkles* and *weizen*, (light, dark and wheat). The beer menu also now includes a non-alcoholic beer, styled after the Weihenstephan "original" brand. Try mixing the two and you will be surprised at what a great-tasting spacer this can make. Also, the brewery is experimenting with a 7.7% alcohol (ouch!) bock wheat beer called "Vitus".

A trip to Weihenstephan can consume the better part of a morning in travel time. Those who enjoy learning more about brewing and the chance to tour an operating plant will gain the most from a visit. So will those who make time for a second Freising stop — the Plantage beer garden.

Waldgaststätte Plantage
Plantage 2, 85354 Freising
Phone: 08161-63155
www.plantage-freising.de

As mentioned at the outset, there is now more to enjoy in Freising to go along with Weihenstephan. Plantage, a 1200-seat beer garden in the middle of the woods, is just the ticket. Getting there from the Freising S-Bahn station, only requires a short bus ride, followed by a 14-minute walk. From the station, take bus 620 or 621 to Wallberg Str. (9th stop) and follow the map. You'll come to a sprawling beer garden smack in the middle of the woods. Plantage (German for "plantation") was once, as its name suggests, filled with rows of apple and cherry trees up until a point about midway through the last century. Around that time, a local

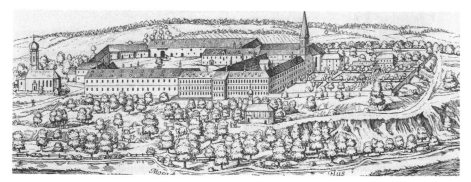

Weihenstephan Cloister, prior to secularization.

The Brüstüberl at Weihenstephan

Waldmeister (forest master) cleared an area to build a forest home and allow for additional recreational opportunities. Hiking through the woods was foremost on that list and at one end of the beer garden today is the head of an informative public nature study trail. Somebody had to be thinking ahead because the 2-mile trail circles back to its starting point and thus back for another round in the beer garden. How convenient is that! As expected, the beer here is Weihenstephan and the ambience is traditional Bavarian.

Weihenstephan Brewery Tour: The "world's oldest brewery" offers one-hour tours for groups of 15 or more, but will accommodate individuals in conjunction with full groups where possible. Tours are 10 a.m. daily, Mon.-Wed., with a Tues. afternoon 1:30 p.m. tour. Reservations can be made by calling the brewery a week in advance at 08161-5360. More information available in English at www.weihenstephaner.de (separate from the Bräustüberl website). The € 6 cost of the tour includes a € 2 credit at the beverage shop.

Although the land and the permanent structures are publicly owned, the restaurant and beer garden are privately operated by proprietor Rochus Möchel and his family. The beer garden is tiered with eight ascending levels, ranging from lower sunlit areas requiring table umbrellas to heavily shaded tables that seem to disappear up the hill into the woods. Sundays and holidays are reserved for live entertainment in the beer garden, including jazz, dixieland and country bands. This is an excellent rural beer drinking experience, with a solid Bavarian look and feel to it. Plantage helps to make the most of a trip to visit the historically significant Weihenstephan. The two Freising venues combine for 3-1/2 beers and a high recommendation to make the day trip to one of Munich's suburbs.

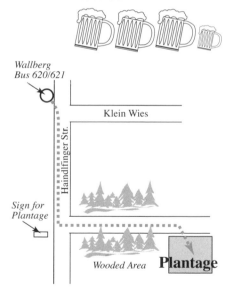

Plantage: Getting there — Take bus 620 or 621 from S-Bahn station to Wallberg Str. bus stop. Walk 6 min. to sign: "Plantage 300 meters". Turn left and walk down hill another 8 min. to beer garden.

Hauptbahnhof
Take S-Bahn 2 toward Petershausen, get off at Dachau.

Dachau S-Bahn Station
Take Bus 720 or 722 to stop for Rathaus. Follow map to beer garden, turning right at the street in back of the Bezirks Museum.

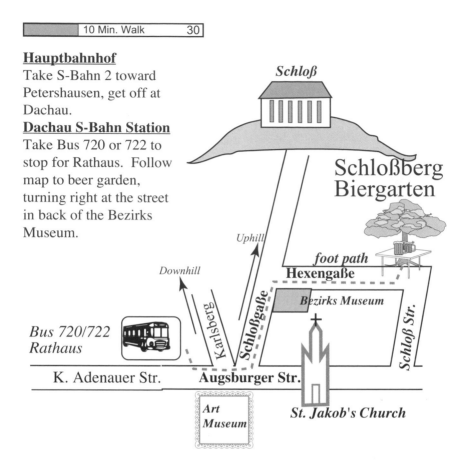

Address ...	Seating ...
Schloßberg Biergarten Schloß Straße 8 85221 Dachau	500 in Beer Garden
Phone ...	**Sounds like ...**
(08131) 614088	'Shloss-Berg Beer-Gar-Tin'
Hours ...	**Web presence ...**
10 a.m. - 11 p.m. (daily, if the weather is good)	www.schlossberg-garten.de
Beer ...	**Rating ...**
Schloßberg, Spaten	3-1/2 Beers

Schloßberg
Biergarten, Dachau

The nearby town of Dachau would hardly seem the place to find one of the region's best beer gardens. But the town forever linked with the terror of the Holocaust is full of surprises and paradoxes. Schloßberg Biergarten is one of them. If years were pages, the history of this Bavarian town would be a thick, 1200-page tome. Yet, a thin 12-page subchapter is all the world knows about Dachau. Yes, the Nazis established their first, and most infamous, concentration camp in an abandoned munitions factory at the outskirts of town. Yes, the townspeople knew it existed, although doubtful they comprehended the atrocities being committed there. And yes, no one questions the terrible legacy the camp left behind from its inception in 1933 to its liberation at the hands of Allied soldiers in 1945.

Certainly, anyone who visits the *KZ Gedenkstätte* concentration camp memorial will be moved and shaken by the telling evidence on display. The museum is filled with photographic images of torture and death at Dachau. And the better known the truth, the less likely it will ever happen again. But visitors should not mistake as callous or insensitive the de-

Schloßberg Beer Garden is an unexpected pleasure in a town better known for its dark page in history.

209

sire of the citizens of Dachau the city to put the brief but horrifying period of Dachau the concentration camp behind them. A day does not pass that they are not reminded of the sins committed in their name during the Holocaust. They are prepared to accept their part of the responsibility.

Dr. Lorenz Reitmeier, former Dachau Lord Mayor now retired, said it best: "We don't run or hide from the guilt of Dachau," he explains. "We do ask that we be allowed to share the guilt with the rest of Germany, and not to shoulder it solely on our own." He has a point. Dachau was a medieval town with a thousand years of history when Adolf Hitler came to power in 1933. (It's worth noting that the Nazi dictator was elected to office without the benefit of a majority vote from the electorate of Dachau.) The city had been the summer palace of Bavaria's dukes for centuries. As an art colony in the late 19th and early 20th centuries, the town played a significant role in the European art movement by launching the *Frei Luft* "open air" style of landscape painting. The writer and poet Ludwig Thoma, one of Germany's most famous and prolific literary figures, began his writings here.

The Nazis ignored all of that history along with the wishes of the local populace when they unilaterally decided to place a concentration camp nearby.

Thousands will visit the KZ memorial, but few will take a slight detour to the city's old town section. Those who do will find a well-stocked art gallery, a folklore *Bezirks* museum and a baroque hilltop castle overlooking the town. The home where Thoma worked is in the area as well, as is one of the German author's favorite watering holes, the Schloßberg Biergarten. Formerly the Zieglerkeller before new management in 2006 gave it a new name, this blue-collar beer garden is one of the most comfortable in all of Bavaria. Schloßberg has immortalized Thoma — as though he needed it — by naming one of their brews after him. A strong märzen dark beer, Ludwig Thoma Bier, is served in a distinctive tall, cut-glass mug. Thoma was a regular at the bräustüberl and beer garden during his time in Dachau, 1894-97. His "Dachau Stories" launched him as a serious writer and captured a turn-of-the-century local lifestyle that the town aspires to today.

As with many Bavarian beer gardens, Schloßberg has its own roots in local

The annual Dachauer Volksfest is a local version of Oktoberfest at half the price.

history. In 1616, a section of the town was set aside as an "economic zone" to support the palace. Later it became a small piece of the royal estate that bounced around from countess to duke to prince until it finally settled with Eduard Ziegler, a mere commoner, who bought the property free and clear in 1876. Ziegler gave it its mission in life along with his name and rebuilt the restaurant portion in 1895. In 1901, the business was handed down to Eduard Ziegler, Jr. and later transferred to the Schloßberg Brewery. Eventually, the entire operation—brewery, next door bräustüberl and beer garden—was bought out by Spaten. Most recently, new management has reduced the number of seats in the beer garden and the restaurant (the "stüben") is only available for private bookings. The good news is that the beer garden is still fully operational most of the year, and is now completely self-service. That usually translates to lower prices, and Schloßberg Biergarten is no exception. The menu is filled with tasty and incredibly cheap gasthaus food as well as Spaten beers to go along with local Dachau brands. Fact is, this part of Dachau is frequented so rarely by tourists that it has yet to suffer the inflated prices and take-it-or-leave-it service that commonly afflict businesses in other well-traveled areas. From the bus stop near city hall (Rathaus), a 10-minute walk down Hexengaße (witches' alley) will deliver you to the well-shaded beer garden. The garden is open in good weather, from spring to late fall, and is best visited when the locally famous Dachauer Volksfest is on (see footnote).

Schloßberg Biergarten, if it were in Munich proper, would be just another excellent beer garden, with lots of Bavarian tradition and warm country atmosphere. A festive beer garden may seem like a strange circumstantial juxtaposition unless you can accept the fact that life goes on for the 39,000 people of Dachau, 90 percent of whom were not even alive when the Nazis were in power. They've learned from the past and they deserve a chance to live for the future. Visit the Dachau camp memorial and join those who will never forget that most important lesson of history. Then raise a beer later in the garden at the Schloßberg and say a toast, and maybe a prayer, for the future. The Schloßberg Biergarten — with its new name, management and service format — still gets a reputable 3-1/2 beers.

Concentration Camp Memorial. From Dachau S-Bahn station bus 724 (only on weekends) or 726 (daily, every 20 minutes) go to the Concentration Camp. If on Bus 724, get off at KZ-Gedenkstätte *Parkplatz* (parking lot); Bus 726 get off at KZ-Gedenkstätte *Haupteingang* (main entrance). Museum hours are Tues. through Sun., 9 a.m. to 5 p.m. English documentary film 11:30 a.m. and 3:30 p.m. Closed Monday. **www.kz-gedenkstaette-dachau.de** Guided tours: **www.dachauer-gaestefuehrer.de.**

Art gallery and folklore (Bezirks) museum hours: Tue.-Fri., 11 a.m.-5 p.m.; Sat., Sun., Hol., 1 p.m.-5 p.m., closed Mon.

Schloß. Open daily except Mon.: Apr-Sep, 9 a.m.-6 p.m; Oct-Mar, 10 a.m.-4 p.m. Schloß Cafe open to 6:30 p.m., daily, except Monday. Small courtyard beer garden in good weather.

The Dachauer Voksfest is held each year around the middle of August (August 15, a local holiday, is always included). Arrive when the fest is in full gear and you'll be treated to an event that rivals the Munich Oktoberfest, only on a smaller scale. Check **www.dachau.de** for precise dates. The 10-day Volksfest runs Sat. through Mon. week, with a huge beer tent, plenty of thrill rides, lots of eats and rivers of flowing suds. The city takes particular pride in holding the line on its prices. The price of a liter at the volksfest is claimed to be the cheapest in all of Germany. At around € 4 for a liter Maß of beer, I'd say they were right.

After Hours

Munich is a city that swings all night. While most beer halls and beer gardens close around midnight, a number of nightclubs, late-night cocktail lounges and dance halls are just cranking up. They keep the lights burning, the music blaring and the beer flowing until the sun comes up. A taxi will take you there and a well-padded pocket book will let you stay awhile. After hours bars and discos in Munich are expensive and cover or entrance charges are the norm. It's not unusual for drink prices to double after the clock strikes 12. Be forewarned that doormen will sometimes deny entrance to those not meeting the prevailing dress codes or representative age groups. Still, these late-night bistros and clubs offer a "no-last-call" alternative for tireless beer-drinkers who can party with the roosters and still soar with the eagles in the morning. Here's a list of the best:

Hotel Bayerischer Hof Nightclub
Promenadeplatz 6
Tel: 212-0994
Hours: 6 p.m.-3 a.m.
Live dance bands, international atmosphere, older crowd. Lots of mixed drinks and expensive. Five minutes from Marienplatz.
www.bayerischerhof.de

Evergreen
Neuhauser Str. 47
Tel: 593-696
Hours: 8 p.m.-4 a.m.
DJ music nightly. Has a dancehall look and feel. Mixed to older singles.

Kultfabrik (formerly Kunstpark Ost)
Grafinger Straße 6 (Ostbahnhof)
Tel: 4900-9070, Hours: 8 p.m.- 6 a.m.
Huge complex of more than two dozen clubs carved out of an old factory. Something here for everybody. Includes Americanos, Boomerang, Kölsch, Temple Bar, Kalinka (Russian) and others. Hours vary and themes as well. A lot to choose from, most with slight cover charge.
www.esgehtweiter.de
www.kultfabrik.com

Master's Home
Frauen Str. 11
Tel: 229-909
Hours: daily 6 p.m.-3 a.m.
Relaxing atmosphere, older crowd. Feels like someone invited you over.
www.mastershome-muenchen.de

Nachtcafe
Maximiliansplatz 5
Tel: 595-900
Hours: 9 p.m.-6 a.m.
50s atmosphere, live listening music. Jazz to folk from midnight on.

Kilian's Irish Pub
Frauenplatz 11
Tel: 2421-9899
Hours: Mon.-Thurs. 4 p.m.-1 a.m., Fri.-Sat. 11 a.m.-3 a.m., Sun. noon-1 a.m.
Around the corner from Andechser am Dom. Darts and Guinness, of course.
www.kiliansirishpub.com

Ned Kelly's Australian Bar
(in Kilian's basement, with similar opening hours) Sharks, boomerangs and Fosters.
www.n-kellys.moonfruit.com

P1
Prinzregentenstraße 1, Haus der Kunst
Tel: 2111-1140
Hours: 9 p.m.-4 a.m. daily (to 6 a.m. Fri.,
Sat.). Upscale and dressed up, one of the
city's best nightclubs. Bring lots of money.
www.p1-club.de

Rattlesnake Saloon
Schneeglöcken Straße 91
Tel: 150-4035
Hours: Tues.-Sun 7 p.m. to 3 a.m.
Country and Western in the music and
menu. Line dancing and Spaten beer. An
odd sight, but fun. S-1 to Fasanerie.
www.rattlesnake-saloon.com

Pusser's New York Bar
Falkenturm Str. 9
Tel: 220-500
Hours: Daily, 6 p.m.-3 a.m.
Oldest bar in Munich. Formerly Harry's
before Harry died. Now run by Bill Deck
and son. Right around corner from
Hofbräuhaus. All ages, great atmosphere,
and relaxing. Try their signature drink,
"The Painkiller." **www.pussersbar.de**

Schumann's
Odeonsplatz 6-7
Tel: 229-060
Hours: Mon.-Fri. 5 p.m.-3 a.m.
Sun. 6 p.m.-3 a.m., closed Sat.
Spin-off of Harry's New York Bar (now
Pusser's) by Charles Schumann, former
bartender at Harry's; "In" bar in Munich,
mixed crowd. **www.schumanns.de**

Here's a Thought
Don't like any of these? Take U-Bahn to
Münchner Freihcit and just walk around.
You'll find plenty to choose from in
Schwabing.

**Kilian's Irish Pub, just around the corner from Andechser am Dom, is a
heavy late-night draw, with Ned Kelly's Australian Bar in the basement.**

Map of the Oktoberfest

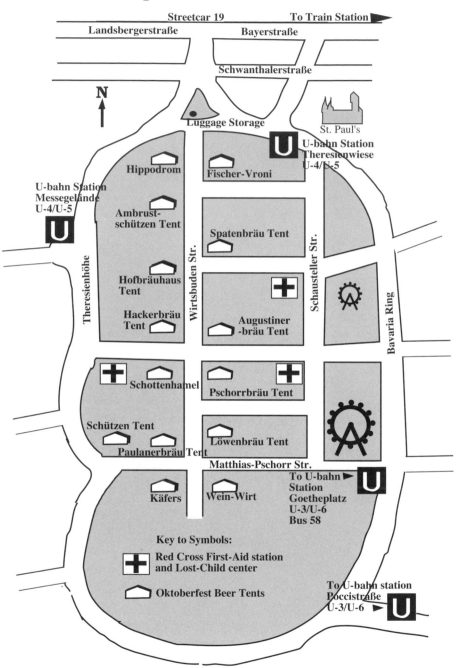

Oktoberfest
and other Keg Parties

In Munich the tradition is to celebrate every day as if it were your last. If the sun rises in the morning, consider it a bonus and time to start all over again. Every day is a festive occasion in the Bavarian capital. From Christmas and New Years and into the strong beer season, through the spring Frühlingsfest and the tri-annual Auer Dults, a quick interlude with the Sommerfest, Bayernmarkt and finally culminating with Oktoberfest — the year is a collage of one fest after another. Here are the most colorful and enticing of the city's annual offerings.

Oktoberfest
(Fall)

This is the grand-daddy of them all, the big beer fest in the sky. It began as a reception for the wedding of Crown Prince Ludwig, later King Ludwig I, to Princess Therese von Sachsen-Hildburghausen, October 12, 1810. What God had joined together, let no man turn asunder, and that included the wedding party. The idea for the royal beer bash is credited to a hackney coachman, Franz Baumgartner. A non-commissioned officer in the Bavarian national guard, Baumgartner sug-

The Oktoberfest in Munich's Wies'n attracts up to a million people a day.

215

gested spicing up the wedding celebration with a horse race to be run in a meadow just outside of town. His idea won royal approval, and a race track was built in time for Baumgartner to enter and win top prize himself. He rode his horse first across the finish line to cheers of thousands of his fellow Münchners, many of whom had bet wisely and heavily on both Baumgartner's ability and his personal familiarity with the track. So huge a triumph in honor of so distinguished a couple called for a victory celebration that lasted through the night and into the next day. Even after the nuptial duo had long departed for the honeymoon, the fest roared on. In fact, the party was such a success the people of Munich insisted it be thrown again the next year. So it was, and so it has been, in the same meadow, named for the bride, *Theresienwiese*, or as the people in Munich say in abbreviated form, *die Wies'n*.

The rest of the world knows it as Oktoberfest, a mad-cap mixture of folklore, festival and frivolity unequaled anywhere else on the globe. The fest has been canceled only 25 times during its two century run: 23 times due to wars, twice (1854 and 1873) due to cholera epidemics. Don't let the name mislead you, the 16-day Oktoberfest usually begins the second to last Saturday in September and always ends the first Sunday in October (see Fest Calendar in this section). It begins with a Saturday morning parade through the center of Munich with horse-drawn carriages hauling the wooden kegs of beer. Once the city's Lord-Mayor successfully plunges a bronze spigot into the first available keg at 12 noon sharp, the call of "O'Zapft Is!" (Hey, it's tapped already!") is made and the first Maß is served.

The tradition of horse racing competition continued for many years, and along with it grew the custom of including a farmer's market and agricultural exhibit. Carnival rides and curious sideshows came later.

The Oktoberfest drew its first 100,000 in 1860, no small feat when you consider that the entire city had only 121,234 population at the time. Beer was there almost from the beginning. By 1890, a number of "beer palaces" were in place and the city's breweries became more and more instrumental in directing the course of the an-

The major Munich breweries sponsor large festival tents (some the size of a multi-story building) as do several private entrepreneurs. Here are names and seating capacities (including beer gardens). Also listed are the phone numbers and addresses of the wirts whereby you can call or write for advance reservations. In some cases the phones aren't activated until about two weeks prior to the start of Oktoberfest.

216

Beer Tent

Hofbräuhaus	9,900	Günter and Margot Steinberg, Innere Wiener Straße 19 81667 München Tel: 44-89-670; FAX: 44-83-587 www.hb-festzelt.de
Schottenhamel (Spaten)	10,000	Festhalle Schottenhamel OHG, Uhlandstraße 3 80336 München Tel: 54-46-9310; FAX: 54-46-9319 www.festzelt-schottenhamel.de
Hackerbräu	9,300	Anton and Christine Roiderer, Tölzer Str.2 82064 Straßlach Tel: 08170-7303; FAX: 08170-7385 www.hacker-festzelt.de
Pschorrbräu/"Bräurosl"	8,200	Georg and Renate Heide, Bahnhofstraße 51 82152 Planegg Tel: 89-55-6353; FAX: 89-55-6356 www.braeurosl.de
Paulaner-Brauerei "Winzerer Fähndl"	10,900	Peter and Arabella Pongratz Keferloh 2, 85630 Grasbrunn Tel: 62-17-1910; FAX: 62-17-1919
Löwenbräu	8,400	Ludwig Hagn and Stephanie Spendler Unions-Bräu Haidhausen GmbH Einsteinstraße 42, 81675 München Tel: 47-76-77; FAX: 47-05-848 www.loewenbraeu-festzelt.info
Augustinerbräu	8,500	Manfred Vollmer, Neuhauser Straße 27 80331 München (Großgaststätte Augustiner) Tel:23-18-3266; FAX: 26-05-379
Ambrustschützenzelt	7,400	Familie Inselkammer, Sparkassenstraße 12 80331 München (Platzl Hotel) Tel: 23-70-3703; FAX: 23-70-3705 www.armbrustschuetzenzelt.com
Spatenbräu "Ochsenbraterei"	7,400	Hermann and Anneliese Haberl, and Antje Schneider Englischer Garten 3 80538 München Tel: 38-38-7312; FAX: 38-38-7340 www.ochsenbraterei.de
Sportschützenzelt	4,400	Eduard and Claudia Reinbold, Perusastraße 5 80333 München Tel: 23-18-1224; FAX: 23-18-1244
Fischer-Vroni	3,400	Johann and Silvia Stadtmüller Konradin Str. 8, 81543 München Tel: 66-10-42; FAX: 65-25-34 www.fischer-vroni.de
Hippodrom	3,200	Josef Krätz Hippodrom KG, Weinstraße 7a, 80333 München, Tel: 29-16-4646; FAX: 29-54-42 www.hippodrom-oktoberfest.de
Käfer's Wies'nschänke	2,900	Käfer GmbH, Prinzregentenstraße 73, 81675 München Tel: 41-68-356; FAX: 41-68-880 www.feinkost-kaefer.de
Wein und Sektzelt	1,900	Doris, Roland and Stephan Kuffler, Residenzstraße 12 80333 München Tel: 29-07-0517; FAX: 29-40-76 www.kuffler-gastronomie.de

nual festival. By 1900 they had divided the territory up by "tents" and introduced live music and the distinctively Bavarian brass *oom-pah* bands.

Each year millions of people overwhelm Munich's permanent 1.3 million population and make their way to Oktoberfest. At the 2006 Oktoberfest, 6.5 million visitors downed 6.1 million liters of beer and 34,000 liters of wine; devoured 494,135 roast chickens; inhaled 144,635 pairs of grilled sausages; intercepted 56,036 pork knuckles; and dismembered 91 oxen roasted whole on the spit. Also, at the end of it all, they no doubt consumed untold quantities of antacid tablets, flavored bromides and jars of aspirin.

A seasonal specialty is the Wies'n Märzen beer, commonly called simply fest or Oktoberfest beer. This is the dark, heavily malted and potent brew that gets its name from centuries ago when religious custom prohibited brewing from April through September. Thus, the dark beer was brewed in March (*März*) to beat the deadline. It was given an especially heavy character that would carry it over until October when it could be properly imbibed. (It was also drunk as soon as it was ready, thus the Starkbierzeit was born.) Now, it might be brewed and dispensed anytime, but during Oktoberfest, it is still a tradition and an alternative to the much more popular *helles* or light (in color) variety.

In addition to the beer, brass bands and the usual armies of buxom mug-toting waitresses, there will be more than 70 carnival rides, including four roller coasters and many others designed with the kids in mind. Most who visit Oktoberfest have world-class fun and an experience they will never forget. A few will leave disappointed. A trip to Oktoberfest should be made with the realization that this is one of the most crowded 104 acres of real estate anywhere in the world, with up to a million visitors in a single day. With 98,000 seats available in the beer tents, it's hard to imagine no room at the inn, but such is the rule, not the exception. Table reservations can sometimes be had through hotels, tourist offices or calling the brewery tents themselves. The phone numbers to the tents (listed on previous page) are in operation from early September. Additional phone numbers and Oktoberfest information can be obtained from the Munich tourist office. There are three main tourist offices in Munich: at the Marienplatz (neuen Rathaus), the main train station, and on Sendlinger Str. The one at the Hauptbahnhof (platform 12) is the most convenient and is open daily from 9 a.m. to 8 p.m., Telephone: (089) 233-96-500; FAX: (089) 233-30-233. For hotel bookings in Munich through the tourist office: (089) 233-96-555. (From U.S. dial 011-49-(drop the 0) 89- phone number.)

Internet:
http://www.muenchen-tourist.de;
e-mail: tourismus@muenchen.de

The Munich tourist office will happily provide a free English-language brochure that answers most questions about Oktoberfest for that particular year.

Here are some worthwhile tips that will make Oktoberfest the positive and memorable experience it should be:

❑ **Take public transportation.** Don't even think about driving. You can't park, and you shouldn't risk driving even after one beer. From the Hauptbahnhof,

218

U-bahn 4 or 5 to Theresienwiese drops you off directly in front of the Oktoberfest grounds, in about five minutes.

❑ **Get there early, preferably on a weekday.** Monday through Saturday, the fest opens at 10 a.m. and an hour earlier on Sundays and holidays. Most beer tents close at 10:45 p.m., but a few stay open to 12:30 a.m. (Hippodrom, Käfer, and Weinwirt). There are no real "slack" times at Oktoberfest, and having someone to share all the fun with is never a problem. Thus, a weekday, say between noon and 4 p.m. is a good time to find an available seat. Once you're settled in, you can stay as long as you like.

❑ **Reconsider bringing young children.** Generally, this is a tough place for kids after 5 p.m. You have trouble keeping track of them in the crush of the crowd. They lose interest and become intimidated by it all. Leave them with a baby-sitter at the hotel and they may thank you for it later. If you bring them, make sure you've made arrangements in case you get separated (it happens). Instruct them not to panic and to seek out a German policeman. He in turn will take them directly to the Red Cross' lost-child station where scores of children are reunited with their misplaced parents every day.

❑ **Have a reserved hotel room waiting.** Many Munich hotels during Oktoberfest are booked a year in advance. Without a prior reservation, expect to stay at least 30 miles out of town. If you're stuck, the best bet is to stand by at a large hotel around 10 to 11 a.m. and hope to get lucky with a cancellation. The hotel accommodations bureau at the Hauptbahnhof can also be of help here.

The Auer Dult seen here in 1905 is still half fest, half flea market and always full of the unexpected.

219

❑ **Bring money.** Oktoberfest is not cheap. Visitors drop nearly a billion euros at the *Wies'n* each year during the 16-day fest. Food, drink and rides will strain the pocket book more than expected. Bring a reserve and don't be surprised if you have to dip into it.

❑ **Don't liberate souvenirs.** Don't even harbor a thought of walking out with one of the glass steins as an Oktoberfest remembrance. They are watching and will be happy to lay a heavy fine on you if you are caught. Each Oktoberfest the city produces a special mug (clay ceramic) with the distinctive thematic design for that particular year. It is sold at numerous souvenir kiosks throughout the festgrounds and makes an excellent memento as well as a good investment.

❑ **There's always next year.** If you absolutely can't get to Munich during Oktoberfest, don't fret over it. That only leaves 349 more festive days to choose from. In Munich, every day is Oktoberfest somewhere.

Auer Dult
(Fall, Spring, Summer)

A festive tradition even older than Oktoberfest is the Auer Dult. For more than 600 years the fest has been staged three times annually: spring, summer and fall. The event has rotated among a number of locations in Munich. However, since 1905 the combination flea market, antique fair and beer fest has found a permanent home at the Mariahilfplatz, in the shadow of Mariahilf Church.

The "Dult," a colloquial root from the original Latin word *indultum* (indulgence), consists of row after row of booths filled with everything from rare, antique books to hand-painted ceramic figurines, to old Munich memorabilia, to plain-but-useful pots and pans. Naturally, there are plenty of carnival rides, a beer tent, and lots of fast-food stands. There's a garage-sale atmosphere here and the diversity of new and second-hand wares is a special treat for those who enjoy a combination shopping spree and scavenger hunt.

The Auer Dult is full of the unexpected and a visitor never knows what curiosity will eventually follow him home. The precise periods of the nine-day (spanning two weekends) Auer Dult vary from year to year. The spring fest begins the last Saturday in April, the summer Dult usually bridges July and August, and the fall event always begins two weeks after Oktoberfest (see Fest Calendar). Exact dates should be confirmed by calling the main tourist office on Sendlinger Straße (089) 233-96-500.

Mariahilfplatz is near the Deutches Museum. The nearest U-bahn stop is Fraunhofer Str. (on the U-1 and U-2 lines out of the Hauptbahnhof), 5 min. walk. Tram 27 or Bus 52 (both stop at Mariahilfplatz).

Frühlingsfest
(Spring)

Locals call it the mini-Oktoberfest and for most visitors it is a suitable alternative when a fall visit is out of the question. It's held in the same area (Theresienwiese) as the Oktoberfest at the end of April (see calendar and again confirm exact dates with the tourist office). The two-week festival is filled with rides and plenty of eats and cold beer. The city's breweries still turn out in a big way for this extravaganza. The crowds are plentiful, yet smaller than the world-renown fest that occurs six months later. Finding an unreserved seat in one of the beer tents (there are usually two) is really much less an insurmountable undertaking at the

Frühlingsfest, without having to compromise any of the fun. It's a festive reminder that keg parties in Munich are a year-round affair.

Sommerfest
(Summer)

As the name suggests, this rapidly growing fest is scheduled each year for the late summer. Held on Coubertinplatz in Olympia Park, the Sommerfest always begins the first Thursday in August and runs through the next three Sundays. There are carnival rides and open-air theaters, as well as musical groups and of course plenty of beer. The second and third Thursdays are reserved for evening fireworks shows.

The Sommerfest has only been around a little more than a decade, so it still has a way to go before matching some of Munich's better known festivals. The beer tents are small but active, and the rides are tame compared to what one finds on the *Wies'n*. There's a little bit of a flea market as well and a sizeable area is reserved for vendors selling their wares. Despite its recent vintage, the Sommerfest is growing steadily and attracting a loyal following. It comes at a perfect time of year, ending just a few weeks before the Oktoberfest begins. To get to the Sommerfest with public transportation, take U-3 to Olympiazentrum. At one end of the parking lot is Lillian-Board-Weg. Take it, walking over the highway to Coubertinplatz. Before or after a visit to the Sommerfest we suggest you also consider two nearby and worthwhile beer gardens of Concordia Park and Taxisgarten. The boredom factor has certainly been diminished with the advent of the Sommerfest, but don't expect to catch your breath too soon, because the next fest, the Bayernmarkt, follows fast on its heels.

Bayernmarkt
(late Summer)

That narrow vacancy between late August and early September has now been filled. The annual Bayernmarkt, the newest fest on the block, is a 17-day — Friday to Sunday fortnight — celebration at Orleansplatz, featuring plenty of food, market wares and of course Munich's favorite beers. Daily entertainment is on tap in an outdoor beer garden atmosphere along with a good dose of Bavarian *Gemütlichkeit*. This is a great addition to Munich's busy fest calendar. To get there, take an S-Bahn to the Ostbahnhof, exit to Orleansplatz and it's just across the street. www.derbayernmarkt.de

Sommerfest in Olympiapark.

221

Fasching
(Winter)

It's tough to find an equal, but the nearest comparison to Fasching is Carnival in Rio, or Mardi Gras in New Orleans. Like the other two festivals, Fasching was originally a religious observance, marking the beginning of lent and a final fling at life's more hedonistic pleasures. In other German population centers — Cologne, Mainz and Düsseldorf, in particular — the celebration is centered on the streets, usually culminating with a Rosen Montag parade (the Monday before Ash Wednesday) accompanied by several days of public partying. In Munich, the season is marked by a variety of indoor masquerade balls, hosted by Munich's more lavish beer emporia. Löwenbräu Keller, Paulaner Keller, and Hofbräuhaus head that list. Munich's brand of Fasching is rowdy and ribald, and if organized properly, down right bacchanalian.

From January 7 to Shrove Tuesday six weeks later, the weekends are taken up with these costumed cotillions. It's a night of music, dancing and legalized carousing, when the married, engaged and otherwise betrothed become suddenly single again, even if for just a few hours. The wilder the costume for men — and seemingly the skimpier for women — the better. The packed pavilions are a veritable hunting ground for the bold and venturesome and, with identities protected, even the most timid wallflowers will bloom with utter abandoned. No one arriving in Munich during Fasching time should ever leave town a stranger.

A full schedule of Fasching balls is published in all the city's major newspapers and tickets can be secured at the door or through local tourist and booking agencies. Most major department stores sell basic costume paraphernalia during the Fasching season. There is no minimum dress code, and a few cosmetic touches are enough to put one in the mood and in proper style to make a night of it at a Munich Fasching ball*.

*Those interested in more elaborate costumes can rent them for the evening from numerous agencies who specialize in such outfitting during Fasching time. Here are several possibilities: Machado Costume Shop, Belgrad Str. 86, Tel: 307-3933; Waltraud Breuer, Hohenzollernstraße 22, Tel: 399-965; Cinyburg Kostüm Haus, Lindwurmstraße 16, Tel: 534-412.

A list of "-ator" starkbiers (Munich and elsewhere):

Aloisiator - Brauerei Alois Gäßl KG, Pfarrkirchen
Animator - Hacker-Pschorr Bräu GmbH, München
Apostulator - Eichbaum Brauerei, Mannheim
Aviator - Ärbräu, Flughafen München
Bambergator - Brauerei Fäßla, Bamberg
Bavariator - Müllerbräu GmbH & Co, Pfaffenhofen
Celebrator - Franz Inselkammer KG, Aying
Cervator - Hirschbraueei A. Welzhofer, Günzburg
Coronator - Brauerei Zur Krone, Tettnang
Delicator - Staatliche Hofbräu München
Equator - Rößlebrauerei Alois Hempfer KG, Laupheim
Fuchsikator - Brauerei Josef Fuchsbüchler, Palling
Hofator - Hofer Brauerei Deiningen-Kronenbräu, Hof
Honorator - Ingobräu Ingolstadt GmbH, Ingolstadt
Impulsator - Privatbrauerei M. C. Wieninger, Teisendorf
Josefator - Brauerei Josef Bachmayer, Dorfen
Jubilator - Schloßbrauerei Maxlrain, Tuntenhausen
Kulminator, EKU Actienbrauerei, Kulmbach

Maximator - Augustiner Bräu Wagner KG, München
Multiplikator - Edelweißbrauerei, Odelzhausen
Optimator - Spaten-Bräu, München
Operator - Schloßbrauerei Odelzhausen, Odelzhausen
Palmator - Brauerei Heinrich Prößl, Pettendorf
Pfaffenator - Brauerei K. Stöttner, Mallersdorf
Poculator - Patrizier Bräu, Nürnberg
Rariator - Münzbräu, Günzburg
Rhönator - Rother-Bräu, Roth b. Nbg.
Salvator - Paulaner-Brauerei GmbH & Co. KG, München
Spekulator - Weissbräu Jodlbauer GmbH, Rotthalmüster
Speziator - Brauerei S. Riegele, Augsburg
Steinator - Schloßbraueei Stei-Wiskott, Bad Reichenhall
Suffikator - Bürgerbräu Röhm & Söhne, Bad Reichenhall
Sympathor - Postbräu, Thannhausen
Triumphator - Löwenbräu AG, München
Unimator - Unionsbräu Haidhausen, München

Starkbierzeit
(Early Spring)

When the snow melts in Munich, the strongest beer begins flowing. The so-called Starkbierzeit, or strong beer time, is generally a two-week period beginning around "Joseph's Day" on the 19th of March. Local beer halls lay on live brass bands and plenty of schmaltz and glitter. Löwenbräu and Paulaner Kellers are especially famous for their generous galas thrown during the potent brew season. In addition to their own famous "-ator" strong brews they dispense with a vengeance, they will also schedule a number of special dances, parties and other events.

A customary attraction is a stone-lifting and tossing contest when hundreds vie for the title of Munich's strongest man. Spectators are content to have spent the day with Munich's strongest beer, a heavily malted libation, from 6-8 percent (vol.) alcohol. The muscle-straining matches are always accompanied by plenty of festivities, music, great food and lots of home-grown *gemütlichkeit.*

The Starkbierzeit is celebrated by most Munich beer halls. Münchners refer to it as the city's "fifth season." It's a seasonal bridge, just before spring, when the indoor beer establishments are about to give way to Munich's army of beer gardens. When that happens, the party moves out doors until late in the fall.

Frühschoppen
(Sunday mornings)

Not exactly a fest, but certainly a custom worth noting, Frühschoppen is the patently Bavarian (Catholic) habit of spending one's late Sunday mornings at the nearest lokal, beer hall or beer garden. The tradition originally began as a sen-

sible diversion for husbands while their wives and family were off in church.

Now, the whole family will show around 10 a.m., having already attended an early Mass. Men share war stories, the women talk about the men and their war stories, the children just bored by it all. It takes place over several *Frühschoppen* (literally "early pints") of beer. Something to remember when quiet Sunday mornings seem to break without much potential: the beer halls and gasthauses just may be full.

Hier kriagst Freund a volles Maßl Aus dem gut bewachten Fassl!

You think Münchners don't take their beer seriously? "Short-pouring" at the Oktoberfest is a criminal offense. This cartoon — a sort of 19th century advertisement — says you'll get a full Maß of beer thanks to our closely watched and monitored kegs. "Beer watchmen" are on duty!

Munich's Fest Calendar

Oktoberfest — www.muenchen-tourist.de

2008	2009	2010	2011	2012
Sep 20 -Oct 5	Sep 19 -Oct 4	Sep 18 -Oct 3	Sep 17 -Oct 3**	Sep 22 -Oct 7

NOTE: **Oktoberfest in 2011 is a day longer, because it includes Monday, Oct. 3, Day of German Unity holiday.

Frühlingsfest* — www.muenchner-volksfeste.de

2008	2009	2010	2011	2012
Apr 11 - Apr 27	Apr 17 -May 3	Apr 16 -May 2	Apr 15 -May 1	Apr 20 -May 6

*Dates for 2009-2012 Frühlingsfest are probable. Precise dates are set a year ahead of time. Confirm with **Munich Tourist Office, Tel:** (089) 233-96-500; **FAX** (089) 233-30-233 (from US dial 011-49-(drop the 0) 89- phone number.) **Internet:** www.muenchen-tourist.de **E-mail:** tourismus@muenchen.de

Sommerfest — www.olympiapark-muenchen.de

2008	2009	2010	2011	2012
August 7-24	August 6-23	August 5-22	August 4-21	August 2-19

Munich's Fest Calendar

Auer Dult
www.auerdult.de

2008	2009	2010	2011	2012
Apr 26 -May 4	Apr 25 -May 3	Apr 24 -May 2	Apr 30 -May 8	Apr 28 -May 6
July 26 -Aug 3	July 25 -Aug 2	July 24 -Aug 1	Jul 30 -Aug 7	Jul 28 -Aug 5
Oct 18 -Oct 26	Oct 17 -Oct 25	Oct 16 -Oct 24	Oct 15 -Oct 23	Oct 20 -Oct 28

Three Auer Dults are held annually, the spring "Maidult", the mid-summer "Jacobidult" and a fall "Kirchweihdult".

Bayernmarkt
www.derbayernmarkt.de

2008	2009	2010	2011	2012
Aug 22 - Sep 7	Aug 21 - Sep 6	Aug 20 - Sep 5	Aug 19 - Sep 4	Aug 24 - Sep 9

Fasching Dienstag (Shrove Tuesday)

2008	2009	2010	2011	2012
Feb 5	Feb 24	Feb 16	Feb 8	Feb 21

Starkbierzeit -Strong Beer Season

Two weeks in March, always encompassing March 19 (St. Joseph's Day). The exact dates are set several months ahead of time.

Beer Songs

Well, sure, you can just hum along and try to lip-synch those great beer songs. If you slosh your beer around enough, wave your arms and mumble just right, you may just be able to fake it. Or, you can check out these verses of some of the more popular songs you will likely encounter during an evening at Hofbräuhaus or any place where the crowd is evenly split between those on and under the tables.

Ein Prosit Der Gemütlichkeit (Always played just before the band goes on break or if beer sales need a boost.)
Ein Prosit, ein Prosit der Gemütlichkeit!
Ein Prosit, ein Prosit der Gemütlichkeit!
Ein, Zwei, Drei, g'suffa. (Take a chugalug at this point)

In München Steht Ein Hofbräuhaus (A well-worn standard at HB)
In München steht ein Hofbräuhaus, eins, zwei, g'suffa.
Da läuft so manches Fässchen aus, eins, zwei, g'suffa.
Da hat schon mancher brave Mann, eins, zwei, g'suffa.
gezeigt, was er so vertragen kann. Schon früh am Morgen fing er an,
und spät am Abend kam er heraus! So schön ist's im Hofbräuhaus!

Eviva España (Watch for the band to put on funny-looking straw hats before they play this one.)
Eviva España, der Himmel weiss, wie sie das macht,
Eviva España, die Gläser, die sind vollerWein,
Eviva España, und bist du selber einmal dort, willst du nie wieder fort.

So Ein Tag, So Wunderschön Wie Heute (A beautiful tune, even if it is a beer song, that will have the whole place swaying to the music and everyone crying in their beer.)
So ein Tag auf den ich mich so freute.
Und wer weiss wann wir uns wiedersehen.
Ach wie bald vergehn die schönen Stunden, die wie Wolken verwehn.
So ein Tag so wunderschön wie Heute,
So ein Tag der dürfte nie vergehn.

Kornblumenblau

Kornblumenblau, ist der Himmel am herrlichen Rheine,
Kornblumenblau, sind die Augen der Frauen beim Weine,
darum trinkt Rheinwein, Männer, seid schlau . . . ,
dann seid am Ende auch ihr, Kornblumenblau.

Wer Soll Das Bezahlen

Wer soll das bezahlen, Wer hat das bestellt?
Wer hat soviel Pinke-Pinke, wer hat soviel Geld?
(Repeat)

Heute Blau und Morgen Blau

Heute blau und Morgen blau,
und Übermorgen wieder,
ich bin Dein und Du bist mein,
und froh sind uns're lieder.
Ich gebe heut mächtig 'ne Welle an,
weil ich das zu Haus nicht so machen kann,
Heute blau und Morgen blau
und Übermorgen wieder,
und wenn wir dann mal nuchtern sind,
besaufen wir uns wieder!

Nach Hause Geh'n Wir Nicht!

Nach Hause, nach Hause, nach Hause geh'n wir nicht,
bis dass der Tag anbricht, nach Hause geh'n wir nicht.
(Repeat)

Der Treue Husar (Our all-time favorite; the haunting melody at close of movie classic, *Paths of Glory*.)

Es war einmal ein treuer Husar
der liebt sein Mädchen ein ganzes Jahr
ein ganzes Jahr und noch viel mehr
die Liebe nahm kein Ende mehr

Du, Du Liegst Mir Im Herzen

Du, du liegst mir im Herzen, du, du liegst mir im Sinn,
du, du machst mir viel Shmerzen, weisst nicht, wie gut ich dir bin,
ja, ja, ja, ja, weisst nicht, wie gut ich dir bin.
So, so wie ich dich liebe, so, so liebe auch mich!
Die, die zärtlichsten Trieve, fühl ich allein nur für dich.
ja, ja, ja, ja, fühl ich allein nur für dich.

Trink, Trink, Brüderlein, Trink

Trink, trink, Brüderlein, trink, lass doch die Sorgen zu Haus!
Trink, trink, Brüderlein, trink, lass doch die Sorgen zu Haus!
Meide den Kummer und meide den Schmerz, dann ist das leben ein Scherz!
Meide den Kummer und meide den Schmerz, dann ist das Leben ein Scherz!

Der Fröliche Wanderer (The Happy Wanderer)
Mein Vater war ein Wandersmann, und mir steckts auch im Blut,
darum wandere ich fort, so lang'
ich kann, und Schwenke meinen Hut.
Valderi, valdera, valderi, valdera, ha, ha, ha, ha, ha,
Valderi, valdera, und Schwenke meinen Hut.
I love to go a wandering, along the mountain track,
And as I go I love to sing, my knapsack on my back.
Valderi, valdera, valderi valdera, ha, ha, ha, ha, ha,
Valderi, valdera, my knapsack on my back.

Böhmische Polka (Beer Barrel Polka)
Rosamunde, schenk mir dein Herz und dein Ja,
Rosamunde, frag' doch nich erst die Mama.
Rosamunde, glaub' mir, auch ich bin dir treu,
denn zur Stunde, Rosamunde,
ist mein Herz g'rade noch frei.
English lyrics:
Roll out the barrel, we'll have a barrel of fun.
Roll out the barrel, we've got the blues on the run.
Zing—Boom—To-ra-ra, sing out a song of good cheer.
Now's the time to roll out the barrel, cuz the gang's all here!

Lili Marleen
Vor der Kaserne, vor dem grossen Tor,
stand eine Laterne, und steht sie noch davor,
so woll'n wir da uns wiederseh'n,
bei der Laterne woll'n wir steh'n
wie einst Lili Marleen,
wie einst Lili Marleen.
(English lyrics)
Underneath the lantern, by the barracks gate,
Darling I remember, the way you used to wait.
'Twas there that you whispered tenderly,
That you loved me, you'd always be,
My Lili of the lamplight,
My own Lili Marleen.

Bier her! Bier her!
Bier her! Bier her! Oder ich fall' um, juch he!
Bier her! Bier her! Oder ich fall' um!
Solle das Bier im Keller liegen und ich hier die Ohnmacht kriegen?
Bier her! Bier her! Oder ich fall' um!

Oh, Du Wunderschöner Deutscher Rhein

Oh, Du wunderschöner, deutscher Rhein,
Du sollst ewig Deutschland Zierde sein.
(Repeat once more.)

Der Schönste Platz is Immer an der Theke

Der schönste Platz is immer an der Theke
ja an der Theke is der schönste Platz.
Ich steh' so gerne dort an diesem schönen Ort
und keine Pferde ziehen dort so schnell mich fort,
denn an der Theke, ja an der Theke,
nur an der Theke is der aller schönste Platz

Schnaps! Das War Sein Letztes Wort

Schnaps! Das war sein letztes Wort,
dan trugen ihn die Englein fort!
Schnaps! Das war sein letztes Wort,
dann trugen ihn die Englein fort!

Bums Valdera

Wir machen durch bis morgen früh und singen:
Bums valdera, bums valdera, bums valdera.
Wir trinken heut' so viel wie nie und singen:
Bums valdera, bums valdera, so viel wie nie.

Das Humta Taterah

Ja, da geht's hum-ta, hum-ta, hum-ta ta-te-rah,
ta-te-rah, ta-te-rah.
Ja, da geht's hum-ta, hum-ta, hum-ta ta-te-rah,
da ruft der ganze Saal: "das selbe noch einmal."
(Repeat until tired)

O, Wie Bist Du Schön!

O, wie bist du schön! O, wie bist du schön!
So was hat man lange nicht geseh'n, so schön, so schön!
(Repeat until bored)

Auf Wiedersehen

Auf Wiedersehen, auf Wiedersehen, bleibt nicht so lange fort,
denn ohne dich ist's halb so schön, darauf hast du mein Wort.
Auf Wiedersehen, auf Wiedersehen, das eine glaube mir,
Nachher wird es noch mal so schön, das Wiedersehen mit dir!

Munich in Winter

Chinesischer Turm — Bernd Zillich, photo

It's below freezing outside, the middle of December and the beer gardens are covered by a blanket of snow. What to do? The quick answer: walk inside and have a beer. But where? Here are a few places that stand out for their interior hospitality, especially in times of rain, wind, sleet or snow, when the beer must go on. We've compiled a cool baker's dozen based on inner atmosphere, spaciousness, and also ease of access, or maybe even egress after a Maß or two. They're presented here in order of winter preference, which may vary slightly from our opinion of them during the summer when beer gardens are open and priorities trend more toward a place in the shade than a corner near the stove:

Hofbräuhaus (pg. 104). First on the list, and definitely where you want to be when it's cold outside. This is always a great indoor option, complete with continuous Oompah band and hordes of fellow beer drinkers any time of year. Team this one with Weisses Brauhaus if the weather is cold and wet. Also worth mention, Augustiner am Platzl and Ayinger am Platzl are two more inside possibilities, just outside the Hofbräuhaus front door.

Augustiner Bräustuben (pg. 46). Completely an inside job, this one has no beer garden at all, save for a few rough sketches to develop a future outdoor service area somewhere up on the roof. Augustiner Bräustuben is easily the most economical

230

(we mean cheap) on this list. We recommend, though, to take the Tram 19 alternative to Holzapfel Str. from the Hauptbahnhof during bad weather to minimize the walking distance. The bottom line is this place does most of its business November through March, so a foul-weather operating model is the rule not the exception.

Augustiner Keller (pg. 52). Little known feature of this world-class beer garden on Arnulf Str. is the cellar beerhall with seating for 300. It's especially inviting during Starkbier season in March and April when *doppelbock* Maximator is flowing from Augustiner's wooden kegs. The Lagerkeller, as it's known, is open 4 p.m. to 1 a.m., Mon.-Sat., with plenty of long benches and lots of spilled beer.

Bräustüberl Tegernsee (pg. 192). A bit of a road trip to get here, this is still one of the best beer halls in all of Bavaria and the one venue on our winter list that is part of the Prosit! Free Beer program. We love this place, come rain or shine, and we think you should too.

Augustiner Großgaststätte (pg. 48). Half restaurant, half beer hall — take your pick when you need to get out of the weather and still want to enjoy Munich's favorite beer.

Andechser am Dom (pg. 70). Get here early because when the weather is bad, this place is good . . . and full. Space heaters in the patio area keep things toasty and big screen plasma TVs keep sports aficionados occupied.

Unionsbräu (pg. 108). Home made brew and a cellar beer hall, all close to the U-bahn stop — a terrific sheltered beer oasis.

Paulaner Keller (pg. 156). This is the county seat for the early spring pre-lent *Starkbierzeit*, strong beer season. Even during the winter months, there's still plenty of chance to try a Salvator (the mother of all doppelbocks) and fire up the innards before venturing forth.

Löwenbräu Keller (pg. 128). Also rockin' during Starkbier craziness, when Triumphator strong beer is flowing. Right next to the U-bahn stop at Stiglmaier Platz.

Max-Emanuel Brauerei (pg. 136). Munich's student beer drinkers have enough sense to know when — and where — to get in out of the rain. "Max-E-Brau" is tops on their list. Also a great place to catch big-screen T.V. sporting events.

Paulaner Bräuhaus (pg. 152). An afternoon to evening selection, with a brewpub atmosphere and decent food. Also, a very short, 5-minute walk to get here.

Weisses Brauhaus (pg. 182). Treat yourself to a Schneider Weisse and warm up to the Hofbräuhaus around the corner. Also, a better selection to enjoy some Bavarian cuisine if you're more hungry than thirsty.

Altes Hackerhaus (pg. 38). A little more restaurant than the others, but certainly a good inside bet. A retractable patio cover will keep out the rain and let in the sun.

The "Wuide Rund'n" Stammtisch (Bavarian for "another round") lives up to its name every weekend at the Hofbräuhaus. This group of experienced beer drinkers has earned its own personalized *Bierdeckel*, beer mat. Helps soak up a little of the overflow when the *Unterhaltung* (conversation) gets a little too deep.

232

Lists

**Weekend Variety Pack
(limited-time itinerary)
Day One:**
 Waldwirtschaft Großhesselohe
 Augustiner Keller
 Hofbräuhaus
Day Two:
 Hirschgarten
 Osterwald Garten/
 Chinesischer Turm/Seehaus
 Paulaner Keller

5-Beer Club:
 Bräustüberl Tegernsee*
 Brückenwirt*
 Menterschwaige*
 Sankt Emmerams Mühle*
 Seehaus*
 **Waldwirtschaft
  Großhesselohe***
 Augustiner Keller
 Hirschgarten
 Michaeligarten
 Augustiner Bräu (Salzburg)

 ***Participating in Prosit!**
beer offer.

Cheapest:
 Airbräu (in the Airport)
 Aubinger Einkehr
 Augustiner Bräu (Salzburg)
 Augustiner Bräustuben
 Concordia Park
 Deutsche Eiche
 Hirschgarten
 Kloster Andechs
 Leiberheim
 Schloßberg Biergarten Dachau
 Spektakel
 Weihenstephan

Biggest:
 Hirschgarten
 Chinesischer Turm
 Augustiner Keller
 Augustiner Bräu (Salzburg)
 Kloster Andechs
 Leiberheim
 Michaeligarten
 Kugler Alm
 Paulaner Keller
 Löwenbräu Keller
 Waldwirtschaft Großhesselohe

**Closest (10-minutes or less walk
from Bahnhof):**
 Park Cafe
 Augustiner Keller
 Andechser am Dom
 Donisl
 Viktualienmarkt
 Augustiner Großgastätte
 Hofbräuhaus
 Weisses Bräuhaus

**Less than a Block to Walk
(from last MVV stop):**
 Airbräu (in the Airport)
 Franziskaner Garten
 Hinterbrühl
 Im Grüntal
 Michaeligarten
 Löwenbräu Keller
 Mangostin
 Spektakel

Best with Kids:
 Am Hopfengarten
 Augustiner Keller
 Augustiner (Salzburg)
 Aumeister
 Hirschgarten
 Leiberheim
 Menterschwaige

233

Best with Kids (Cont.):
Michaeligarten
Seehaus
Siebenbrunn
Waldwirtschaft Großhesselohe

Under-30 Crowd:
Augustiner Bräustuben
Chinesischer Turm
Andechser am Dom
Max-Emanuel Brauerei
Park Cafe
Bräustüberl Tegernsee

Wild-and-Craziest:
Hofbräuhaus
Paulaner Keller
Chinesischer Turm
Waldwirtschaft Großhesselohe
Bräustüberl Tegernsee
Augustiner Bräustuben

Most Traditional:
Augustiner Großgastätte
Augustiner Bräu (Salzburg)
Franziskaner Garten
Hofbräuhaus
Hinterbrühl
Kugler Alm
Leiberheim
Sankt Emmerams Mühle
Zum Flaucher
Menterschwaige
Hirschgarten
Bräustüberl Tegernsee
Schlosswirtschaft
Oberschleißheim

Close to Water (the beer garden not the beer)
Seehaus
Michaeligarten
Seehof
Brückenwirt
Insel Mühle

Brewed on the Premises:
Paulaner Bräuhaus
Forschungsbrauerei
Weihenstephan
Kloster Andechs
Liebhards
Löwenbräu Keller
Paulaner Keller
Augustiner Bräu (Salzburg)
Schlossberg Biergarten
Dachau
Unionsbräu
Bräustüberl Tegernsee

Best-tasting Beer:
Forschungsbrauerei's
Blonder Bock
Augustiner (Munich)
Paulaner
Augustiner (Salzburg)
Ayinger
Hofbräuhaus

By the Beer:
Löwenbräu
Am Hopfengarten
Brückenwirt
Concordia Park
Flaucher
Löwenbräu Keller
Mangostin
Max-Emanuel Brauerei
Menterschwaige
Michaeligarten
Park Cafe
Paulaner Bräu
Am Rosengarten
Im Grüntal
Paulaner Bräuhaus
Paulaner Keller
Seehaus
Hacker-Pschorr Bräu
Altes Hackerhaus
Donisl

Hinterbrühl
Heide Volm
Spektakel
Waldheim
Hofbräu
Chinesischer Turm
Zum Aumeister
Fasanerie
Hofbräuhaus
Hofbräu Keller
Schlosswirtschaft
    Oberschleißheim
Seehof
Zur Schwaige
Augustiner Bräu
Alter Wirt
Aubinger Einkehr
Augustiner Bräustuben
Augustiner Großgastätte
Augustiner Keller
Deutsche Eiche
Hirschgarten
Insel Mühle
Spaten Bräu
Franziskaner Garten
Hirschau
Kugler Alm
Waldwirtschaft
    Großhesselohe
Osterwald Garten
Sankt Emmerams Mühle
Schlossberg Biergarten
    Dachau
Siebenbrunn
Taxisgarten
Ayinger Bräu
Liebhards (Aying)
Kaltenberger Bräu
Hirschgarten
Münchner Haupt'
Erhartinger Bräu
Leiberheim
Maisaicher Bräu
Bienenheim
St. Jakobus
Forschungsbrauerei
Schneider Weiss

Weisses Bräuhaus
Herzogliche Brauhaus Tegernsee
Hirschgarten
Bräustüberl Tegernsee
Augustiner Bräu (Salzburg)
Augustiner Bräu (Salzburg)
Andechser Special
Kloster Andechs
Andechser am Dom
Herrnbräu (Ingolstadt)
Kraillinger Brauerei
Weihenstephaner Bräu
Bräustüberl Weihenstephan
Plantage
Various
Bier und Oktoberfest Museum
Biergarten Viktualienmarkt

Upgrades (from fifth edition):
Am Hopfengarten
Franziskaner Garten

Downgrades:
Am Rosengarten
Kraillinger Brauerei
Schlossberg Biergarten (formerly
    Zieglerkeller, Dachau)

Dropped:
Haus Der 111 Biere (closed)
Landsherger Hof (closed)
Günther Murphy's (After Hours,
    closed)

New:
Airbräu
Andechser am Dom
Aubinger Einkehr
Bier und Oktoberfest Museum
Donisl
Kilian's Irish Pub/Ned Kelly's
    Australian Bar (Late Night)
Liebhards (Ayinger Bräu)
Plantage
Schlossberg Biergarten (formerly
    Zieglerkeller, Dachau)
Seehof

235

Glossary

Bayrischer Abend - Literally "Bavarian evening," a traditional folk theater program of music, folk dancing, skits and unintelligible humor.

Biergärtler - Those who consider the enjoyment of Munich's beer gardens to be a modern science.

Blasmusik - Rousing folk music, played by a brass band, often featured in Munich's beer halls. Great to drink beer by.

Bräustüberl - Usually a bar within a restaurant or larger complex. Much like a lokal.

Floß - Party rafting. About 60-70 beer lovers hire a raft, a bar and a band for an afternoon float down the Isar River. Viewed at Brückenwirt, Hinterbrühl beer gardens.

Gasthaus, Gaststätte, Gasthof, Raststätte, Wirtschaft - A restaurant and/or beer garden complex. All used interchangeably.

Gemütlichkeit - No real English translation, it means warm atmosphere, tradition and hospitality all wrapped up in a single word.

Glühwein - Hot, cinnamon-spiced wine. Usually served in winter or on cold evenings.

Keller - Literally a "cellar", but usually refers to a beer garden.

Kneipe - Another name for a lokal; usually a small, neighborhood establishment.

Krug - German word for beer mug (stein means a rock). "Die Krüge hoch!" is the call to raise mugs for a *prosit*, or toast.

Lederhosen - Traditional Bavarian-style suspendered leather (originally deerskin) shorts. Don't wear them unless you're a native.

Lokal - (Pronounced "low-cal") A bar or a pub that caters to a loyal clientele.

Maß - A liter of beer, usually light or "helles" unless you stipulate something else.

Oom-pah band - Bavarian brass band (plays Blasmusik); standard musical program in most beer halls and some beer gardens.

Radler - Half beer and half lemon-lime soda. Termed a *radler* (bicyclist) because they're a favorite of bike riders who must navigate their way home.

Russe - Half Weissbier (*weizen* or wheat beer) and lemon-lime soda. Especially popular on hot days.

Schmankerl - Bavarian fast-food. Lots of sausages, roasted chickens, salads and cream-cheeses. Typical beer garden fare — marginally nutritious, heavy starches high in carbohydrates. Naturally, it's delicious.

Selbstbedienung - Self service. Sometimes abbreviated SB. Tables without tablecloths usually mean you can bring your own food and serve yourself to the beer.

Spezi - Half coca-cola and half orange soda. It sounds terrible, but it's actually pretty good. Kids and women love it.

Stammtisch - A table set aside for regulars. If you're not sure whether you're a regular, you're not. Usually marked by a sign (Go away unless we know you!) to warn you.

Wirt - The proprietor of the business. The boss. (Also, **Pächter, Direktor**.)

Index

237

238

Prosit!

Buy One-Get One Free
A Special Offer from
5-Beer Club Members

Our Five-Beer Club has become a tradition at The Beer Drinker's Guide. In this sixth edition, the competition for the maximum suds honor is stiffer than ever. The honor of being selected is worth celebrating and several of our members have chosen to say Prosit! and Willkommen through a special offer: Buy one beer (Maß or half-liter) and get a second one of equal size and value free. Just show a copy of the BDG2M at the time you order your beer at these establishments and present the waiter or waitress with a coupon below. The offer is also good for one beer at half the regular price or can be applied to a non-alcoholic drink as well.

When the weather is warm and the throat is dry, there is no better alternative than Seehaus.

Five-Beer Club Member

SEEHAUS im Englischen Garten

Validation:

Pächter
Stephan Kuffler

Seehaus im Englischen Garten · Kleinhesselohe 3 · 80802 München

Willkommen!
Present this coupon to your server and display a copy of this book for a free beer (1 ltr. Maß or smaller) with your purchase of a beer at the regular price, or one beer at half-price. (Offer valid to substitute non-alcoholic beverage for beer. Limit one per customer)

Wa-Wi, the "Jazz Beer Garden", is a mix of the best of old German tradition and modern day musical enjoyment.

Five-Beer Club Member

Waldwirtschaft Großhesselohe

Validation:

Pächter
Josef Krätz

Waldwirtschaft Großhesselohe · Georg-Kalb-Str. 3 · 82049 Großhesselohe

Willkommen!
Present this coupon to your server and display a copy of this book for a free beer (1 ltr. Maß or smaller) with your purchase of a beer at the regular price, or one beer at half-price. (Offer valid to substitute non-alcoholic beverage for beer. Limit one per customer)

Sankt Emmerams offers a slice of life to the rich and famous and just plain commoners who also love a great beer.

Five-Beer Club Member

Sankt Emmerams

Validation:

Pächter
Karl-Heinz Zacher

Sankt Emmerams Mühle · St. Emmeram 41 · 81925 München

Willkommen!
Present this coupon to your server and display a copy of this book for a free beer (1 ltr. Maß or smaller) with your purchase of a beer at the regular price, or one beer at half-price. (Offer valid to substitute non-alcoholic beverage for beer. Limit one per customer)

241

The outside courtyard "beer garden" was standing room only in the Hofbräuhaus of the early 1900s.

Sehrgeehrte(r) Kellner(in),
Der Pächter, dessen Unterschrift auf der Rückseite dieses Coupons zu lesen ist, hat dem Träger des Coupons ein Sonderangebot genehmigt. Der Besitzer dieses Coupons bekommt entweder ein Bier (bis 1 Liter groß) gratis nach dem Kauf eines Biers zum normalen Preis, oder ein Bier zum halben Preis. Dieses Angebot gilt auch für nichtalkoholische Getränke. Heißen Sie bitte diesen Gast willkommen und halten Sie die Verpflichtung, die der Pächter des Seehaus akzeptiert hat, ein. Richten Sie bitte Ihre Fragen an Herrn Stephan Kuffler.

Sehrgeehrte(r) Kellner(in),
Der Pächter, dessen Unterschrift auf der Rückseite dieses Coupons zu lesen ist, hat dem Träger des Coupons ein Sonderangebot genehmigt. Der Besitzer dieses Coupons bekommt entweder ein Bier (bis 1 Liter groß) gratis nach dem Kauf eines Biers zum normalen Preis, oder ein Bier zum halben Preis. Dieses Angebot gilt auch für nichtalkoholische Getränke. Heißen Sie bitte diesen Gast willkommen und halten Sie die Verpflichtung, die der Pächter des Waldwirtschaft Großhesselohe akzeptiert hat, ein. Richten Sie bitte Ihre Fragen an Herrn Josef Krätz.

Sehrgeehrte(r) Kellner(in),
Der Pächter, dessen Unterschrift auf der Rückseite dieses Coupons zu lesen ist, hat dem Träger des Coupons ein Sonderangebot genehmigt. Der Besitzer dieses Coupons bekommt entweder ein Bier (bis 1 Liter groß) gratis nach dem Kauf eines Biers zum normalen Preis, oder ein Bier zum halben Preis. Dieses Angebot gilt auch für nichtalkoholische Getränke. Heißen Sie bitte diesen Gast willkommen und halten Sie die Verpflichtung, die der Pächter des Sankt Emmerams Mühle akzeptiert hat, ein. Richten Sie bitte Ihre Fragen an Herrn Karl-Heinz Zacher.

Prosit! Buy One-Get One Free

Buy one beer (Maß or half-liter) and get a second one of equal size and value free. Just show a copy of the BDG2M at the time you order your beer at these establishments and present the waiter or waitress with a coupon below. The offer is also good for one beer at half the regular price and can be applied to a non-alcoholic drink as well. If the waiter or waitress appears unfamiliar with the offer, point out the German translation on the back of the coupon for further details.

Menterschwaige was the stage of a royal love affair, but now it's a sweetheart of Munich's beer garden lovers.

Gutshof-Biergarten Menterschwaige

Five-Beer Club Member 🍺🍺🍺🍺🍺

Willkommen! Present this coupon to your server and display a copy of this book for a free beer (1 ltr. Maß or smaller) with your purchase of a beer at the regular price, or one beer at half-price. (Offer valid to substitute non-alcoholic beverage for beer. Limit one per customer)

Validation:
Director
Christian Schottenhamel
Gutshof Menterschwaige · Menterschwaige Str. 4 · 81545 München

---

The Bräustüberl in Tegernsee is a day trip not to be missed to visit one of the best beer halls in all of Germany.

Five-Beer Club Member 🍺🍺🍺🍺🍺

Herzogliches Bräustüberl Tegernsee

Willkommen! Present this coupon to your server and display a copy of this book for a free beer (1 ltr. Maß or smaller) with your purchase of a beer at the regular price, or one beer at half-price. (Offer valid to substitute non-alcoholic beverage for beer. Limit one per customer)

Validation:
Director
Peter Hubert
Bräustüberl Tegernsee · Schloßplatz 1 · 83684 Tegernsee

The rest of the world might float on by, but Brückenwirt is the place to relax and enjoy a great beer on the Isar River.

Five-Beer Club Member 🍺🍺🍺🍺🍺

Gasthof Brückenwirt

Willkommen! Present this coupon to your server and display a copy of this book for a free beer (1 ltr. Maß or smaller) with your purchase of a beer at the regular price, or one beer at half-price. (Offer valid to substitute non-alcoholic beverage for beer. Limit one per customer)

Validation:
Director
Erich Müller
Gasthof Brückenwirt · Grünwalder Brücke 1 · 82049 Höllriegelskreuth

www.beerdrinkersguide.com

Come visit our website for updated information on fest dates and beer drinker's memorabilia like beer mugs, T-shirts and screen savers with scenic beer garden shots and daily reminders that won't let you forget when the next Oktoberfest begins • Join our Beer Drinker's Field Research Team and start contributing to the next edition of the BDG2M. Now, Munich's beer drinkers have a home on the Web.

Sehrgeehrte(r) Kellner(in),
Der Pächter, dessen Unterschrift auf der Rückseite dieses Coupons zu lesen ist, hat dem Träger des Coupons ein Sonderangebot genehmigt. Der Besitzer dieses Coupons bekommt entweder ein Bier (bis 1 Liter groß) gratis nach dem Kauf eines Biers zum normalen Preis, oder ein Bier zum halben Preis. Dieses Angebot gilt auch für nichtalkoholische Getränke. Heißen Sie bitte diesen Gast willkommen und halten Sie die Verpflichtung, die der Pächter des Gutshof Menterschwaige akzeptiert hat, ein. Richten Sie bitte Ihre Fragen an Herrn Christian Schottenhamel.

Sehrgeehrte(r) Kellner(in),
Der Pächter, dessen Unterschrift auf der Rückseite dieses Coupons zu lesen ist, hat dem Träger des Coupons ein Sonderangebot genehmigt. Der Besitzer dieses Coupons bekommt entweder ein Bier (bis 1 Liter groß) gratis nach dem Kauf eines Biers zum normalen Preis, oder ein Bier zum halben Preis. Dieses Angebot gilt auch für nichtalkoholische Getränke. Heißen Sie bitte diesen Gast willkommen und halten Sie die Verpflichtung, die der Pächter des Bräustüberl Tegernsee akzeptiert hat, ein. Richten Sie bitte Ihre Fragen an Herrn Peter Hubert.

Sehrgeehrte(r) Kellner(in),
Der Pächter, dessen Unterschrift auf der Rückseite dieses Coupons zu lesen ist, hat dem Träger des Coupons ein Sonderangebot genehmigt. Der Besitzer dieses Coupons bekommt entweder ein Bier (bis 1 Liter groß) gratis nach dem Kauf eines Biers zum normalen Preis, oder ein Bier zum halben Preis. Dieses Angebot gilt auch für nichtalkoholische Getränke. Heißen Sie bitte diesen Gast willkommen und halten Sie die Verpflichtung, die der Pächter des Gasthof Brückenwirt akzeptiert hat, ein. Richten Sie bitte Ihre Fragen an Herrn Erich Müller.